49/00

FRANZ A. RŒDELBERGER – VERA I. GROSCHOFF
and 70 wildlife photographers
present

AFRICAN WILDLIFE

in 250 photographs with 24 colourplates

ENGLISH VERSION BY NIETER O'LEARY AND PAMELA PAULET
WITH AN INTRODUCTION BY BRUCE CAMPBELL

CONSTABLE · LONDON

THE VIKING PRESS
NEW YORK

LONGMANS GREEN
TORONTO

Original title: BELAUSCHTE WILDNIS / PARADE ANIMALE

© 1963 Buchverlag Verbandsdruckerei Ltd. Berne as well as by the contributing photographers
English text © 1964 Constable Company Ltd., 10 Orange Street, London WC 2

PRINTED IN SWITZERLAND

INTRODUCTION
by BRUCE CAMPBELL

Sometimes I feel as if I am the only naturalist who has not been to Africa, but in fact there must be thousands who can learn about the wildlife of the great continent only at secondhand from television programmes, films, and photographs such as Franz Rœdelberger and Vera Groschoff have assembled in this book. This is not the first book of pictures of African animals, nor will it be the last, but it has a vital job to do by reinforcing three points: that these animals form a unique and spectacular fauna, that many of them are threatened with extinction, and that it is our duty to preserve this heritage.

Although Africa is famous for its big animals, the skill of the modern photographer is enabling us armchair travellers to realise the beauty and diversity of other groups of fauna: birds, reptiles, fish and insects. All these are represented in this book and many of the photographs are of real biological interest. Look, for example, at the astonishing pages from 179 onwards devoted to insects or to the birth of the baby Dorcas gazelle on pages 80–81. This latter was actually photographed in Germany, and makes another important point: that to preserve species and study them it may be necessary to keep a stock in semi-captivity. The remarkable plan now in operation to save the Arabian oryx by building up a herd under suitable conditions in America is perhaps the outstanding example of this technique, which can also be seen in Britain at the Wildfowl Trust, where over half the world population of nenes or Hawaiian geese walk unconcernedly round the feet of visitors.

The book rightly includes some pictures which shock, of the way man is still killing animals for greed or gain. The author's lucid and concise text supports the photographs with telling statistics, showing how this wonderful wildlife has been reduced to the danger limit, so that a number of species survive only in reserves and sanctuaries.

What can be done about it? One of the hard lessons we have learned, both at home and abroad, is that we cannot sit back in the comfortable expectation that "they" are doing something, that "the matter is in hand". There are devoted men and women working to save a heritage that is as irreplaceable as the great buildings and works of art in Europe, but they are few and face all sorts of odds. In the World Wildlife Fund we have an international agency which exists not only to find the money the cause of conservation so urgently needs, but to give the people in the forefront of the struggle the heartening feeling that there are millions of others wishing them well.

Bruce Campbell

Part of the proceeds from the sale of this book will be donated to The World Wildlife Fund, 2 Caxton Street, London, S.W. 1

Africa and Europe are, for better or worse, bound together by remorse for the past and hope for the future.

The wisdom of the early Egyptians fertilised the Mediterranean cultures, and, thousands of years later, that basic knowledge, through the inventiveness of the northern peoples, flourished into technical science. From the Renaissance onward, lured by the prospect of gain and animated by feelings of superiority, Europeans set out to conquer the Dark Continent. Wherever they appeared, they uprooted or enslaved the natives and drove out the animals. What had begun on the coast spread deep into the interior, following the tracks of the explorers. White settlers claimed the best land and drove the pastoral tribes into the steppes, once the realm of migrating herds. The harm done to the balance of Nature by this sudden intrusion was threefold: Africa's peoples had to skip several stages in their development; her sun-scorched earth suffered through exploitation; and, finally, the coming of firearms drastically depleted her animal wealth. The sin against Nature cannot be concealed under the veneer of progress, and the independent states of Africa have been left a problematical heritage, a legacy they are expected to manage more intelligently than did the white man. The world gives aid to these new states and anticipates that they will follow the good example rather than the bad; to make up for past neglect and bring to fruition what began too late. They are not only expected to nurture and educate 258 million people, but also to preserve life in its entirety. Will the Africans understand what the Europeans never recognized, that the Age of Man is also the Age of Mammals, that *Homo sapiens* should not be master but custodian of the animal kingdom? The next decades will decide if Africa's fauna can escape the fate to which other continents have condemned their living heritage.

Seen from the air above the swamp-lands of the Nile in southern Sudan, this herd of 180 elephants seems to prove that the grey giants are far from extinction. However, there is no denying the fact that Africa's elephants were reduced in the 19th century from 3 million to 300,000. Recovery has come only in the past 50 years.

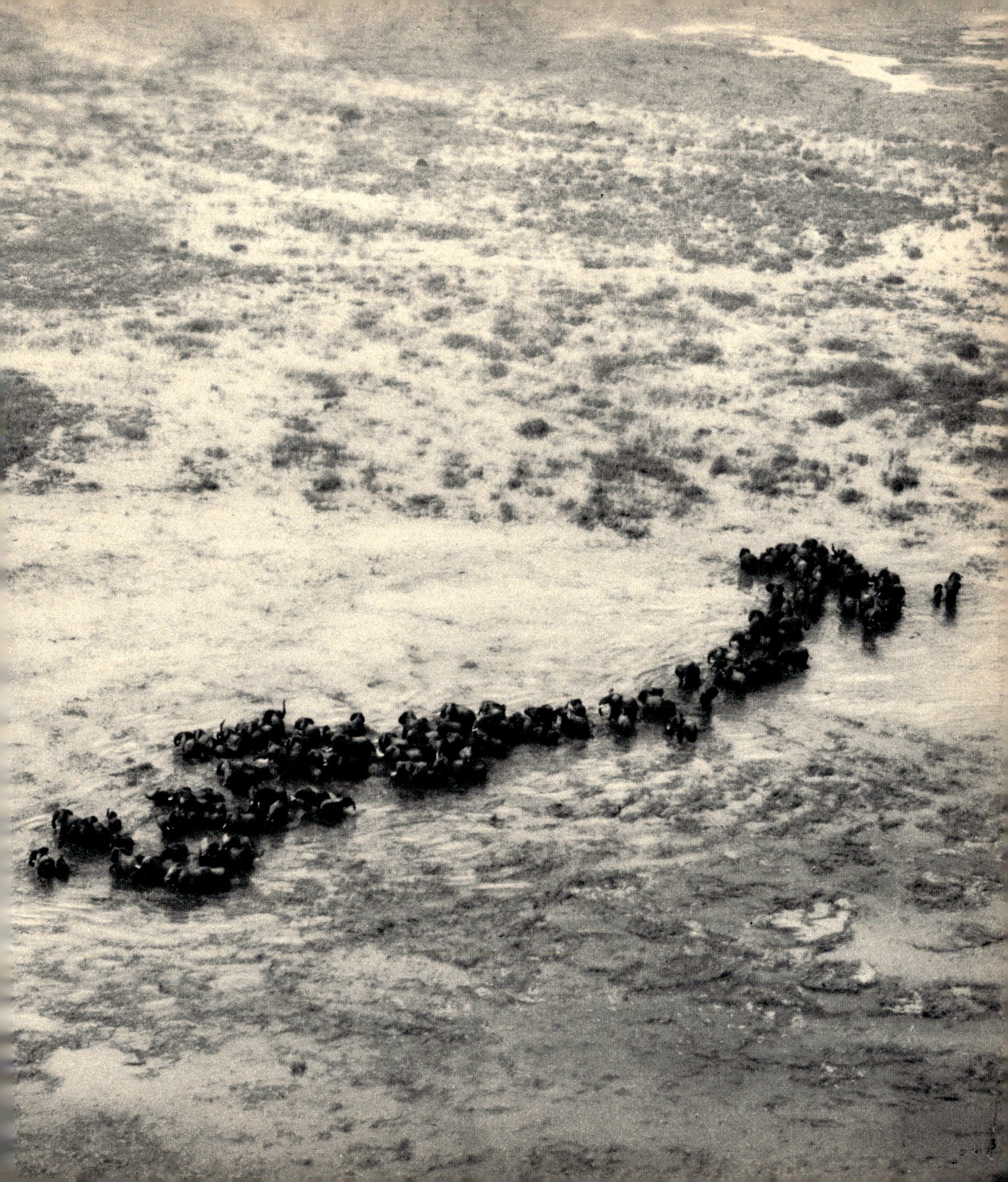

Hundreds of Lechwe Waterbuck *(Kobus leche)* move through the lush grasslands of the Caprivi marshes between eastern Angola and Bechuanaland.

Aerial photographs of plains teeming with wildlife invite us to go and see this abundance with our own eyes. Will our grandchildren contemplate these pictures solely as historical documents? While sentimental pessimists give up everything as lost, realistic optimists the world over work for the future of African fauna and hence for man too, that he may live *w i t h* animals. Wild animals have mediators in high places, for nature conservation has become a world problem and every nation, young or old, is called upon to render an account of the actual state of its fauna. UNESCO considers the spiritual relationship between man and animals to be an important part of its educational and cultural programme;

FAO lists wildlife among the natural resources; the International Union for the Conservation of Nature, UICN, urges the accomplishment of practical schemes; and the World Wildlife Fund and other private organisations help to provide financial aid in cases of emergency. The Lechwe Waterbuck in the upper reaches of the Zambesi have not, so far, been threatened, though their North Rhodesian relatives are in danger. In 1934, about 250,000 head were still living in the valley of the River Kafue and another 150,000 round Lake Bangweolo. To-day, Lechwe in these territories have been reduced to one-tenth of their former number. Such figures are more eloquent than words.

Near the mouth of the Zambesi (Mozambique): a flock of white Cattle Egrets flies over a fleeing herd of Cape Buffalo *(Syncerus caffer)*.

"The fauna is as much a part of a country's wealth as the fertility of its soil." This adage, tardily voiced by modern ecologists, finds a strong echo in Africa's élite, for deep in his innermost being the native has ever been aware of this truth. But the white man goes from one extreme to the other: treating wild ungulates yesterday as a menace to agriculture, and to-day declaring them a treasure not to be tampered with. Each time a new state is born, and bloody tribal feuds break out, the world is afraid for the indigenous animals. And yet, in spite of atrocity stories of ravaged national parks, it cannot be denied that the new independent states are doing their best to protect wildlife reservations; doing so not only for love of animals, but for speculative purposes... We should not chide them, for the colonisers did not create the reservations out of magnanimity, but out of sheer remorse. But neither laws nor fine words from white or black, can build protective walls round territories as large as Hawaii or half the size of Wales. What is needed are facilities for the training of native game wardens; also roads, jeeps, and small aircraft for a better control service. Hitherto, only the city of Philadelphia has volunteered to be godmother to a small coastal reservation in Kenya. When will other cities follow this worthy and practical example?

Hippopotami *(Hippopotamus amphibius)*, Pelicans and Cormorants. Semliki-Nile region, Kivu (Albert) National Park, Congo (L.) Republic.

Time was when all African river banks and lake shores presented a paradisaic picture of teeming wildlife communities, but to-day the big mammals are confined within sanctuaries. Only birds can ignore artificial boundaries. In a continent which man has divided into farm and virgin land, they seek in unhindered flight the most favourable habitat. Thus, at the end of their breeding season, the water birds leave their nesting places on other shores and, moving in small flocks, spread over the whole lake region. Pelicans and Cormorants prefer to enter the game reservation and to settle close to the herds of hippopotamus, for wherever these gigantic vegetarians browse and digest, their dung stimulates the metabolism of aquatic life, which in turn promotes an abundance of fish. At present, about 35,000 hippopotami live in the two national parks flanking Lake Edward on the border between Congo (L.) and Uganda. On many other shores these placid giants have been foolishly exterminated. All along the Nile, from the Delta to Khartoum, the hippopotamus, the biblical "Behemoth", has vanished, shot from pleasure steamers by travellers to whom the subtler thrill of hunting with a camera was as yet unknown.

Odd neighbours in the Caprivi marshes: Glossy Ibises *(Plegadis falcinellus)* search for food near the Crocodiles *(Crocodylus niloticus)*.

To-day only aerial photographs of remote marshlands — blind-alleys to the crocodile hunters — can convey an idea of what all the great rivers must have looked like a hundred years ago. In the arid north and south the crocodile was hated more than elsewhere as a treacherous enemy in the life-giving waters, and was exterminated so that thirsty camels and cattle could drink in peace. Since many rivers outside the equatorial forests are now free of saurians, it is difficult to understand why flocks of Ibises, able to choose better "company", should, as seen here, settle so close to the basking reptiles. Herodotus and Pliny both wrote of the little bird *Trochilos*, searching for leeches and particles of meat in the yawning jaws of those *Leviathans*. In fact, these feathered "toothpicks" were the little Egyptian Plovers. The larger waterfowl are all too often snapped up on the surface. Do Ibises feel safe in the daytime because they can make off to the trees when their dangerous neighbours start hunting after sunset? Or is the Caprivi region so abundant in fish that the giant reptiles need no supplementary diet? It would seem that young crocodiles dare not go too near their cannibalistic parents, otherwise some smaller saurians would be seen basking on the sandbank.

"A garland of roses..." "A living ribbon of fire..." "The waters aglow with rosy wings..." Thus did famous African explorers describe their first impressions of the flamingo lakes. But to-day, scientists who fly their small aircraft over the bird colonies do more than contemplate beauty alone; they try to estimate the numbers of the flocks and observe which lakes provide the best environment for sustenance and propagation of the species. Out of an approximate world population of six million flamingoes, over half live in East Africa, between Lake Rudolf in northern Kenya and Lake Rukwa in south-western Tanganyika. Flamingoes are not drawn to the huge freshwater lakes, for it is only in water containing salt and soda that they can filter the plankton on which they feed, out of the mud. For this reason, the largest flocks gather around small mineral-saturated crater lakes, as in Naivasha. ➤ However, an assembly of some hundred thousand birds does not mean that the lake is suitable for breeding. If the water is too deep the birds cannot build their mudhill nests far out in the shallows where eggs and young are safe from predators. Hence the flamingoes come from great distances to breed in the shallow waters of Lake Natron on the borders of Kenya and Tanganyika. When its water level rose unexpectedly in 1962, two million birds made for Lake Magadi, where, in early autumn, 800,000 chicks hatched. This lake had been avoided hitherto because of its exceptionally high concentration of soda which now became a perilous hazard for the young flamingoes. Nearly 10 per cent of the chicks were in jeopardy because the soda crystals stuck to their legs in heavy, paralyzing lumps. Only by the efforts of zoologists and soldiers from East Africa, and with financial aid given by bird lovers all over the world, were a hundred thousand young birds driven out of the danger zone. Thirty-eight thousand chicks had to be freed from their lethal burden by means of light hammer strokes and freshwater baths. Thus man, at the cost of one penny per bird, has paid at least part of his debt — a debt incurred during the centuries in which he took a heavy toll of Old World flamingoes. But the days are gone when ten birds were killed for just o n e meal of flamingo tongues.

➤ Lesser Flamingoes *(Phoeniconais minor)* on the crater lake Naivasha, Kenya.

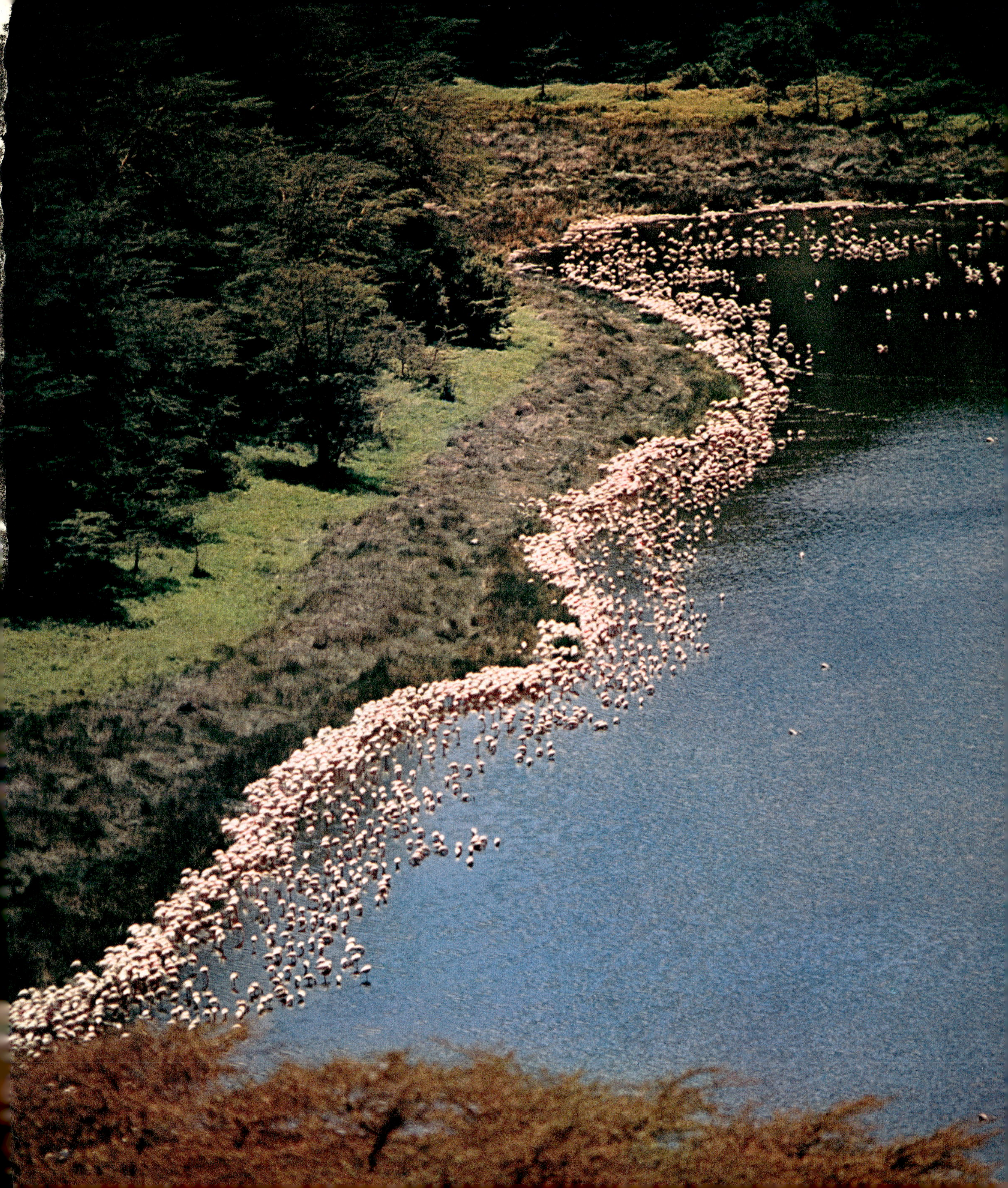

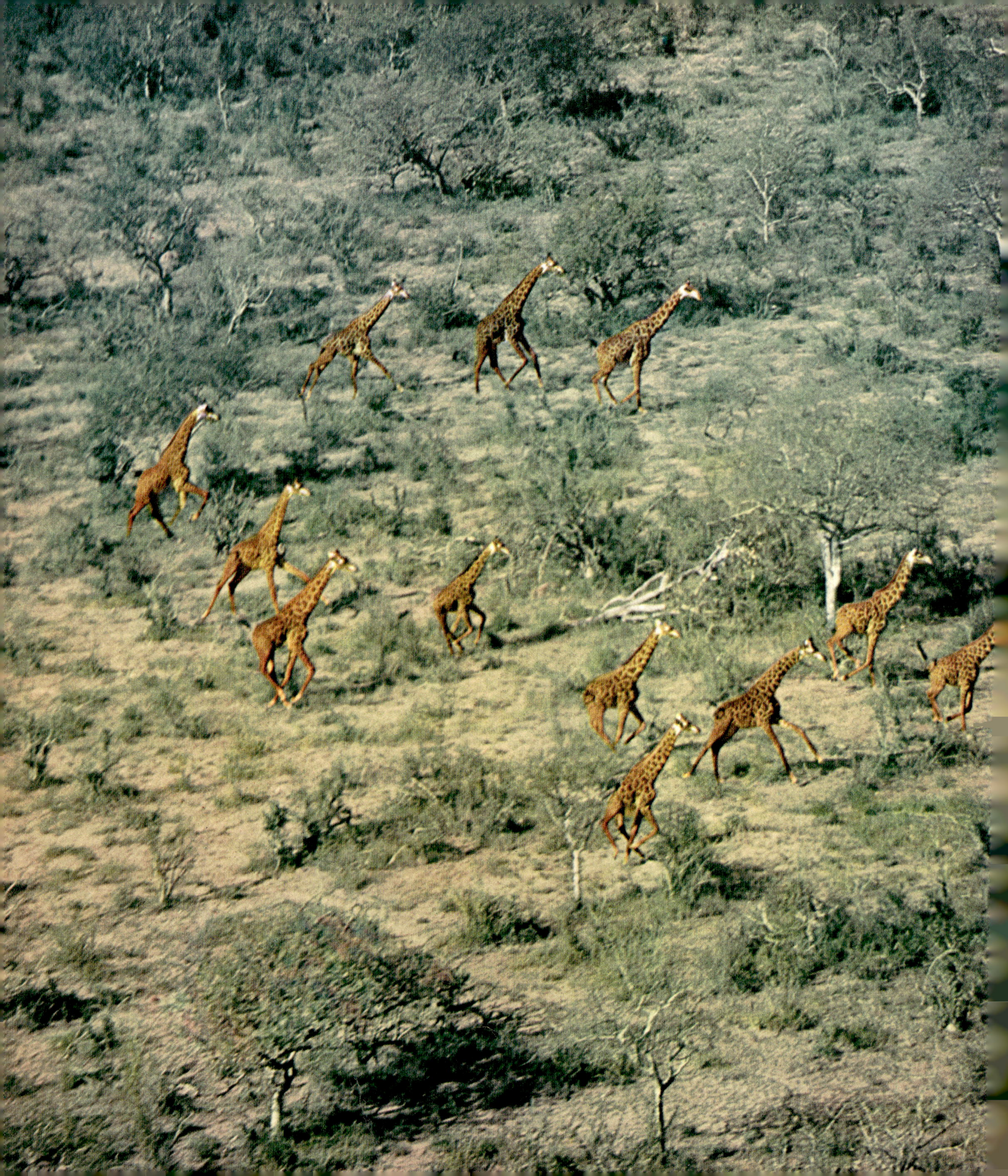

When an airplane hums overhead giraffes lose their sedate calm and show one of the rare spectacles of fleeing giants. This aerial photograph, which freezes the movement of the herd against the background of a sun-drenched savannah, resembles prehistoric cave paintings. Rock drawings of giraffes discovered in the centre of the Sahara indicate how their habitat has shrunk because of climatic changes. To-day, these long-necked animals are a symbol of Africa, but fossil remains prove that at the end of the tertiary period, 16 species of giraffes lived all over the Black Continent *and* from South China to Greece and Italy. They were described in Greek writings as early as 2,000 years ago, but it was not until 1826 that a young giraffe was shipped to Europe. The animal was a gift from the Sultan of Egypt to Charles X of France and had to walk all the way from Marseilles to Paris. In 1828, another specimen hoofed along the road from Venice to Vienna. Since then the wondrous animals, whose Arabic name, *Zrafa*, means "the graceful one", have gained world fame. Ninety-five per cent of European and American children have seen giraffes in picture books, in zoos or at the movies, but many African youngsters have never seen the tallest creature of their Continent. Most African children know only the story of Baronga, the flute player, who hid himself in the "Smithy of Life" of the Creator. There, legend has it, he fashioned from the leftovers of dromedaries, leopards, and antelopes, the curious giraffe. Africa's youngest generation, growing up in territories which have been shot almost empty by Europeans, must learn to love the animals of their homeland in order to understand the need for game preservation. School trips into National Parks, new zoological gardens for cities, posters and film shows for villages — all this costs money which only subscriptions and endowments can help to meet. The finest rewards for active animal-protection propaganda are the touching essays and drawings by African school children when they are allowed to discover *their own* wonderful fauna.

◂ Fleeing Giraffes (*Giraffa camelopardalis*) in the Serengeti, Tanganyika. The change from an amble (synchronous movement of both left legs and right legs) to a 30 m.p.h. run (alternate lifting of hind and front legs) is quite a problem of balance for an animal 15 feet high. With their awkward gait they hardly seem to move, but in fact each leap takes them 15 feet forwards. As they move, they whip their flanks with their tails and rock their necks to and fro like ships' masts on a rough sea.

➤ Prehistoric rock drawings from Libya prove that during the European glacial age the Sahara was a green savannah which supported big game and tribes of hunters. *Above*: Giraffe mother and young (at El Greiribat north of Murzuk). *Centre*: Elephant. *Below*: Ostriches (both from the valley of Gonoa in the Tibesti).

Two photographs from the Serengeti National Park in northern Tanganyika: Thomson's Gazelles and Boehm's Zebras browsing peacefully...

Through "Serengeti Shall Not Die" the whole world heard the battle cry of the zoologists Professor Bernhard and Michael Grzimek. The son gave his life for the animals of the Serengeti, but his father and all determined conservationists will continue to defend this wildlife sanctuary against all political interests. The controversy which rages around the Serengeti — the richest spot on earth for game and the home of 170 species of mammals — is symptomatic of the fate of wild animals throughout Africa. During the years that Tanganyika, a former German colony, was a British Mandate, the administration placed the wishes of the natives above the natural rights of wild animals, in order to keep the peace. Theoretically, Serengeti National Park was created in 1940, but it was not until 1951 that absolute immunity of wildlife was enforced by law. Yet the Masai were still allowed to graze their cattle in the Ngorongoro Crater and on its edge. This proud tribe, which lives on milk and cattle blood, would never have interfered with the wild ungulates had their herds not increased, through veterinary care, to 250,000 head. From then on, the Masai regarded the wild ruminants as competitors for grazing land and water and, by protests, succeeded in 1959 in getting the Ngorongoro Crater and other regions detached, for their own benefit, from the Serengeti Park.

...together while Lions sleep. Their resting places on the Seronera River are a big attraction for camera-safaris.

It is not lions that threaten the survival of zebras and antelopes in the Serengeti; it is man. Zoologists, by aerial surveys of wild game migrations, have proved that the new boundaries of the National Park — 4,450 square miles — are too confined. When the plains to the east of Lake Victoria have been grazed bare, the animals must, unfortunately, move to those regions where the enormous cattle herds of the Masai have already denuded the land and spoiled the water holes. Aerial observation has shown that the one million head of game which have been optimistically assumed to live in the Serengeti, have already decreased alarmingly. Grzimek's famous census revealed only 360,000 head of big game. Later statistics indicate a total of 416,150 subdivided thus: 100,000 wildebeest, 60,000 zebras, 40,000 Grant's gazelles, 200,000 Thomson's gazelles, 1,500 ostriches, 850 giraffes and 14,150 miscellaneous ungulates. What will happen next? In spite of considerable financial aid, the native agents of the Conservation Authority have not been very successful. Will the Government of independent Tanganyika proclaim the threatened regions "Masai Parks", thereby adopting Sir Julian Huxley's wise suggestion? Thus, a new sense of responsibility, and a share in the profits yielded by tourism, would convert the Masai from enemies into supporters of the good cause.

Three symbols of Africa! They crop different levels of vegetation, thus not competing with one another. When they meet at the watering places they respect the rights of the first-comers. Patience and harmony are the twin columns of this paradise... but the earth does not belong to the vegetarians alone.

This impressive picture was taken in Wankie National Park in Southern Rhodesia. In this very industrialised country of subtropical Africa there are no longer wild animals outside the 3 big and 11 small National Parks. Nature conservancy organisations have urged that Wankie Park, an area of 5,010 square miles, should soon be enlarged by the creation of an extension into neighbouring Bechuanaland. To-day, Wankie Park alone harbours 50 kinds of game, including 2,000 elephants.

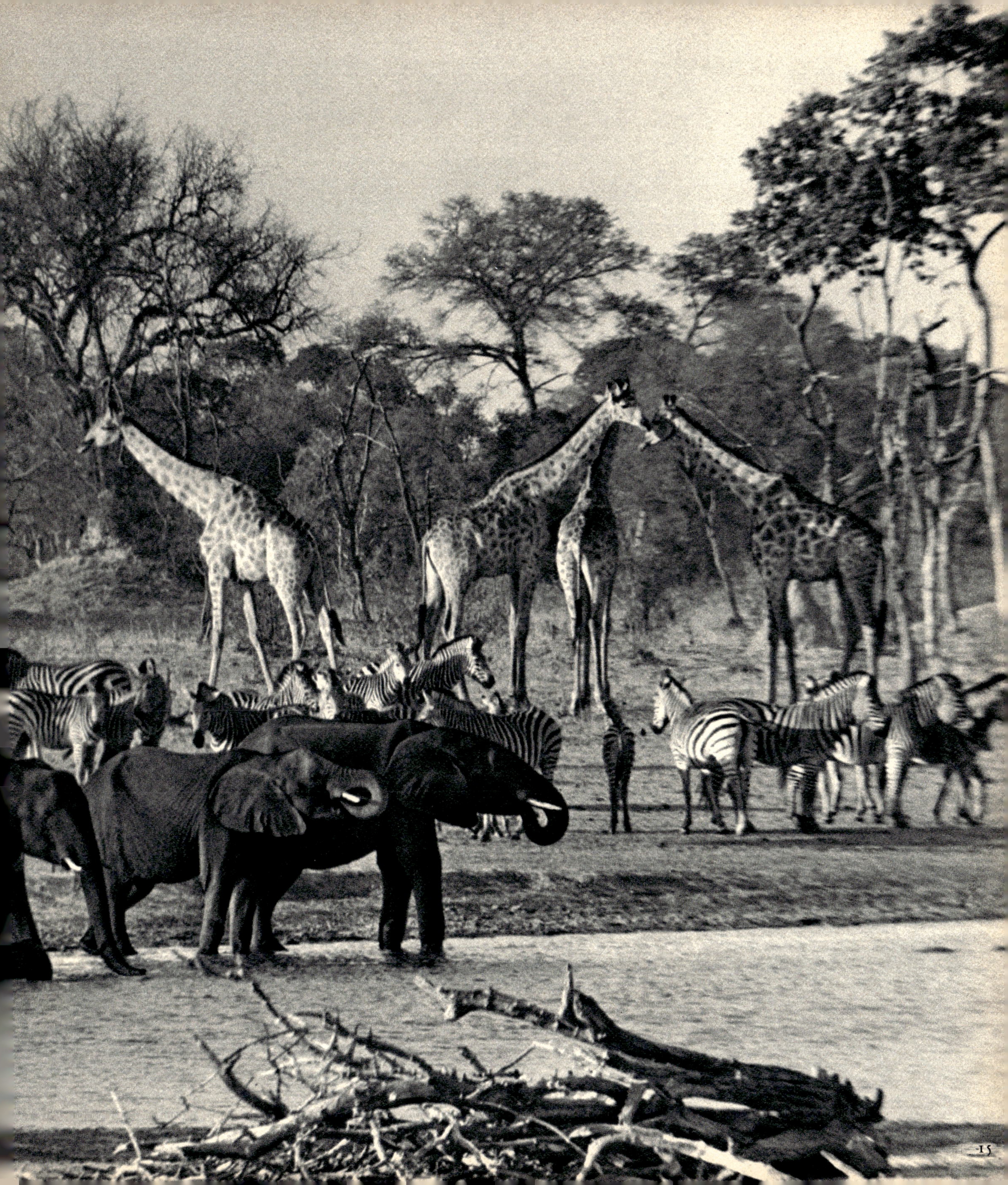

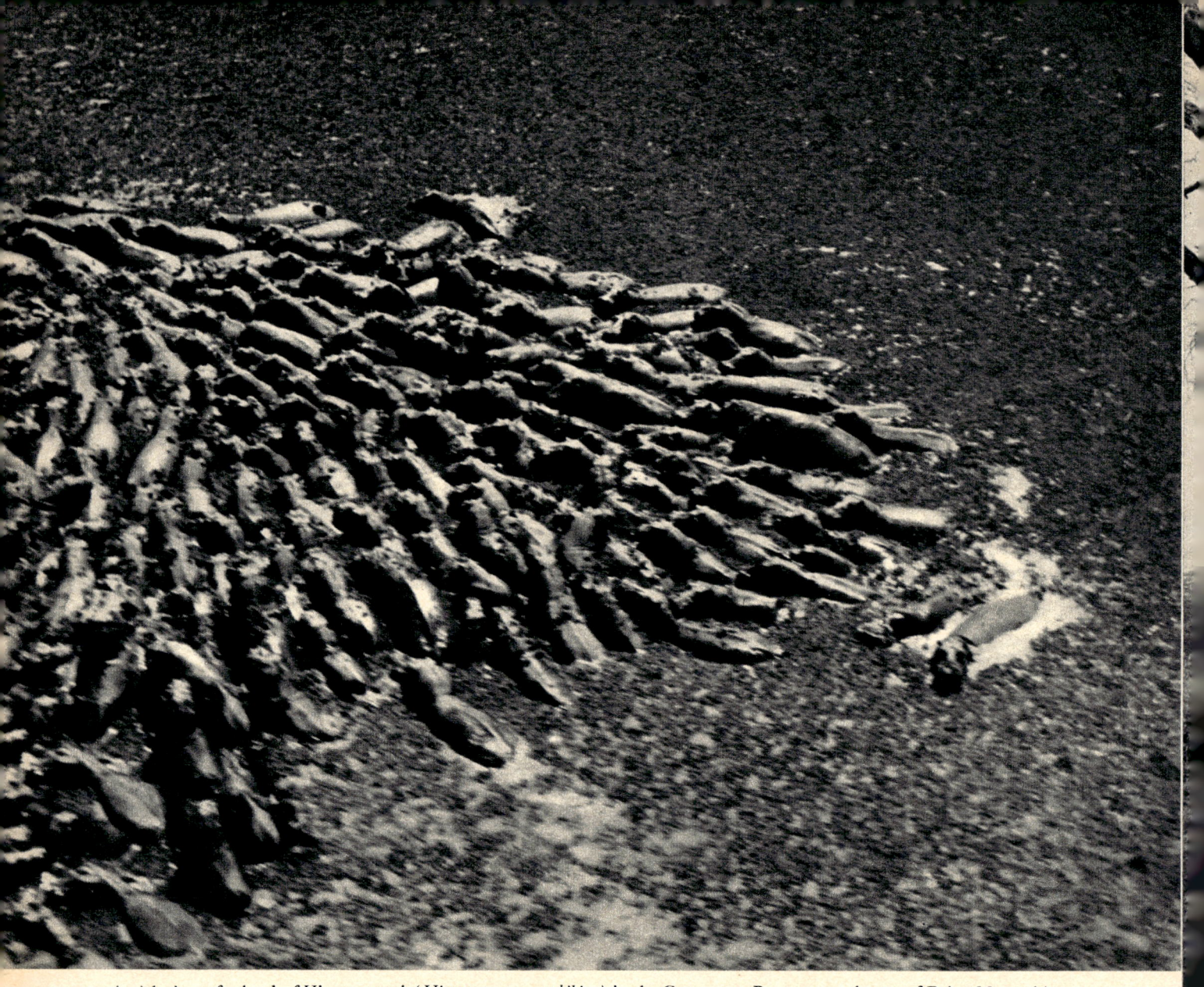

Aerial view of a herd of Hippopotami *(Hippopotamus amphibius)* in the Gorongoza Reserve, northwest of Beira, Mozambique.

From the air a mass of hippos looks like an island of flesh surrounded by a green carpet of Nile cabbage. During the dry season, with the general water level sinking, smaller groups of hippopotami merge into huge herds and crowd into the deepest pools. Extreme drought has often claimed hundreds of victims because the heavy giants cannot drag their bodies out of the sticky mud. When catastrophic drought and epidemics reduce the excess population in a reserve it seems as though Nature were in opposition to conservancy. When the carcasses float down rivers or lie on the banks, disdained by overfed predators and satiated vultures, the natives ask with reason how it makes sense to forbid hunting, while all this meat lies rotting away. Zoologists, game wardens, and ecologists have, therefore, made plans for a more utilitarian animal husbandry, whereby hippos can be both *protected a n d utilized*. In Queen Elizabeth Park in Uganda, the annual surplus of 1,000 hippos could be converted into dried or canned meat. The yearly production of some 1,400 tons of preserved meat would satisfy the proteïn requirements of 40,000 undernourished natives. At the same time, overgrazing and damage to the vegetation on river banks, to the detriment of other animals, would be prevented.

Elephants *(Loxodonta africana)* on migration: Aerial photograph from Mozambique (Gorongoza) showing only a small part of the herd.

A hundred years ago, some three million elephants still roamed the "Dark Continent". At a time when the grey giants still had the right of way, herds of a thousand head moved with the seasons, crossing mountain ranges, wading through swamps, and swimming rivers to reach the green savannahs during the rainy season, or to return to the forests with the onset of drought. There was enough food then for all the elephants in Africa. Each one ate his daily 5 to 8 hundredweight of green fodder on the way, and vegetation had time to recover after the trek had passed. But when the great change from virgin land to cultivation began, this idle feasting came to an end. When owners of trampled plantations cried out for revenge the ivory hunters rejoiced. Between 1880 and 1910 they shot over 2 million elephants. To-day, the depleted herds have grown again to about 300,000 head. From man's point of view, modern Africa cannot support more. The concentration of elephants in reserves damages much of the vegetation to their own detriment and that of other animals. In accord with the new "protection a n d utilisation" theory, the various countries are trying to adjust the surplus culling to local conditions and to use the meat for native consumption.

All elephants extant are the highly developed descendants of the 60-million-year old family of *Proboscidae*. Since the Tertiary era, 113 species have lived in every continent except Australia. *Moeritherium*, the original form, was not much bigger than a tapir and had neither trunk nor tusks, but had four incisors lengthened into fangs. As later forms grew larger and larger the proportionately growing fangs, or tusks, which were then bent backwards, hindered the animal when feeding; so the nose and upper lip evolved into a trunk. The giant of the primitive elephants was the 15-foot high *Dinotherium*, who was followed by the no less monstrous Swamp Elephant who scooped up waterweed with enormous shovel teeth. At the beginning of the glacial period, the clumsy Mastodons gave way to the shaggy Mammoths, until these 12-foot high creatures, the game of ice-age man, died by the thousands during the rainy period which followed the receding glaciers.

Elephants could only survive in areas that were unaffected by drastic changes in climate. The two living species, the African and the Asian, differ greatly — one might say as much as lion and tiger differ — but they resemble each other in their perfect adaptation to their respective habitats. The trunk, unique in the animal kingdom, has helped in the development of their mental faculties; inventiveness was necessary to utilise its many possibilities. The trunk is used not only to suck up water and to hold things, to pick fruit and break branches, but also serves as a trumpet, as a weapon, as a shower and a dust spray to keep insects off the skin, as a "helping hand" in case of accidents, as well as a weather vane — when the elephant blows dust skywards he can detect the direction of the wind. Tusks serve the grey giant not only as a weapon but also as a sturdy tool with which to uproot trees and loosen earth. On the move this colossus is surprisingly agile, and when necessary, he can be almost noiseless, for the elastic "cushions" of his huge feet take his weight like shock absorbers. The chief attribute of the African elephant is his big ears, without which he could hardly live in the hot savannah. He waves them like enormous fans to cool the blood in them, thus regulating his body temperature. But should *Sama* spread his ears like great sails and at the same time raise his trunk to test the air, he has discovered a hunter or a photographer and may charge at any moment.

Driving close to fighting bull Elephants in the open plain is far less dangerous than travelling on foot and meeting a herd in the thick undergrowth of a forest. This colour photograph, taken in the Manyara Reserve (Tanganyika) is, therefore, a rarity. ➤

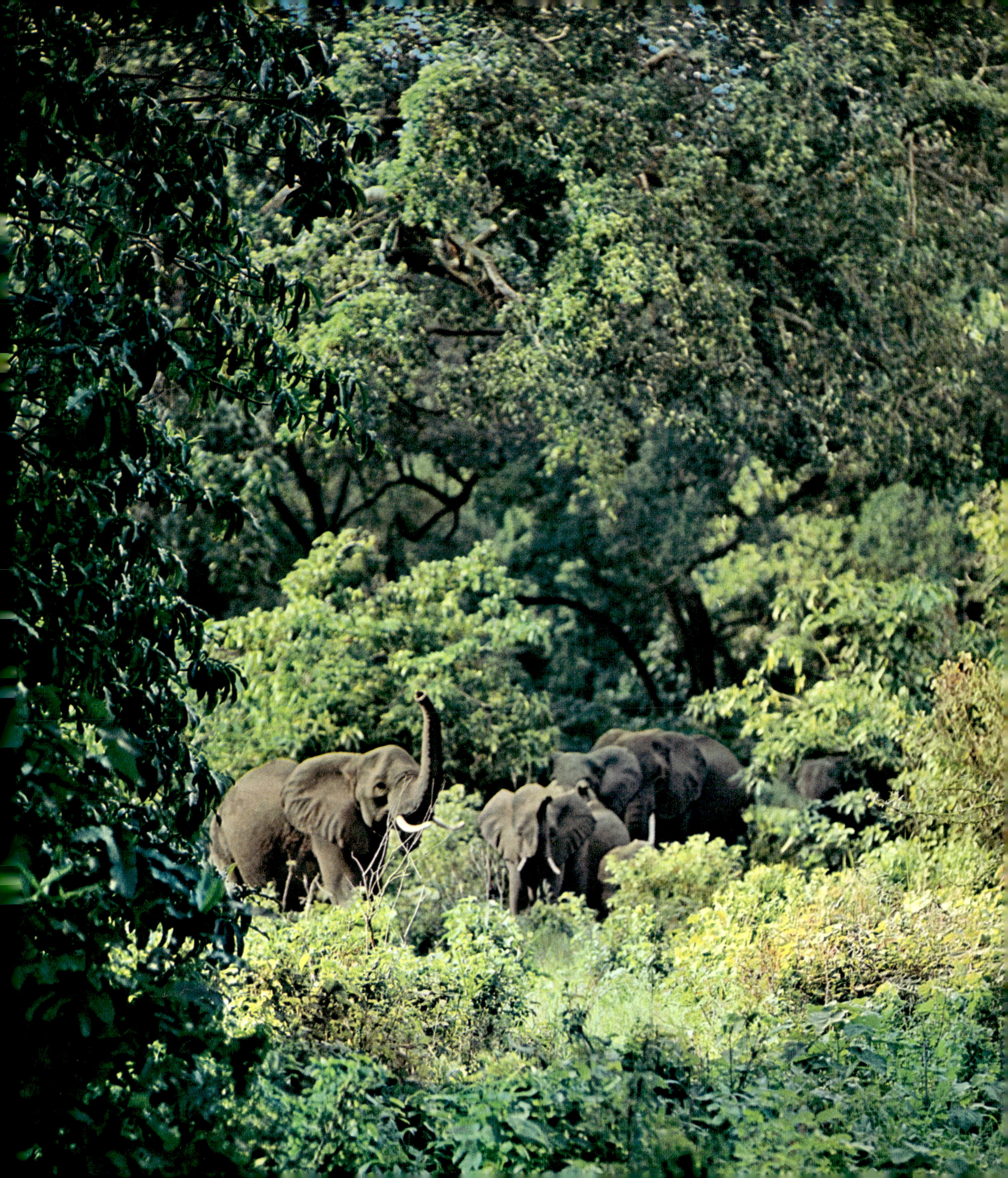

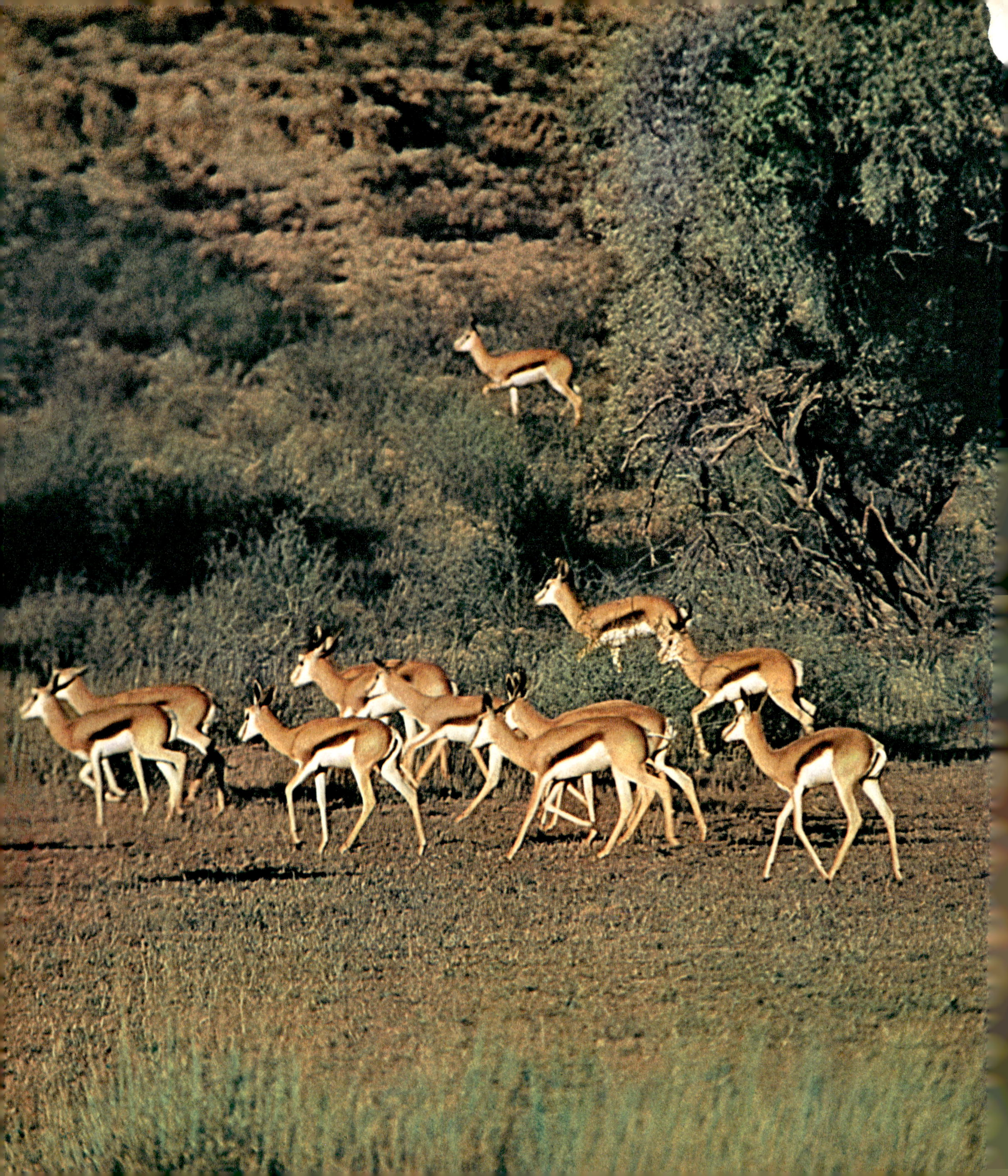

The Kalahari is green only during a few weeks of the year. Hundreds of thousands of Oryx and Springboks once lived in this South African semi-desert, and the vast natural phenomena of their migrations aroused the admiration of the first Boer settlers. To-day, in South West Africa and the Republic the survivors of this former abundance live in the great conservation zones of the *Kalahari Reservation* and the *Kalahari Gemsbok National Park*. Herds of 1,500 Springboks still wander there although the annual rainfall is usually only 5 ½ inches. During the dry season, on their way from one water pump to the next, the animals have nothing but the dew and chamma pumpkins to slake their thirst as they move slowly and steadily through the land. However, when these small gazelles scent one of the last remaining Kalahari lions and scatter in wild flight, they live up to their name (Springbok) with their graceful 12-foot leaps. — No lion can keep pace with the speed and endurance of fleeing gazelles. This sensational high-speed photograph shows a lioness attacking a herd of Impala. Springing suddenly from her hiding place she makes a hundred-yard dash, trying to separate one member of the herd from the rest. Generally lions avoid the risk of hunting singly; they hunt in groups, one lion going off to startle the herd and drive it towards his hidden companions.

↗ Fleeing Impalas *(Aepyceros melampus)*, East Africa.

◄ Springboks *(Antidorcas marsupialis)* in the Kalahari, South West Africa. In old French bestiaries the Springbok is called "the gazelle with a satchel": when excited Springboks display a ruff of white hair which normally is hidden in a fold of skin on their backs.

Under Kilimanjaro (19,565 feet) a lion *(Panthera leo)* watches his kill while the jackals wait at a respectful distance...

Ever since man has existed, he, the *Lord of the Earth*, has admired and feared the lion, the *King of the Beasts*. In fable, in heraldry and in sculpture, the lion is bound up with art and folklore since antiquity; the Bible calls him by ten different names. — During the glacial age the hunting grounds of the lion still extended over the whole of Europe and Asia. It was not until after 200 BC that he vanished from Greece, while in Rome the emperors let *leones* by the thousand fight and bleed to death in their arenas. Therefore, even in early times, the lions of North Africa were quickly decimated, while to-day "the strangler of herds" *(Sabaa)* or "the tumult provoker" *(Essed)*, as the Arabs once called him, spreads terror no more. Thus the Atlas or Berber Lion became extinct a hundred years ago, and only in the reservations south of the Sahara can *Simba* survive, for his true home is the steppe, where game is abundant. — The Negroes did not call the lion "*King of Beasts*", for they had already given this title to the elephant... Lions duly avoid elephants and rhinos and also shun encounters with buffaloes. If driven by hunger the carnivore will attack even large prey and take the risk of having his bones broken by a kicking bull giraffe...

... the following day the vultures will have the remainder, while the giraffes move on, less the one that had to die yesterday.

...nevertheless there are lions who like to lie in wait at regular crossing places of giraffes. The long-necks can keep up a speed of 30 m.p.h. for only a few minutes of their flight. Taken unawares, young or weakened giraffes especially are easily put off balance so that they stumble, fall and break their necks. When that happens the lion has to jump aside so that he is not crushed by the weight of his falling prey. The panting victor first refreshes himself with the blood and intestines and then gorges himself on 30 to 60 pounds of flesh. As he cannot deal alone with what is left, he willingly allows the others of his tribe to have their share.

Meanwhile, the jackals wait patiently nearby. The banquet for the carrion eaters begins only when the lions have fully satisfied their appetite. All night the cadaver is surrounded by hyaenas, and during the next day it is covered with vultures... but the last shreds are left to the ever-present ants. One life has been extinguished to fan the vital spark in other creatures — only man kills senselessly. The giraffes hardly notice the loss from the herd, and continue to follow the same trail where the same dangers lie in wait. In the wild, "yesterday" and "to-morrow" have no meaning. Animals give themselves up entirely to the beautiful, irretrievable "to-day".

White-backed Vultures *(Gyps ruppellii)* and African Vultures *(Gyps africanus)* in the Wankie National Park, Southern Rhodesia.

"Vulture trees" are a characteristic of the African landscape: it is not only in the wilderness where the services of these carrion birds are needed. Proper sanitation is known only to a small part of the Dark Continent, and in many habitations these feathered cleaners and scavengers are even nowadays the only effective substitute for modern methods of hygiene and sewage disposal. Ancient civilised peoples and primitive hunting tribes alike held the ugly servants of death in awe, knowing full well that only the vultures could prevent the accumulation of filth round their dwellings. The little White Egyptian Vultures nest in the middle of the villages where they eat everything — even the most unspeakable offal — and feed their young on regurgitated garbage. The great Griffon Vulture, White-backed Vulture, King Vulture and Bearded Vulture, however, keep their distance, building their nests on the steep sides of the mountains or in high trees out in the wilderness. From these strongholds they fly in groups, gliding on their 8-foot wing-span, to spy out every cadaver in the steppe. As soon as one vulture lands, the others follow in a steep dive. When these rapacious hosts have gorged their crops, nothing remains of the carrion to pollute the air or to become the birthplace of an epidemic.

At dusk the Pelicans *(Pelecanus rufescens)* retire to their tree dormitories. Lake Naivasha, Kenya.

There exists in man the tendency to see reflected in all other creatures some aspect of his own character, and while he dreads the vulture as a symbol of death, he loves the pelican for being good-natured and humorous. Legend, too, gives only praise to these great birds. The Muslims believe that, ordered by Allah, the pelicans once brought water in their beak pouches for the building of the Kaaba in Mecca. In spite of all the adulation, bird hunters and egg robbers have brutally decimated the flocks of pelicans. In the quiet bays along the Red Sea and on the Nile, where a hundred years ago these birds occupied many square miles, to-day only a few thousand remain to breed. Along treeless shores they will build their nests in the rushes, although they prefer to nest at a safe height, even if they have to fly long distances to the water to get their daily 25 pounds of fish for the family. Communal fishing starts early in the morning. Then until the afternoon the whole colony devotes itself to the pleasure of preening their feathers. In the early evening they set out again to fish, forming a chain to drive their silver prey into the shallow water where every bird can fill its pouch to its heart's content. Because of their air-retaining plumage and their bone structure, pelicans of the Old World cannot dive for the fish in deep waters like their cousins on the coasts of Latin America.

Sentry at dusk. An Olive Baboon *(Papio anubis)* on a thorn acacia in the Nairobi National Park, Kenya.

The baboons of East Africa are driven to their sleeping quarters in the trees long before dusk by a primeval terror of the dangers of the night. Their cousins, the mountain-dwelling Abyssinian Hamadryads and the South African Chacmas, retire to inaccessible, high rocky caves. However, quiet undisturbed sleep is unattainable in either place and so a third of the horde is always keeping watch. Not only the threat of predators and snakes frightens the sleepers in the trees: they are also plagued by an atavistic nightmare of "falling down". When morning comes they feel unrefreshed and angry screeching starts up immediately. After much bending and stretching they climb down from the trees and form themselves into an organised troupe. Then the horde, comprising anything from 80 to 200 animals, moves off, the females with their infants clutched to their bodies, marching safely in the middle, together with males of the highest rank. Vanguard, rearguard and protective flanks are made up of youngsters and males of the lower rank. No baboon dares to cross open ground without the security which is offered by such military discipline.

Carefree climbing and playful jumping. Baboons *(Papio cynocephalus)* in the Gorongoza Reservation, Mozambique.

From whatever direction danger strikes, a rank of growling male baboons will form instantly between the attackers and the troupe. Even bloodthirsty Hunting Dogs retreat before a superior force of these snarling, death-defying creatures. After such encounters the baboons indulge in an excited palaver; their language even has special warning sounds for specific enemies. Baboons consider cheetahs to be comparatively harmless, but a battle with a leopard usually leaves several of the front-line defenders dead. Any sign of a lion will send them screaming to the safety of the trees; this is the reason why baboons shun treeless steppes like the plague. A look-out on a high tree can anticipate danger. Antelopes, zebra and wart-hogs are aware of this and like to browse in the neighbourhood of monkeys — the baboons in their turn profiting from the more acute sense of smell of such neighbours. Before the heat of high noon the baboons move on to their own particular tree-surrounded water-hole. If harmless animals are already drinking there, the troupe throws caution to the wind, but if the scene is deserted, great care is exercised. The thirsty horde will wait in trees until scouts report "All clear of lions".

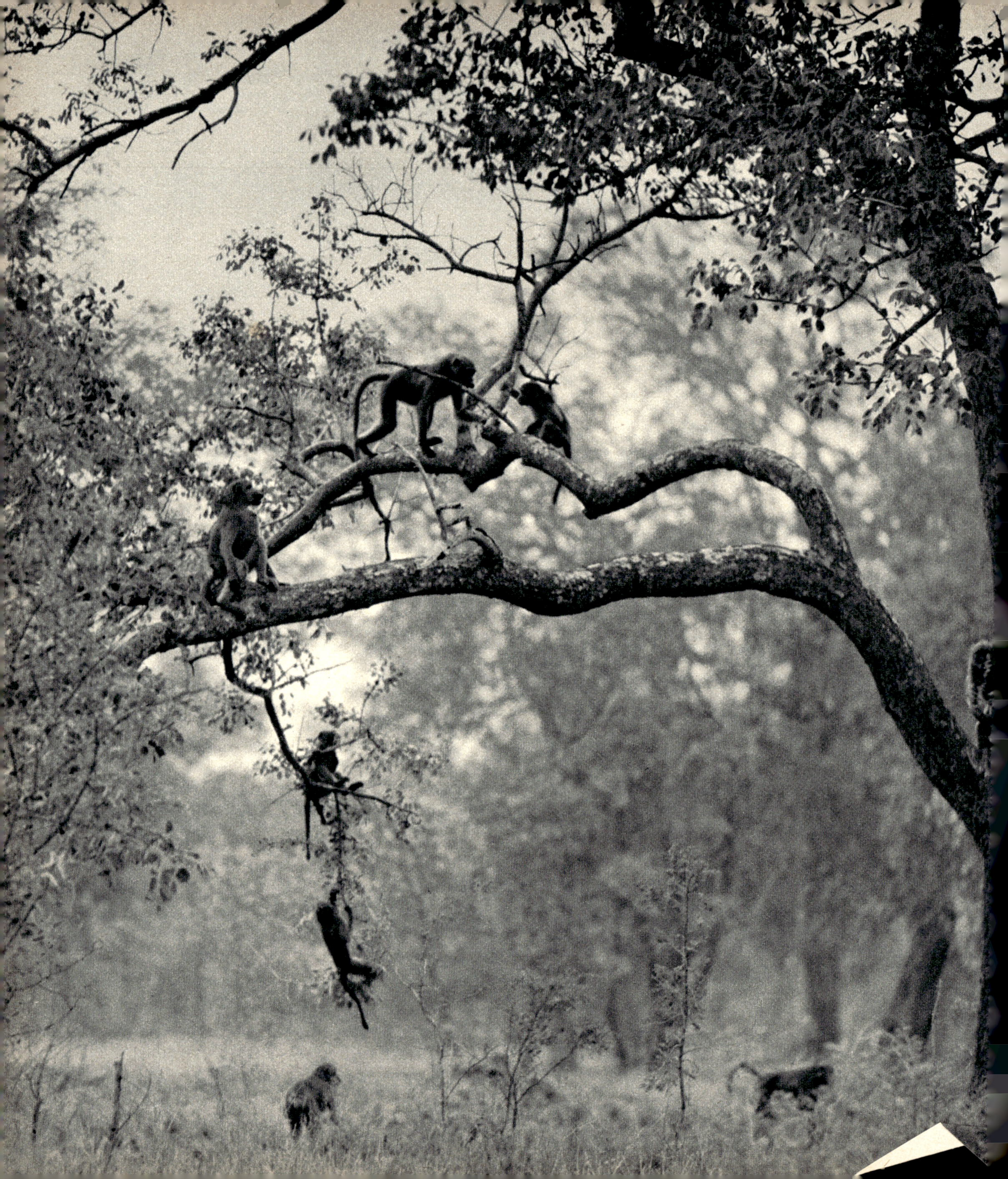

Only in childhood are baboons allowed to be playful; but the graceful Vervet monkeys remain so throughout their whole lives. In their loose family groups, the latter live in friendly relationship, whereas the baboons have to submit to the authority of higher rank. When baboons and Green monkeys meet, the weaker species, with foresight, flee out on to the thinnest branches. As long as both find sufficient green-stuff, fruit and insects, baboons tolerate messmates in their territory. Should these delicacies become rare, a troupe of baboons will brutally drive the Vervets away, even eating their wounded. But neither is popular with farmers. Again and again they organise raids on orchards and plantations, not only to satisfy their hunger but, it would seem, out of sheer wanton destructiveness. When the noisy gang is taken by surprise they hurry to stuff their cheek pouches full and carry away armfuls of maize or grapes.

◄ Baboon mothers with their unruly offspring in the Kruger National Park, Transvaal.

➤ Vervet or Green Monkey (*Cercopithecus aethiops*), Kenya.

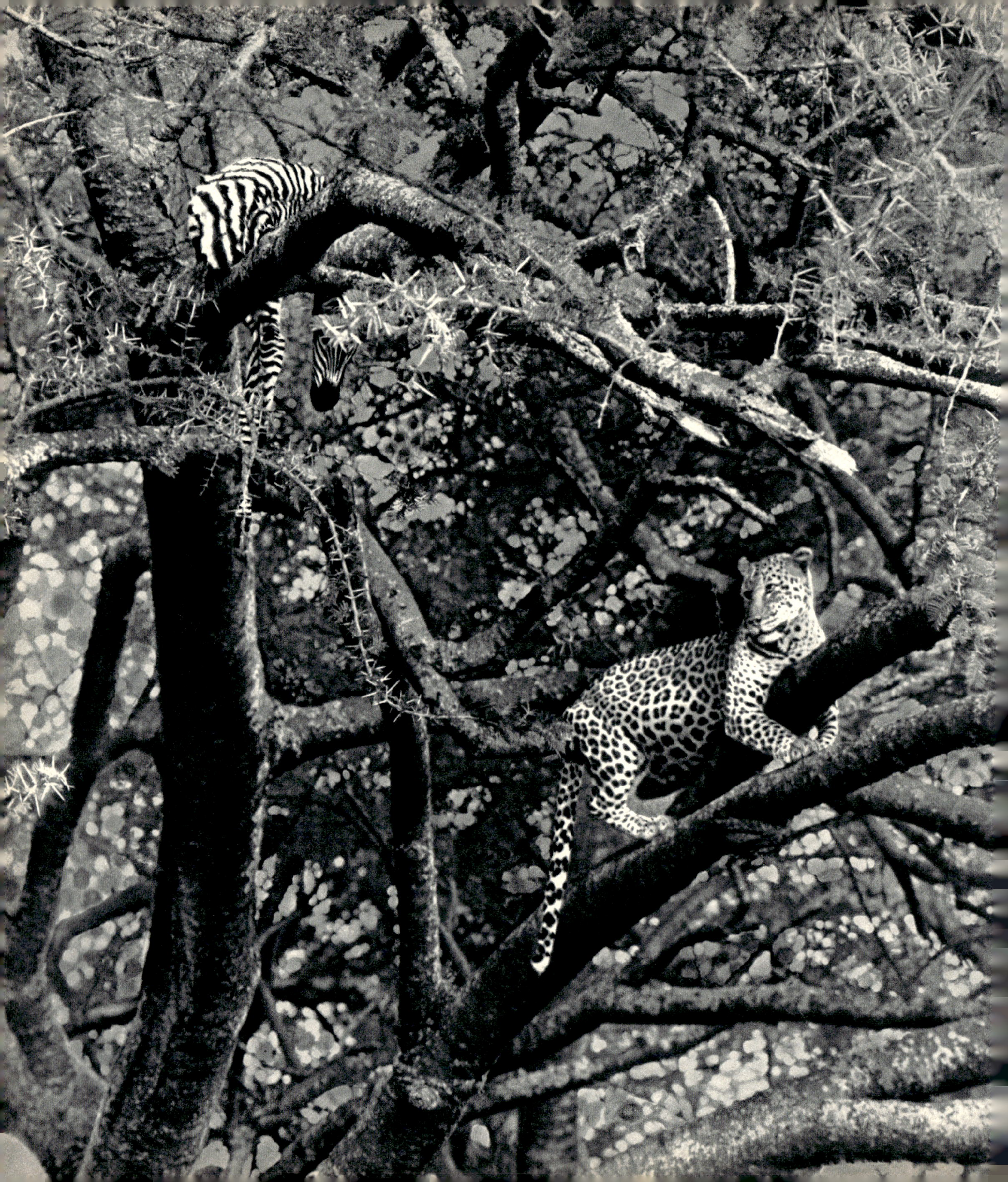

Plagues of monkeys are known only in places where there are no leopards. Farmers learned too late that to let the leopard take a few sheep or calves, was not too great a price to pay for reducing the numbers of shameless harvest-thieving monkeys. Natives understood the connection but did not wish to make the sacrifice. On the one hand, they set traps for the cattle-thief, yet on the other, they buried a piece of leopard skin to keep baboons away from their fields. It is understandable that they should have feared the sly cats which inflicted terror on whole villages, when occasionally "mistaking" a crawling baby for a small baboon. But certain tribes should have blamed themselves: Being afraid of death and disease, they abandoned their aged and sick out in the bush... and thus the leopard was educated to become a man-eater. Apart from such temptations the leopard hunts fairly, striking down his victims quickly and painlessly with one well-aimed leap. Only rarely does he attack a full-grown animal, for his prey must always be light enough for him to hide it in a tree beyond the reach of lions and hyaenas.

Two scenes from the life of *Panthera pardus*, in the Serengeti. ➤ The supple, camouflaged hunter glides down a tree trunk. ◂ Satiated and lazy he guards his food reserve, a zebra foal, in a thorn tree.

For centuries natives have fought the leopard by simple means. With bleating lambs they lured him to baited traps, or arranged strings on the trails near water-holes in such a way, that on touching the strings, poisoned arrows would be released from concealed bows. By these methods *Chiru* was kept within bounds but not exterminated. Only when the white hunters came were these lithe cats shot in their thousands, yet because they saturated the market the hunters received only low prices for the beautiful skins. — People have always been fascinated by leopard skins with their black rosettes on a golden ground. Because many pure black panthers occur in India and Abyssinia it was believed in Europe in the Middle Ages that the leopard was a cross between a panther and a lioness, or a lion and a pantheress. In fact the camouflaging spots are the true colouring of leopards while the black panther is a mutation, for Nature knows no hybridisation between lions and leopards. However, it has happened in zoological gardens... a short time ago spotted "Leopons" with the suggestion of a lion's mane were born in Japan. Colour variations in the leopard are not exceptional: the heavier forest and mountain leopards are golden or ochre coloured with big black spots ➤ ; the smaller leopards of the plains have light yellow ground colouring which shines through the centres of the black rosettes. ⋎

➤ Gorged to bursting point, the leopard's belly hangs between the branches of a yellow thorn tree. This particular leopard has experienced how man's outlook has changed during the last decade. Because he lived in a settled area with little game he made himself unpopular, being a cattle-thief. He was not shot but caught by game wardens, and transported over 600 miles to the Tsavo National Park in South Kenya where he now lives as a free hunter.

⋏ Whether domestic or wild — the young of the feline race are carried by the scruff of the neck so gently that one forgets all about the parent's dangerous fangs.

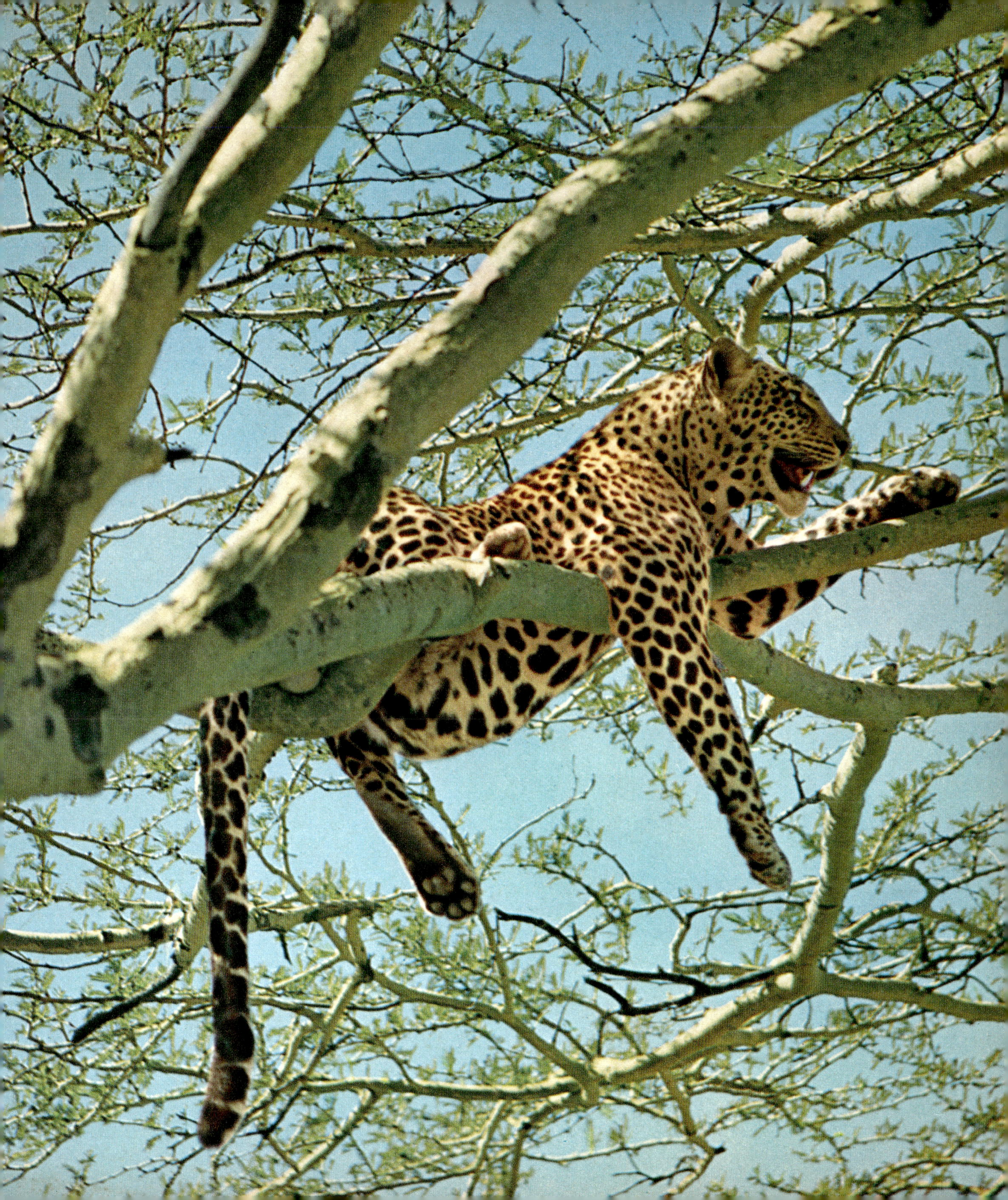

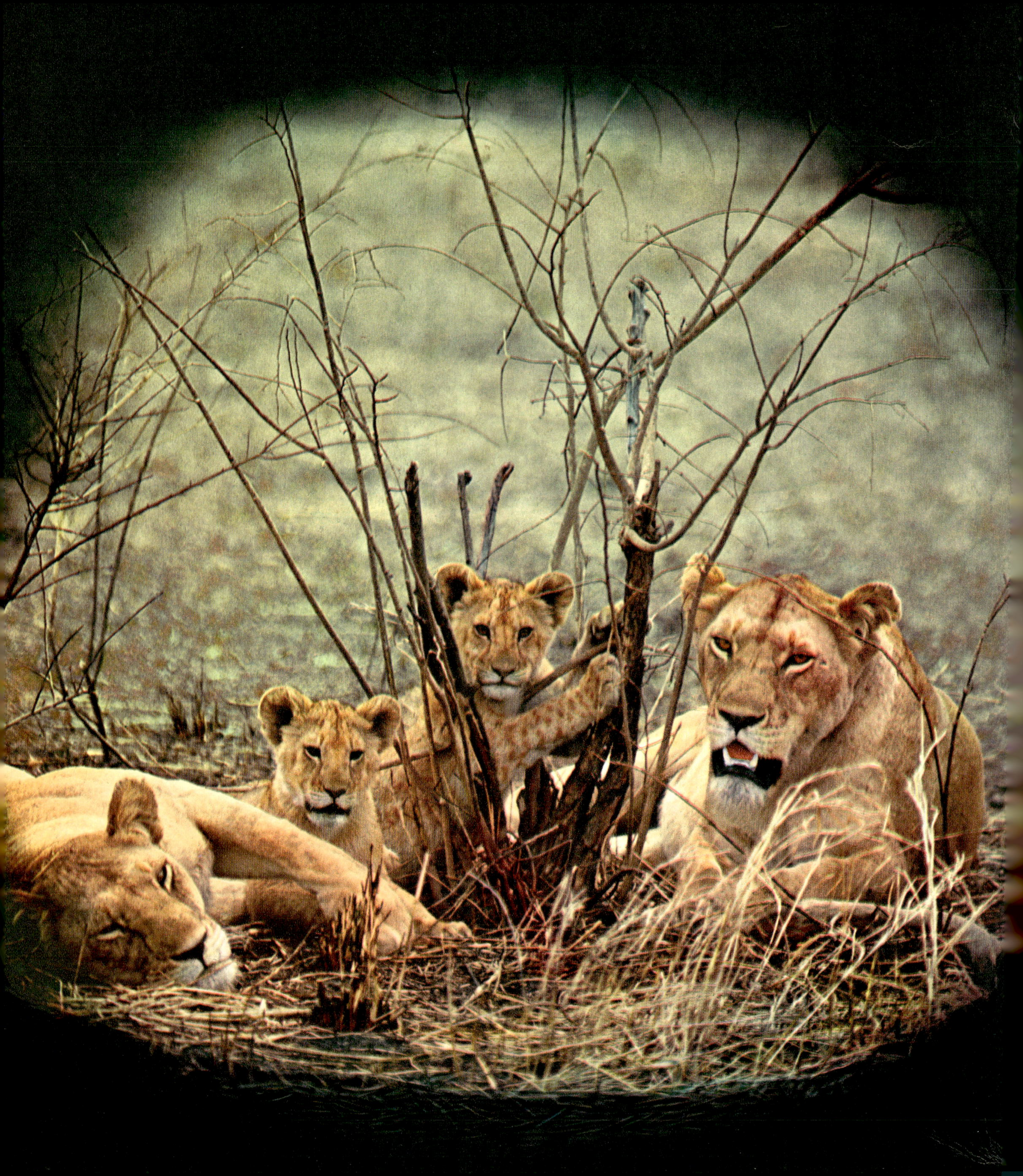

Because lions are the only members of the cat tribe to live in groups, a pregnant lioness can usually count on help. In the last weeks of a gestation period, lasting 102 to 112 days, other lionesses will bring her food, and when she retires to a cave or into the bush to give birth, an "aunt" may soon appear to guard the cubs. Difficulties arise in territories where only a few lions live as isolated couples. If the male has been killed or wounded and there is no one to provide food for the family, the lioness herself has to hunt; fortunately she is able to retract her vulnerable mammary glands. But if a lioness should be overtaken by labour far from any cover or the shelter of a cave, she will soon be surrounded by hyaenas. If, by chance, a game warden passes by, he may with a few shots and some cans of water provide the stricken lioness with food and drink and scare away the menace.

Lion cubs are at first quite helpless and only begin to stumble around in their second month. It is some time before they make the acquaintance of their father, and then he will suffer their clumsy games patiently, and growls only when they pull his mane too hard. At 6 weeks they already begin to lick and worry at the fur of the prey, but it is not until the 6th to 8th month that their mother's milk dries up completely. At this time the cubs slowly loose their baby spots, although the mane of the males does not grow before the third year. During all this period the playful offspring are dependent on their mother's care and teaching. For this reason lions in the wild produce young only every three years.

◄ The long-focus lens picks out an idyllic tableau of a lion family group.

▲ This lioness carries a gnu calf to her hiding place. Lions can carry weights only up to that of a medium-sized antelope. It takes all their strength to drag larger animals a few yards. Exaggerated reports that lions were supposed to have carried full-grown cattle over 10-feet-high thorn hedges stem from the fact that lions which have penetrated a kraal stampede the cattle until one of them leaps over the hedge and is killed by other lions waiting outside. With nothing to carry a lion can leap across a chasm 36 feet wide.

Panthera leo at the kill. The svelte lioness and the muscular lion show their excitement by the nervous twitching of their tails.

Although we may be horrified at the sight of a gory predator meal, we must remember that everywhere, at every second, millions of small and big predators are killing, each after its own fashion, so that life may continue. They all gorge themselves with the same elementary greed on an organism that has become food. Whether the victim be a midge or a zebra ... death comes too swiftly to be painful. The lion is a master of surprise attack. He fells small antelopes with one blow of his paw and immediately cuts the throat with a single bite. A zebra he tries to throw with one leap, dragging its head down so that it falls and breaks its neck at once. Only young lions who lost their teacher too early in life are sometimes driven by hunger to prey for food before their hunting and killing technique is sufficiently developed. Then, the victim may suffer; but all animals in the wild seem to be born with an inherent submission to fate. — It has been calculated that a troupe of 4 or 5 lions kill about 80 to 90 animals annually. That is to say one lion kills only about 19 animals in a year. Therefore he does not hunt every day. When he is satiated and dozes in the shade zebras and antelopes browse quite close to him.

When the lion arrives to quench his thirst the screeching monkeys in the trees warn all other animals to stay away.

A lion in his prime tends to behave as an absolute monarch. To the chief of the clan belong the best bits of the feast, even if he has not actually contributed to the success of the hunt. When lions press round a kill cuffs are dealt out to the younger ones who do not respect the privileges of the master. But should a seven-year-old threaten to become a rival, he is driven not only away from the kill, but right out of the family group. It sometimes happens that during the mating season an even stronger lion will wander in, and after a furious battle, take over the clan. The vanquished chief slinks away and will loose weight visibly because during his comfortable life as pasha he has lost his cunning as a hunter. This rivalry among lions accounts for senile lonely males soon ending up in the stomachs of Wild Dogs, while the group continues to support lionesses weakened by age. But a healthy lion is a truly majestic creature. After dusk when he raises his voice all animals are silenced; only from the far distance other lions answer. A roaring lion lowers his head to the ground, and the sound carries for miles and rumbles in the distance like thunder. With this solemn, almost ritual demonstration the *King of Beasts* informs his kindred: "As far as my voice carries, this is my territory."

Two exceptional photographs taken in the Amboseli Reserve, Kenya. A satiated lion sleeps near his giraffe kill which he guarded for 3 days...

If one compares earlier eye-witness accounts with those of to-day it might well be believed that lions have changed their character during the last hundred years. However, the "rapacious beasts" have not suddenly become "tame photographic models"; it is man's attitude towards them that has radically altered. To the first white settlers a lion hunt was indeed full of danger. Ramming powder sacks and percussion caps into a muzzle loader while on horseback, the hunter often suffered the fate of the vanquished. When these white marksmen moved in, the lions, who had paid little attention to the natives, learned to fear man as a dangerous enemy. — From time immemorial the initiation rite into lion hunting was a test of courage for the Masai youth. Many days before the ceremony scouts went out to track down a *Simba*. In the meantime, the young initiates built up their strength with all kinds of magic brews. Finally 20 to 30 of these would-be heroes set out naked, without any impeding finery, to surround the lion. Although spear thrusts would suffice, proof of manhood required that the lion killer should first jump on to the beast or pull its tail. — The Arabs, however, used to set traps in the middle of their encampment and divide the heart of *Essed* among the boys so that they, too, should become strong and courageous. Every member of the tribe carried some hairs from the mane which were supposed to give protection in case of attack by lions.

...while an angry lioness drives off a jackal who had dared to come too soon to claim his usual right to the bones and remains.

Angered by big-game hunters, an unusual number of East African lions turned into man-eaters at the end of the 19th century. When the Mombasa-Arusha Railway was built, the assaults along the track, which now runs through the Tsavo National Park, made tragic headlines all over the world. The same occurred in 1924, during the building of the Uganda Railway, when 84 labourers fell prey to the lions. Transgression on such a large scale is rare. Indeed, it happens only when a lion becomes unfit to hunt and sets a bad example, or when healthy lions acquire a taste for easy game, as they did with wounded during the First World War in the German East African battles.

The twenties and thirties were the worst decades for all game of the plains, carnivores and ruminants alike, for then the hunters, mounted in jeeps and armed with modern rifles, began shooting from their travelling fortresses, killing off in a few hours more creatures than they could have stalked in a month. To-day, hunting from cars is prohibited and the new generation of lions, growing up in the safety of reservations, allow Landrovers to come quite close, seemingly regarding the "creature on wheels" as completely harmless. Now, in the Amboseli National Reservation, hundreds of tourists take souvenir pictures of apparently tame lions, but only game wardens and local photographers have enough time and patience to come across such real-life camera studies.

Half-grown Cheetahs (*Acinonyx jubatus*) lurk playfully beside the road in the Kruger National Park, Transvaal.

The cheetah is an oddity among the big cats. His lithe body combines the best characteristics of both the dog and the cat, while his movements give the impression of a long-legged greyhound in a leopard skin. He is the only cat who cannot retract his claws, and the points, therefore get worn down like those of a dog. He has lost also much of the cat's ability to climb and for this reason avoids the dense forest. He is so fast and agile that cover for protection is unnecessary and he does not shun the daylight. At one time his hunting grounds extended over the wide steppes and savannahs of the whole of Africa, Mesopotamia, Persia and India, but now this much-hunted animal is rarer in the reservations than the lion. In the Kruger National Park one can count 1,000 lions but only 160 cheetahs, while their Asiatic cousins have found a last sanctuary in Turkmenistan. The cheetah would be able to support himself everywhere because he never hunts with lust for killing but only because of hunger; nor does he carry his prey away, but savours it on the spot, first gorging himself with blood and "vegetables" — the grass-filled intestines. Unlike the lion or panther he never returns to a kill.

Four young Cheetahs fall hungrily upon a Thomson's Gazelle that their mother has just killed for them.

Young cheetahs have to go through a long training period before they can master the peculiar hunting methods of their kind. When three or four half-grown young go out hunting with their mother they are not distinguishable from her by their size but only in their behaviour. Like all children they are easily diverted and will play with each other or chase their tails rather than concentrate on the prey. Here and there they may catch a hare or a bird on the ground but the main meal must be provided by the parent. From her example the young learn not to lie in wait or stalk, but to rely on speed in the chase. The cheetah first moves up to a game trail and follows a herd of antelope at a distance of about 300 feet, without apparent interest. As soon as she has selected a victim her gait changes from an easy lope to a bound of lightning speed. Like a released arrow she overtakes even Thomson's gazelles fleeing at 40 m.p.h., but she does not spring at her prey as big cats usually do. She throws a small gazelle down with blows from her paws and then goes for her prey's throat. In contrast to the abundance of 500,000 Thomson's gazelles in East Africa hardly 1,000 cheetahs remain.

Is the cheetah really the fastest mammal on earth? Sceptics checking the often-reported speed of 85 m.p.h. against the speedometer of a Landrover have found that the wonder-animal barely touched 30 m.p.h. Of course, such calculations are worthless because only the hunting fever spurs the cheetah to his fastest sprint. When about to kill he will accelerate to 34 yards a second, nearly 70 m.p.h., but as this effort pays only when close to the prey, he needs such speed for distances of not more than 300 to 500 yards. He is no marathon runner like the African Hunting Dog; he cannot, indeed, he does not want to, run his victim to a standstill. If he miscalculates his spurt he has to give up and rest. He is not an engine, but an animal, and one can measure his performance with a stopwatch, but not with a tachometer. The ancient Egyptians, Indian Princes, and Mongol rulers knew that their trained "hunting-leopards" were no hounds of the chase. They carried their cheetah hooded on horseback and removed the hood only when game was in sight. Then the rested cheetah took off like the wind after the fleeing herd and made sure of a kill for his lord and master.

➤ A cheetah, unaware of the observer, slakes his thirst at Lake Naivasha, Kenya. He has no urge to take to the water. Cheetahs swim only from absolute necessity.

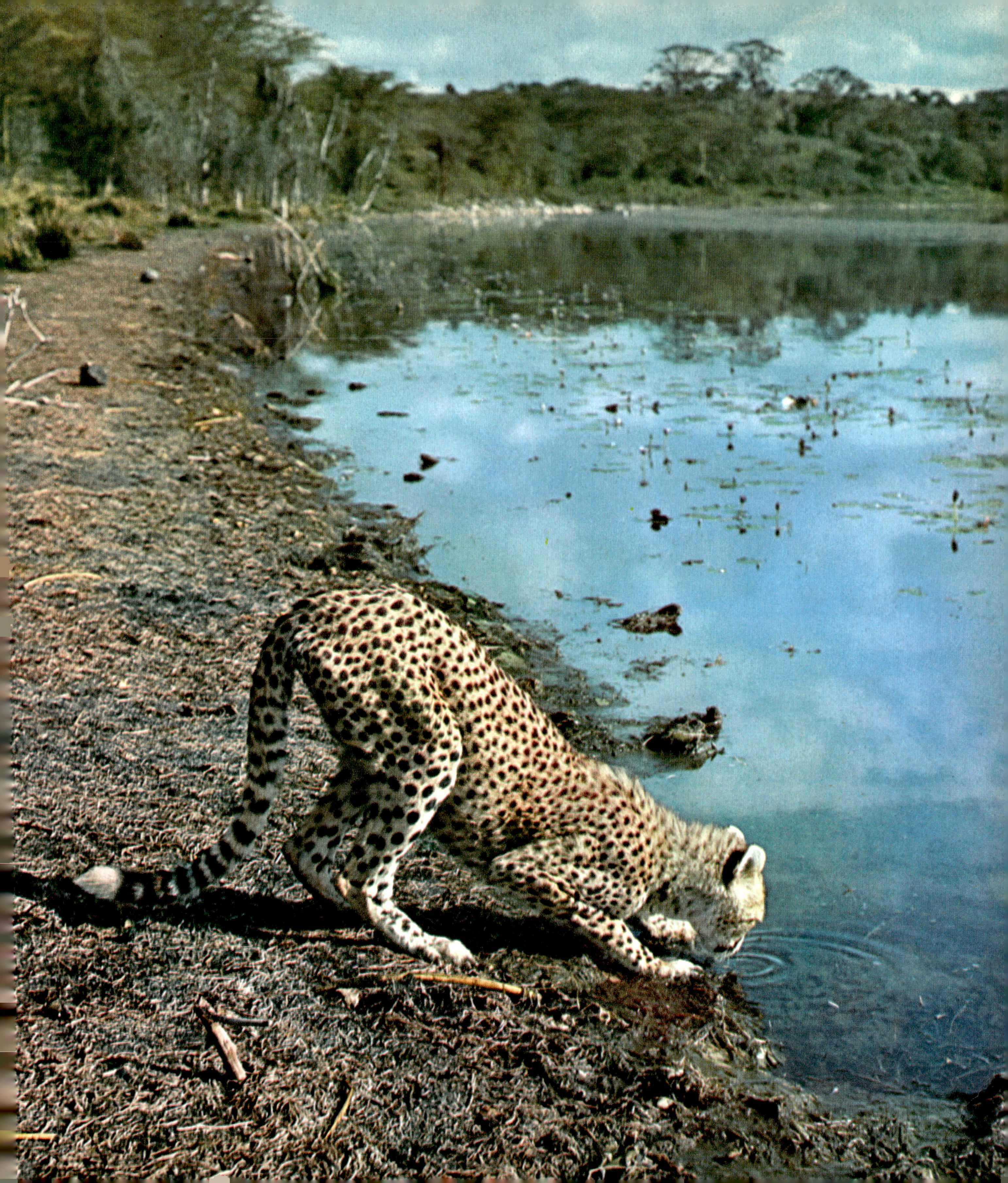

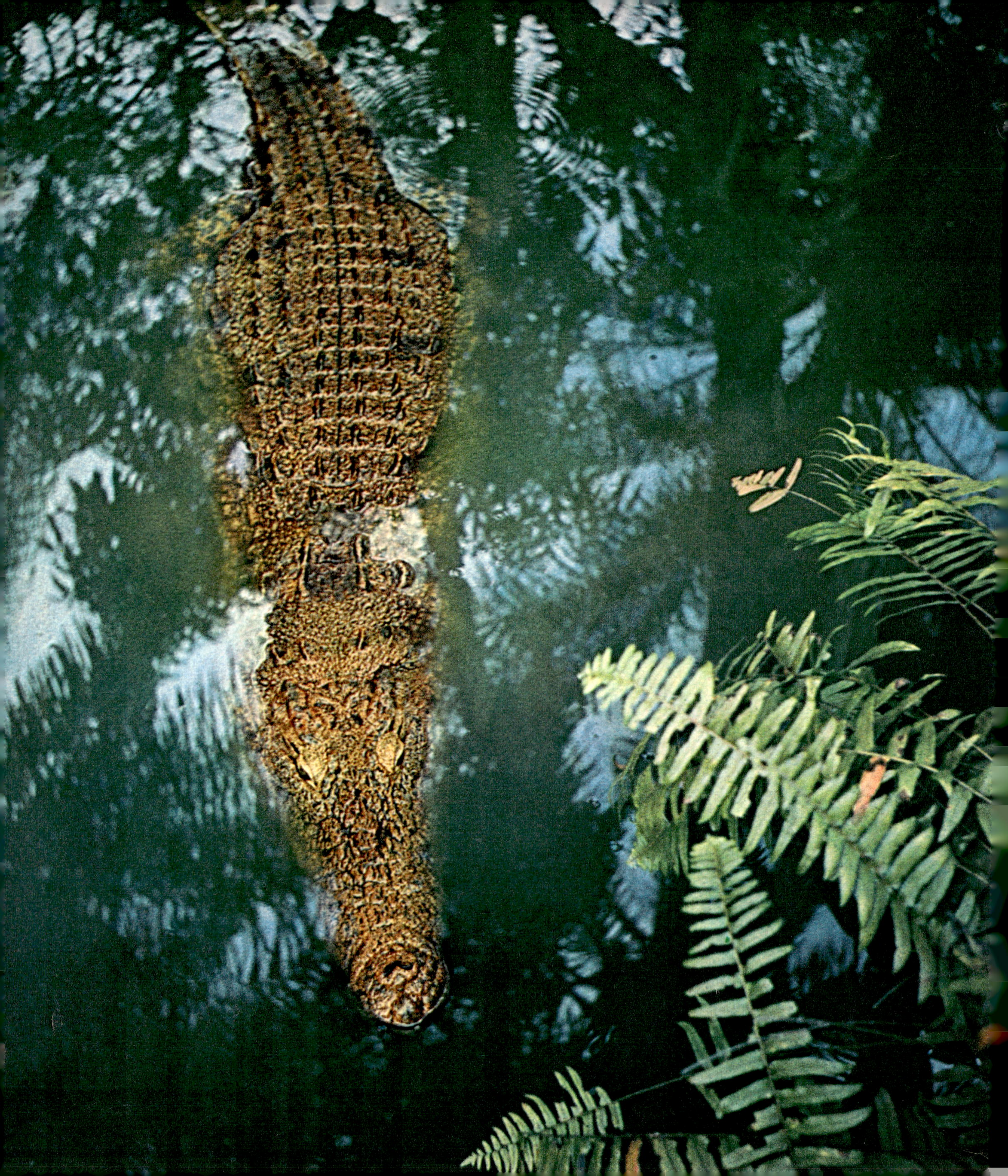

The great predatory reptiles were, for millions of years, masters of the world. Their last descendants are few, but a fully-grown crocodile is still a master in its "territory", too powerful to be threatened by enemies in the animal kingdom. In the dawn of civilisation even Man felt no animosity towards crocodiles, as mummified reptiles found in Egypt and images of the crocodile-headed god Sobek prove. On the islands of the great East African lakes there still live negro tribes who try to lure their "own" particular crocodiles ashore for play, by singing traditional songs which have a certain hypnotic quality. Only the threat of modern firearms has thinned the ranks of these armour-plated reptiles. In Egypt hardly any are left, and in South Africa they have been exterminated. In the African tropics, too, hunters no longer leave the green crocodile time enough to grow to the age of 80 years and a length of 26 feet like his less persecuted cousins in Madagascar. Even young specimens have to give their lives and skins for the leather industry, and as long as there are no laws to protect the last amphibious saurians, their survival as a species cannot be guaranteed. This is the more alarming since Nature herself takes her toll from the family of crocodiles, and only a few reach maturity. Although the female watches over the 30 to 50 eggs she buries in the sand or in fermenting heaps of leaves, Mongooses and Monitors plunder as much as they can. When the foot-long, newly-hatched crocodile infants crawl into the water, either alone or led by their mother, most of their number end up in the jaws of their own kind, are swallowed by Marabus and Whale-headed storks or carried away by other predatory birds. The survivors grow about a foot each year but are sexually mature only when they reach 8 feet, 7 to 10 years old. The rate of growth then slows down but does not stop completely even in old age, unless a bullet should end the life of the great beast sooner.

◄ Blunt-nosed Crocodile *(Osteolaemus t. osborni)* in a quiet backwater of the River Congo below the Stanley Falls. These crocodiles live exclusively on fish and crayfish and grow no longer than 6 feet.

▲ Newly-hatched African Crocodile *(Crocodylus niloticus)*. Hatching out in the heat of the sun, the tiny crocodiles croak inside the egg to attract their mother's attention. The negroes imitate these infant voices in the hypnotic songs referred to above. In the water the young at first paddle vertically like seahorses, but later on they swallow stones to adjust their balance.

An African crocodile *(Crocodylus niloticus)* comes back to its booty — a gnu — which it killed some days before. Wankie National Park, Southern Rhodesia.

A hungry African Crocodile is a cunning adversary. No matter how cautiously game animals come down to the water, now and again they fail to see the half-submerged eye-bulges and nostrils of a silently approaching crocodile... and suddenly strong jaws snap unexpectedly at the muzzle of a drinking gnu. No resistance is possible against this vice-like grip and a powerful swipe of the reptile's tail unbalances the victim which is then pulled into the water and drowned. But some time must elapse before the crocodile may enjoy its meal. Larger prey cannot be eaten until putrefaction sets in, so the cadaver is dragged back on to the land and the killer has to live on fish for a few days. — Even the biggest crocodiles move with incredible agility when submerged. Their larynx and oesophagus close up with a skin valve and in order to swallow their prey they have to lift their heads out of the water. After their nocturnal hunting the sated reptiles crawl up the shore and lie basking themselves with wide-open jaws. They are so sluggish now and peaceful that the little Egyptian Plover can pick between the terrifying teeth for leeches and remnants of food. — Because of the strong evaporation the salt content in the blood of amphibious saurians rises and the excess is eliminated through the eye glands as "crocodile tears".

An African Monitor (*Varanus niloticus*) in the Congo River. This dark-green, yellow-striped reptile grows to a length of 6 feet.

Movement on land is not easy for the crocodile, so only when forced by necessity will he undertake a long journey. When the water level of his immediate habitat falls he would rather "hibernate" in a deep cave than go searching for deeper waters elsewhere. The African reptiles next in size are the big Monitors which are not only good swimmers and persevering divers, but also fast runners and skilful tree climbers. With their long tongues, sharp teeth and dangerous claws they hunt for fish, small mammals, birds, lizards and snakes. This probably accounts for the Tuareg custom of carrying the head of a Desert Monitor as protection against snake bite. The monitor's hey-day begins when there are crocodile and tortoise eggs to dig up. The females gain so much experience during this egg robbing that when their own breeding time comes they try to give their brood better protection. They lay 50 eggs (having parchment-like shells) in a termite hill which they break open, thus assuring their offspring a rich larder during their first weeks of life. Until the young can defend themselves with angry snapping and tail-swiping they live in great peril... later, if they survive infancy, they are hunted for their tender flesh and beautiful skins.

A carpet of water lettuce *(Pistia stratiotes)* makes ideal camouflage for Hippopotami. Lake Edward, Queen Elizabeth Park, Uganda.

Where there are waters rich in plant life the hippopotami can devote themselves entirely to an aquatic existence. The daily ration of three to four hundredweight of green fodder literally grows into their mouths. But even hippopotami cannot deal with the water lettuce which periodically chokes up many rivers and lakes, as they do not seem to like it. Thick carpets of water hyacinths, just as unwelcome, already cover the new artificial lakes in Rhodesia, but it is no use to clear away this unwanted vegetation by introducing the choosey hippopotami. To avoid using expensive chemicals, possibilities of making industrial use of the vegetable fibre are being investigated. It is even planned to introduce the Manatee from British Guiana to help combat the rampant plant growth. Hippopotami do not like such wild rankness and effectively "mow" their underwater meadows so that there is always fresh growth to be harvested. They fetch up a big mouthful to the surface, spread it out on the water and then munch it at their leisure. Where the lake-bottom does not offer food enough, their trampled-down paths lead inland, sometimes up to a distance of three miles, to favourite meadows which they visit after sundown. On such long wanderings their skins get dry and they appear to sweat blood because the skin glands exude a wine-red mucus which compensates for the lack of humidity in the surrounding atmosphere.

Fighting Hippopotamus bulls *(Hippopotamus amphibius)*. Fully grown they can be 12 ft.long, weigh up to 4,000 lbs.and live to 47 years of age.

When battling for supremacy hippopotami bulls, who are usually placid, become furious monsters. If a stray bull invades the territory of another out of the mating season, the disputes can be settled by a ritual in which the opponents "shoot" with bowel ammunition, propelling their tails to shower dung over their rival and spread a veritable cloud of odour. During the mating season, however, such skirmishing is but the prelude to a terrible battle which is accompanied by snorting, neighing and roaring that can be heard for miles around. After some hours of embittered struggle the deeply wounded loser drags himself away from the victor's domain. Their powerful, constantly growing tusks are dangerous weapons, but it is for these six pounds of fine-grained ivory that the hippopotami have been butchered by greedy hunters. The hippos use their tusks only against their own kind. From the second year onwards they have, apart from parasites, no enemies in the animal kingdom. Even lions and crocodiles cannot penetrate the thick skin; only the young are at all vulnerable. The offspring are born and suckled under the water and have to come to the surface to breathe after every mouthful of milk. It is some time before they learn to walk on the shallow lake-bottom, or to accompany their mothers on to dry land where the leading cow, in a maternal defensive mood, can run down a hunter.

As if from the darkness of primeval times, the horned colossi step out into the flashlight of 20th-century photography.

White Rhinos *(Diceros simus)* in the 69,000-acre expanse of the Umfalosi Reservation, Zululand, South Africa.

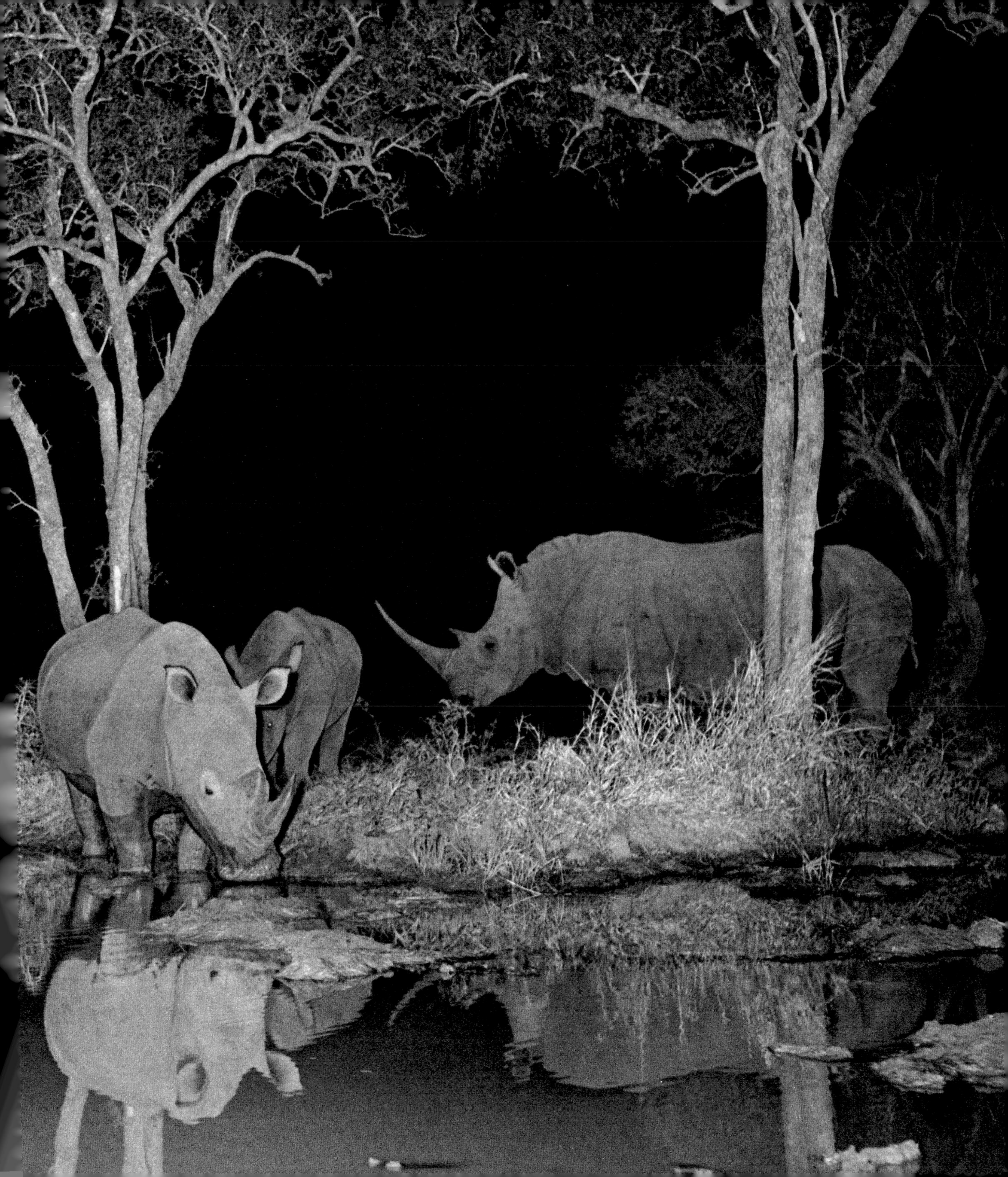

Black Rhinoceros *(Diceros bicornis)* with her young. This rhino cow subsequently lost her abnormally-formed four-foot-long horn in a fight with an over-passionate admirer.

34 species of rhinoceros, some as small as badgers and others 15 feet high have left their fossilised remains in the earth of four continents. All were victims of tremendous climatic changes as was the European woolly rhinoceros which died out after the last glacial period. Only five species remain in Africa and Asia, yet during the last 150 years *Homo sapiens* has almost driven them off the face of the earth. In India, Java and Sumatra only some 800 survive under the strictest protection. Rescue came to the African rhino at the eleventh hour. The White Rhinoceros of South Africa *(see pages 50/51)* suffered particularly. They were discovered by Boer hunters in 1812 and from then on "*Witrenoster*", as they were called, were shot by the thousand. The sociable grass-eaters were an easy prey in the open plains between the Okavango, Zambesi and Orange Rivers. Barely a hundred head escaped the massacre. In 1897, their last refuge on the banks of the Umfalosi River was declared a nature reserve and they have since increased to six hundred head. But in 1907, the big game hunters found a new thrill when 20 degrees to the north, in the valley of the White Nile, another sub-species of white rhino was discovered. The small number left from the resulting intensive killing for "trophies" is now divided between the game reserves of the Sudan, Northern Congo and Uganda... but to-day hardly 3,000 White Rhinos remain.

A colossus weighing 1½ tons on the move. This rhino bull lives in the Ngorongoro Crater, Tanganyika, which has been irresponsibly separated from the Serengeti National Park and ceded to Masai herdsmen.

The rarity of an animal is truly reflected by its catalogued price. A zoo will have to pay over £ 4,000 ($ 12,000) for a White Rhinoceros, and a young Black Rhino will cost £ 1,200 ($ 3,500). In Central and East Africa 11,000 to 13,500 Black Rhinos still exist thanks only to their way of life. In the thorny bush where they pluck leaves from the branches with their prehensile upper lip, these solitary browsers are better camouflaged than their gregarious grass-feeding relatives, the White Rhinos. It was much easier, and less dangerous, too, to take pot shots at the placid "*Witrenoster*" than to expose oneself to an easily angered Black Rhino. Nevertheless, the apparently large number of these latter rhinos seems alarmingly small to far-sighted zoologists. This dwindling race is further decimated by Nature herself. They are extremely conservative in their choice of locality and keep to their trails between feeding and resting places, and to their water-holes, with such inflexibility that during periods of drought they would seemingly rather starve and die of thirst in whole groups than migrate to a more suitable habitat. In any event, wide rivers are an obstacle to these heavy beasts because they cannot swim far. However, mud-holes and shallow ponds are their delight, for there the turtles will rid their thick hides of the ticks with which ox-peckers could not deal.

A victim of organised poaching. The poisoned arrow can be seen on the shoulder of this Black Rhino. The "miracle working" horns have been removed with an axe.

In spite of the strictest conservation laws poachers still slaughter every year about a fifth of the rhinoceros herds. A birth rate of 5% cannot compensate for such losses. Rhinos are particularly threatened because both sexes carry the horns coveted by poachers, so that even pregnant cows, or those with young offspring, fall victim to wire nooses, traps and poisoned arrows. Negroes once hunted rhinos only for the flesh and leather. However, when the Asiatic rhinoceros was nearly exterminated, the search for the allegedly aphrodisiac horns spread to Africa. Black market groups comprising hunters, dealers and seamen were organised and even to-day a pound of rhino horn will fetch £ 4.15s ($ 14) at the port of exit. How much more will the owners of harems eventually pay for one ounce of this supposed love-potion? Even herdsmen as the Masai are tempted by the market demand to kill the *Kifaru*. The only possible way to stop poaching is to impose a collective fine — equal to a number of head of cattle — on the tribe so that the "business" no longer pays. In regions where rhinos are in danger, evacuation to safe reservations, after temporarily paralysing the animals with darts carrying anaesthetic, has been tried. But poachers soon reappeared and in their haste took only the horns, leaving the meat to rot. So rhinos have to die because of their ornament and weapon, a boneless structure of compressed hair, which is worth 3 ½ times as much as ivory, and which — if it could be removed from the living animal — would always grow again.

Before birth came death. The most brutal hunter must surely feel remorse when his bearers cut his victim open and reveal the unborn calf inside the mother.

The easiest, but also the most tragic death is that of the unborn. Was it a rich white man who could afford the costly elephant hunting-licence, or was it a profit-hungry black poacher? Whether licensed or unlicensed, even unintentional killing of the unborn is a crime. — There have always been many different ways of hunting elephants, and the oldest were by no means the most humane, but through the centuries hunting Negroes hardly thinned the ranks of the huge pachyderms. In the Nile valley it was customary to dig deep traps across elephant paths and spread over them a deceptive covering of dung. The leading animal was thus made to believe that another herd had already passed in safety. By contrast the Njamnjam and other tribes, a thousand warriors strong, went out with drums beating and set the savannah on fire to drive the grey giants together. But the true *elephant-eaters* live in Central Africa. They approach to dangerously close quarters and cut the sinews of the hind legs with sharp bush knives. This, of course, is justified only if the fallen colossus is killed immediately to feed an entire starving village. Of greater cruelty is the uncontrolled *modern* method of a wire noose from which the elephant often struggles free only to stagger round with deep suppurating wounds. Yet the scorned native poachers cannot understand why the white man penalises them since he himself set the example for mass murder when, between 1889 and 1909, he exported 7,000 tons of ivory from the Congo region alone, and even in 1946 still exported a further 274 tons.

55

Elephants prefer a full evening bath to a mere shower from the trunk. Four "students" from Epulu Camp (Congo) splashing to their heart's content.

Thousands of years ago the animal-loving Indian mahouts had already mastered the difficult art of making wild elephants docile by patient encouragement. In 333 BC under the Persian King Darius III serried ranks of war elephants were drawn up against the armies of Alexander the Great. Much later the Carthagenians used Mauretanian elephants as their battle allies, but the Romans abandoned the use of these "living tanks" because the nervous colossi spread confusion in their own ranks. During the next centuries the services of African elephants were finally dispensed with, but around 1900 King Leopold II of Belgium wanted to prove that "big-ear" could be tamed. In the Congo elephant camps, Indian mahouts have since tried giving to Assandeh Negroes an understanding of elephant psychology. These tribesmen in their turn have endeavoured to discipline the pachyderms, but the working elephants of Gangala-na-Bodio and Epulu have lost their economic importance in this motorised age. It has been the experience of Indian experts that man alone is an ineffective teacher if he is not aided in the instruction of novices by trained working elephants. An elephant as a worker is, in any case, difficult to please. He will cheerfully transport heavy loads only if his strength is not abused — a matter in which he himself is the final arbiter — if he is never driven, and if, apart from much loving care, he gets at least four months holiday every year in his natural habitat.

Loxodonta africana by the Victoria Nile. Each sucks up a trunkful of water and squirts into its mouth some 10 to 20 gallons a day.

Elephants delight in places where there is an abundance of water. They suffer greatly during times of drought, but – unique among wild animals – they have developed the capacity of water divining. It is assumed that they can sense water even to a depth of 180 feet although they cannot reach it. When they break up the hard earth crust of dried-out river beds with their tusks and then deepen the holes with their front feet and trunk, ground-water will soon collect, which not only keeps the elephants alive, but aids other thirsty animals as well. With the same intuition and endurance the huge beasts dig for salt and laxative types of earth to rid themselves of their many intestinal parasites. It can happen that during this digging a tusk breaks off close to the root and an inevitable inflammation of the nerve sets in. This in turn induces infestation by the dreaded flesh eating parasites which penetrate every open scratch and plague also healthy elephants. The pain-racked creature weakens and eventually looses even the energy to heave itself out of a soothing mud bath. Because numbers of tusks were often found in swamps, the myth arose that these places were elephant cemeteries. The truth is that, whenever ivory seekers stumble upon such treasure, they have discovered either a poacher's hoard or the remains of some natural catastrophe which once wiped out a whole herd, similar to the mounds of well-preserved mammoth tusks which have come to light in the Siberian tundra.

In the past, when elephant herds were still vast and their stamping grounds unlimited, the bulls roamed in exclusively male contingents. To-day, they prefer family unity and assume the protection of the herd which is led by an experienced cow. When a birth is about to take place several matrons gather round the expectant mother, and their trumpetings join in her cries of pain. The elephant baby, which is born after a gestation period of 20 to 23 months, weighs two hundredweight and is the heaviest newborn of all land mammals. For the first few days of life it hides between the column-like legs of its mother and the herd browses and waits until the youngest member is strong enough to keep pace. At every halt, and even on the march, the little one keeps folding back its tiny trunk as it tries to get its lips to its mother's teats which are situated close to the forelimbs. The milk continues to flow for two years, but the young will stay close to their mothers until their twelfth year. Elephants are sexually mature only at the age of 16 after which they have periods of irritability and aggressiveness. Growth of both body and tusks goes on into old age. However, the days are gone when a hunter could obtain a booty of ivory weighing 200 pounds from an elephant standing 14 feet high and weighing 6 tons. Because of over-hunting, the average age is decreasing rapidly. Without the menace of Man, elephants, especially the cows in the safety of the herd, could live for about 100 years. There are numerous, rather touching stories of how the grey giants support their wounded and lead them to safety, and how piously they honour their dead, covering them with fallen leaves.

➤ Young and old on the move: East African elephants between cactus-like tree euphorbias.

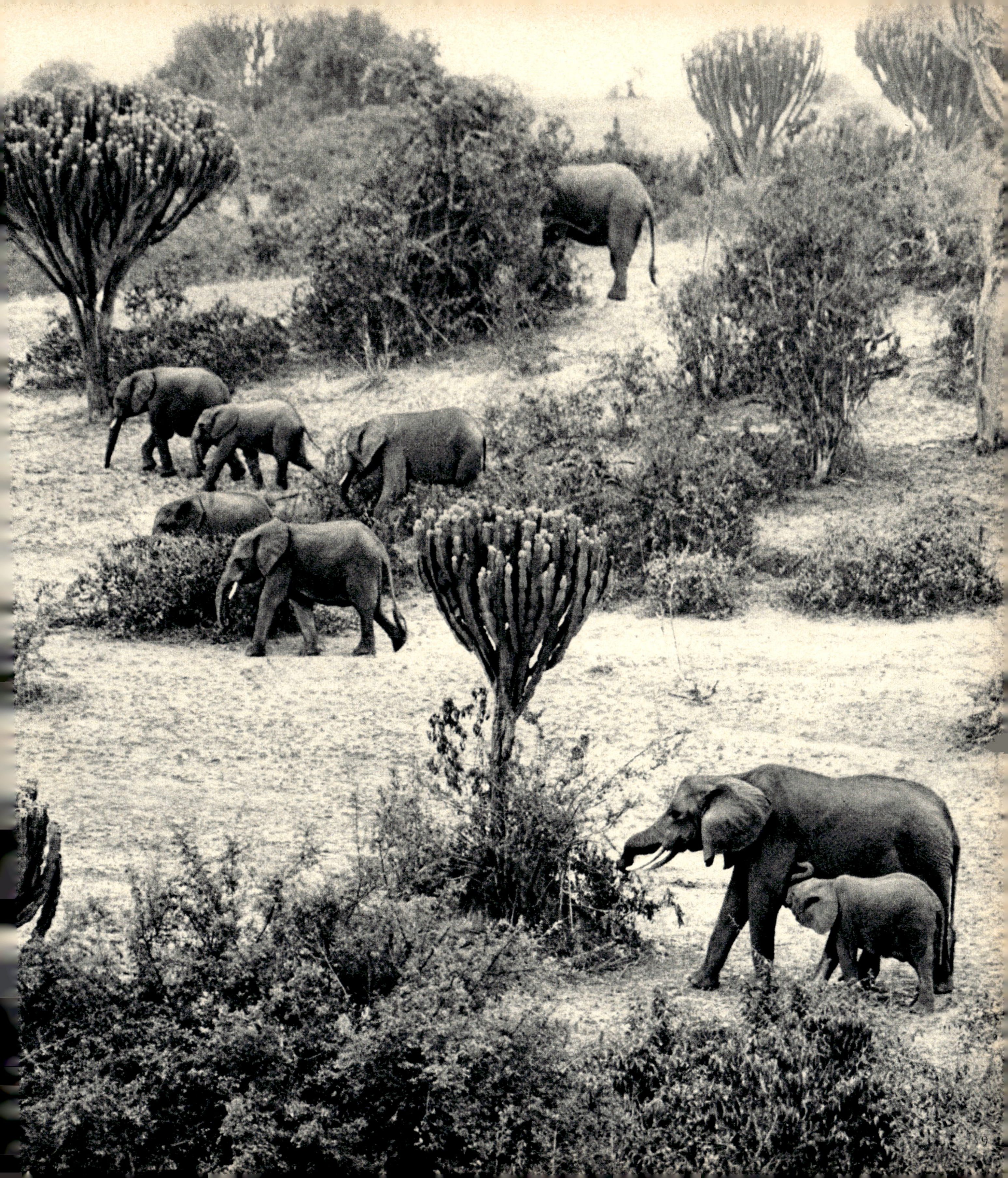

Siesta in the wild. Like the lion, the Buffaloes *(Syncerus caffer)* seek the cool shade of the trees.

In regions where the balance of power is important, the "*King of Beasts*" is only a part of the familiar landscape, and co-existence between the strongest members of the animal kingdom is a matter of course. In youth, the lion learns from the example of his kind that it is wiser to leave adult elephants, rhinoceros, hippopotami and buffaloes in peace. Hungry predatory cats who forget this lesson usually come to an unfortunate end. Game wardens have reported that on one of the rare occasions when a buffalo had been attacked by a lion and lioness, all were fatally wounded; on another occasion when three lions fought against a buffalo the result was a draw. *Simba's* only hope of overpowering an old bull weighing a ton is to attack in a force of eight to one. A wounded buffalo does not fall into the weakness of blind fury. Craftily he pretends to retreat in order to avenge himself with utmost malice. Some hunters who have followed a trail of blood closely, being too sure of their quarry, have been taken unawares, hurled into the air and then trampled to death. When left in peace the buffalo leads a dull ruminant life, spending the day in the shade but preferring to wallow in a mud-hole, and grazing only by night. During the dry season the many buffalo troupes in South and East Africa unite to form enormous migratory herds. With the onset of the rainy season they disperse again. In contrast the small West-African Dwarf Buffaloes move quietly and timidly through the forests in family groups.

A rare picture taken in the Wankie National Park, Southern Rhodesia. Seven Greater Kudus *(Tragelaphus strepsiceros)* meet at a water-hole.

Among big game hunters a buffalo trophy with a yard span is valued as the prize for a foolhardy encounter with a formidable quarry, whereas the twisted horns of the Greater Kudu are treasured as the award for endlessly stalking through thorny bush. To-day, there are hunters who after completion of their collections have the insight to change the rifle for a camera. Frankly, the photographer is often more fortunate than the man with the gun. Although the Greater Kudu is distributed from the Cape to Lake Tchad and Eritrea, only the natives know where the proud antelope hides in the bush or the foothills. Anyone undertaking this exhausting search can be disappointed, for there are only a few unhorned females *(left)* to show themselves, while the 8-foot-long and 5-foot-high bulls remain mostly invisible. This makes the proportion of the sexes at the water-hole — as in the photograph — all the more astonishing. No one has yet succeeded in taking wildlife-pictures of the Greater Kudus at the height of the mating season. In zoos, however, it has been possible to observe how the bull demonstratively throws his horns on to his neck to pursue the fleeing female and then lays his head on her back. After this ritual an exciting game follows when, running at full speed, the admirer tenderly rubs his cheek against the flank of the female and makes gentle clicking noises. He then pushes his neck across hers and the caress is enhanced by the soft waving of his mane.

A stampede in the Savannah. Thomson's Gazelles *(Gazella thomsoni)* fleeing helter-skelter over the Serengeti, Tanganyika.

Even to-day, when the many-thousand-headed herds have dwindled to a fraction of their former wealth, Africa can still be called the Continent of Antelopes, the Land of Gazelles. Among the most charming inhabitants of the East African game reserves are the graceful Thomson's Gazelles, 200,000 of which live in the Serengeti alone. Only 24 inches high, weighing barely 50 pounds, both sexes carry magnificent horns; the record measurement is 18 inches. Being afraid of lions they avoid the high grass, and during the rainy season move behind the columns of gnus who leave enough grazing for the small camp followers. The picture shows *Tommies* in full flight seen from a Landrover on a photo safari. It is wrong to startle animals in a National Park, but to please tourists, some safari leaders do so to comply with demands for a chance to get exciting pictures, although, because of jolting over the rough roads, snapshots are frequently unsatisfactory. In the Kiswahili tongue to go on "*safari*" really means to travel by "Shank's pony", but in the economic balance of East Africa safari-tourism has become an important factor, accounting for an annual income of some £15 ($42) million. The greater the number of visitors the more valuable the natural heritage will prove to the newly-established States. Anyone who can afford the spectacular satisfaction a safari can offer should travel to the Land of Gazelles and help thereby to maintain the reservations and safeguard the future of the wild animals.

Life on the edge of the desert. Fleeing Dama Gazelles *(Gazella dama)* and White or Scimitar Oryx *(Oryx algazel)* in the Ennedi region, Tchad.

Every big mammal which manages to thrive in the desert is a miracle of natural adaptability to an environment inimicable to life. To hunt in these regions is a double crime because the biological balance will be disturbed by even the slightest interference with this tenuous existence. In North Africa, in spite of this, military garrisons and the staffs of oil companies have presumed to regard the gazelle herds as meat supply. Thus the white Oryx has been almost exterminated and the Dama Gazelles are reduced to living in small groups along the fringes of the Sahara. On their dusty trails they find spots of sparse vegetation nurtured by subterranean springs. In the interior of the great desert, some ruminants — the small Dorcas Gazelle *(page 80)* and the magnificent Addax Antelope *(page 87)*-also manage to survive. How is it possible that big creatures, such as the Addax, whose body, like that of all animals, consists of 80% water, can even survive in this hopeless land of sand dunes without drink; and not only survive but even suckle their young? The thorny grazing of the Addax seems drier than wood shavings. Addax are never seen at the oases but will trek for 600 miles in search of the green vegetation which sprouts in the desert for a short time after every thunderstorm. For a wanderer in the desert an encounter with an Addax means deliverance from death by thirst, because a drinkable fluid can be squeezed from the spongey stomach walls. This mysterious liquid reserve is the result of a metabolic process which biochemists are as yet unable to explain.

No one knows when the wild dromedary *(Camelus dromedarius)* was tamed to be the "ship of the desert"; no history book can say whether it was three or perhaps five thousand years ago. But certainly without the help of the camel, the wide expanses of sandy waste from Mauretania to the Middle East would still be empty of man. To-day, there seem to be more discarded petrol cans than camel skeletons lying beside the desert tracks, but for the nomadic Arabs of Africa their four million dromedaries are the wealth and the hub of their life. Camels carry their riders through the scorching heat of sun and sand storms. They bear heavy loads of palm fruit and salt to the coast and return to the oases with millet, sugar, tea and ready-made goods. They feed man with their milk, provide dung as his only fuel for the cold desert nights; they are currency when buying a bride or alimony in case of divorce. Finally, they give meat and fat for food, wool for clothing and carpets, leather for shoes and straps. In return for all this they ask only a minimum of care, and a handful of dates now and again; a rest to browse without haste among the salty herbs and thorny scrub, and in good times, every 4 to 5 days, enough water to fill their bellies, as they are seen doing here by the Nile in the Sudan.

The young dromedary grows up quite unaware of its future toils. Rich herd owners let the mares browse with young without doing any work, but Bedouins, the poor sons of the desert, strap the foal to its mother's back until it can keep pace with the caravan. Only in its fourth year will the young animal begin its training as a beast of burden. The one-humped camels give their best service from the age of 6 to 15 years. In the form of highly-bred *Maharis* they carry their riders 60 to 80 miles a day at a swaying amble, and as tough *Jamels* they plod, for month after month, on horny-soled feet over sand dunes and stony ground at 3 m.p.h. bearing loads of 3 to 4 hundredweight. Even sand-storms will not hinder their progress, for they are able to close their nostrils, and additionally they have heavily-lidded eyes with long protective eyelashes. When they set out on a journey, their hump is big and firm, but at the end of a dry trek it hangs wrinkled and flaccid. Its fat has been organically changed to liquid for supplying the spongey cells of the first stomach and the salivary glands with juices to digest the thorny vegetation. From both his environment and man the dromedary has learned patience. Only in winter, in the mating season, will the males rear up viciously and throw off their loads to a bubbling roar. Then they are dangerous to rival males and cameleers alike.

The younger the giraffe, the easier it drinks! When, after a gestation period of 14½ months, the man-high baby slides from a height of 6 feet to the ground, its neck wobbles helplessly and only after many attempts can the little one get up onto its stalky legs to be just tall enough for reaching its mother's milk. Three days after birth it can skip about playfully, and at the end of the first month, it is already feeding on grass and leaves from low shrubs, in addition to milk. Six months later the little giraffe is weaned and becomes a fully active ruminant. Neck and legs grow continually and from then on the green fodder at lower levels belongs to smaller nibblers. With their powerful blue tongues which are 16 to 24 inches long, giraffes strip the foliage off the spiny twigs of acacias and mimosas and can go without water for days. These giants appear at water-holes only when the leaves have been parched by drought. When they bend their necks from a height of 12 to 18 feet, valves in their veins prevent a sudden rush of blood to the head. However, the luxury of a refreshing drink is not only uncomfortable but also dangerous. Often a lion is lying in wait to surprise a giraffe in his "doing the splits" attitude.

Two different races of Cape or Southern Giraffe *(Giraffa camelopardalis)* showing variations of patch pattern.

◂ In the wild it is only rarely possible to surprise a mother suckling her young.

▸ Thirsty half-grown giraffes. Both pictures were taken in the Kruger National Park, Transvaal.

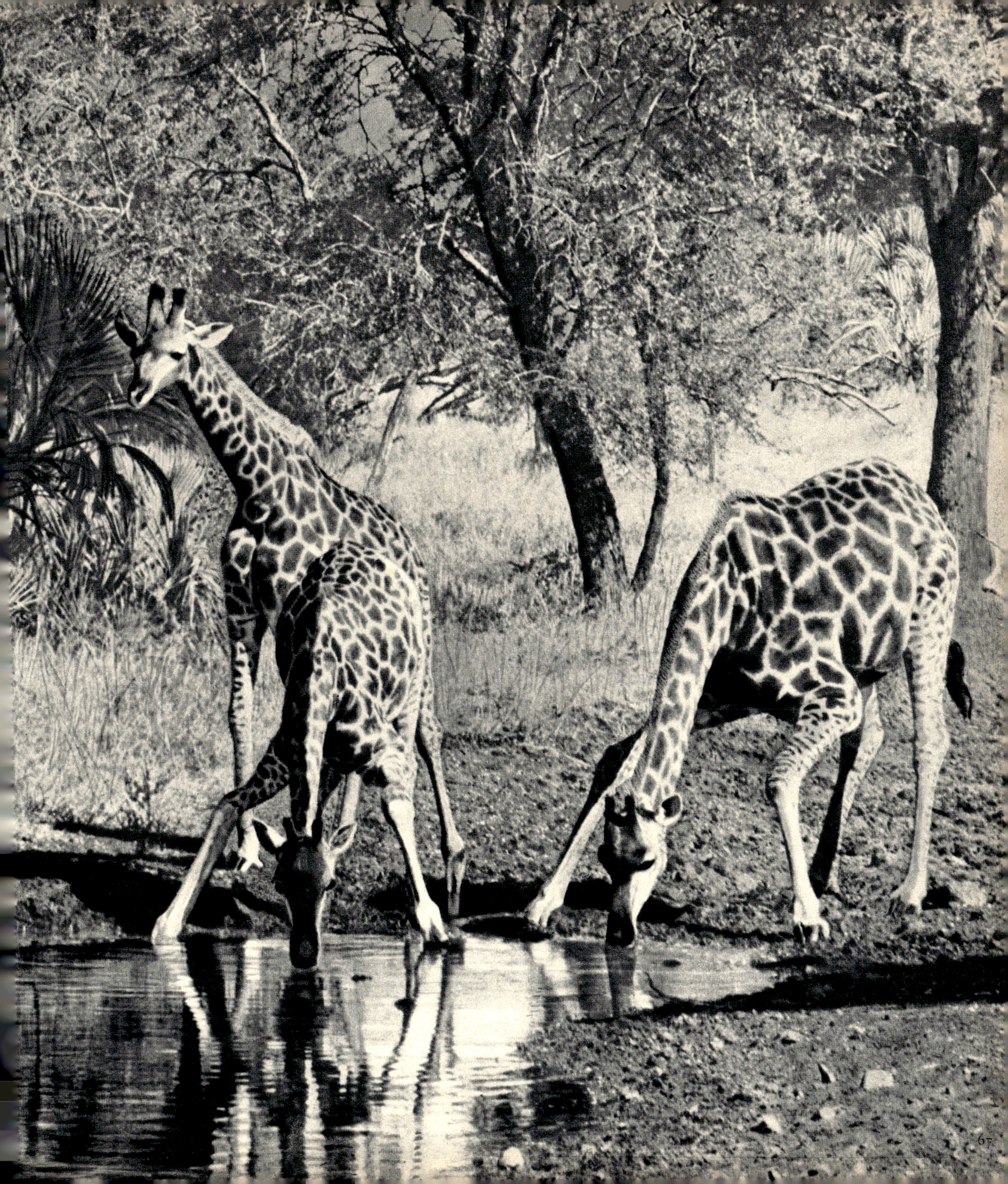

Whenever two giraffe bulls argue over a long-necked beauty it is more a matter of honour than a real fight, for neither would allow himself to use his shattering hooves against one of his own kind. The ritual demands that the rivals stand close to one another as if rooted to the spot. Then begins a sudden weaving and winding of necks; at first probing, then evading, as in the similar love play, but with increasing vigour and violence. Finally hard blows upon neck, back and flanks are delivered in quick succession and each bull tries to knock the other with the horny protuberances on the forehead. This curious adornment, which is neither horn nor antler, is covered with skin during the whole lifetime, but in old giraffes it develops branch-like lateral growth. Some species grow a third "peg" between the eyes, and the rare Rothschild Giraffe found in the region of Mount Elgon between Kenya and Uganda even wears a five-pointed coronet.

◀ The argument takes place in the middle of a track. Today, the strictly protected giraffes cross the "roads" in reservations with confidence, because they have almost overcome the fear of man.

During the mating season when giraffes snort, puff and bleat, one wonders if their usual muteness has something to do with the great distance between the "bellows" and vocal cords. Their tower-like anatomy is unusual enough. The metatarsus alone is nearly a yard long but the sky-scraper neck has only seven tube-like vertebrae — the same number as in man. However, the supply of blood to such heights requires a pressure thirteen times that of man. It is believed that the white coat-markings between the dark patches indicate the interlocking of a special system of blood vessels which accelerates the reduction of body temperature; but whatever the reason, these features are the trade marks of the various races. Only the reticulated or northern giraffe has sharply defined dark brown multi-angular patches, while the 4 southern sub-species have more irregular light brown leaf-like markings. Pure white giraffes are as rare as albinos of any other genus, but because of their size they are more conspicuous and are always a delight to the naturalist with a camera.

➤ Only the eye-witness can judge by the sequence of action whether giraffes are fighting or just indulging in love play. This picture shows a specially animated duel between two "Masai"-Giraffe bulls.

Zoologists who believed that the inventory of the great mammals was complete were astonished when, at the turn of the century, a ruminant was discovered which the pygmies called *O'kapi*. In 1882, in a Congo forest, the famous explorer Stanley got a fleeting glimpse of an unknown animal which he thought was a wild ass. Sir Harry Johnston who was Governor of Uganda at the time, followed up the "sighting", and in 1900 was able to send a strip of okapi skin to the *British Museum of Natural History*. There it was thought that the skin samples came from a forest zebra. Only the study of a skull and a whole skin revealed that the okapi is a link between the present-day giraffes and their extinct ancestors; in other words a living fossil. Already in 1902, the administrators of the Belgian Congo were astute enough to protect the "new" forest giraffe. When, after the First World War, okapis were transported to the North by river steamer, freighter and cattle truck, they never survived the hardships of the journey. Only the creation of the animal acclimatisation camp at Epulu in the Ituri Forest has made it possible to prepare the delicate forest giraffes for a change of diet. Nowadays, okapis are flown to Europe and America, and since 1950 their healthy offspring have given great pleasure in a number of zoological gardens. During the Congo crisis it was feared that only the thirty-five captive okapis in all the zoos of the world could preserve the species from extinction. In fact, the Epulu Station has not been burnt down as it was reported; neither have hungry Congolese eaten all the okapis.

◄ *Okapia johnstoni*: a pair of okapis at Epulu capture station some 300 miles east of Stanleyville (Congo Republic).

➤ The okapi cow "Bibi" with her young, "Heri" ♂ who was born in the Basle Zoo in 1960.

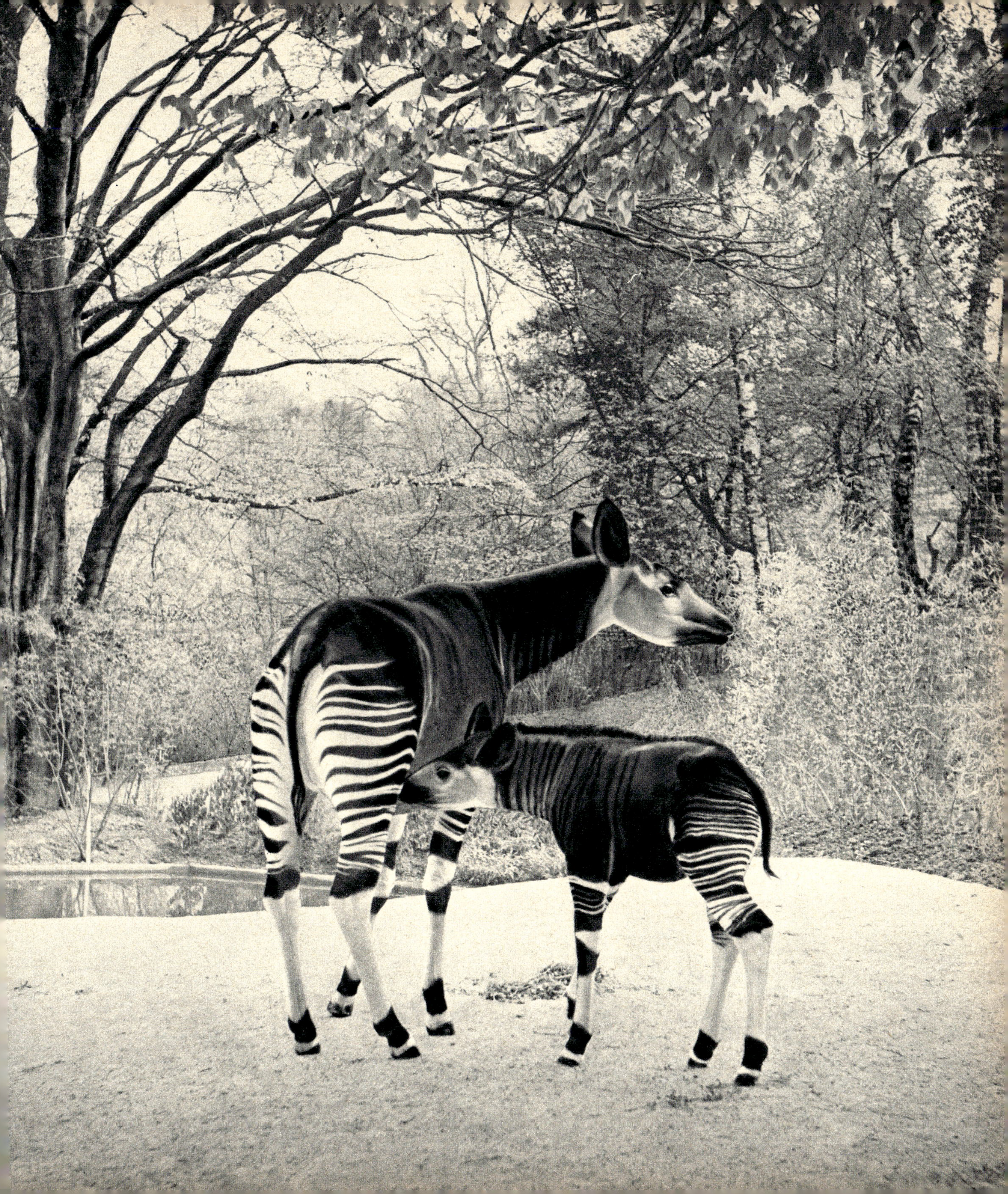

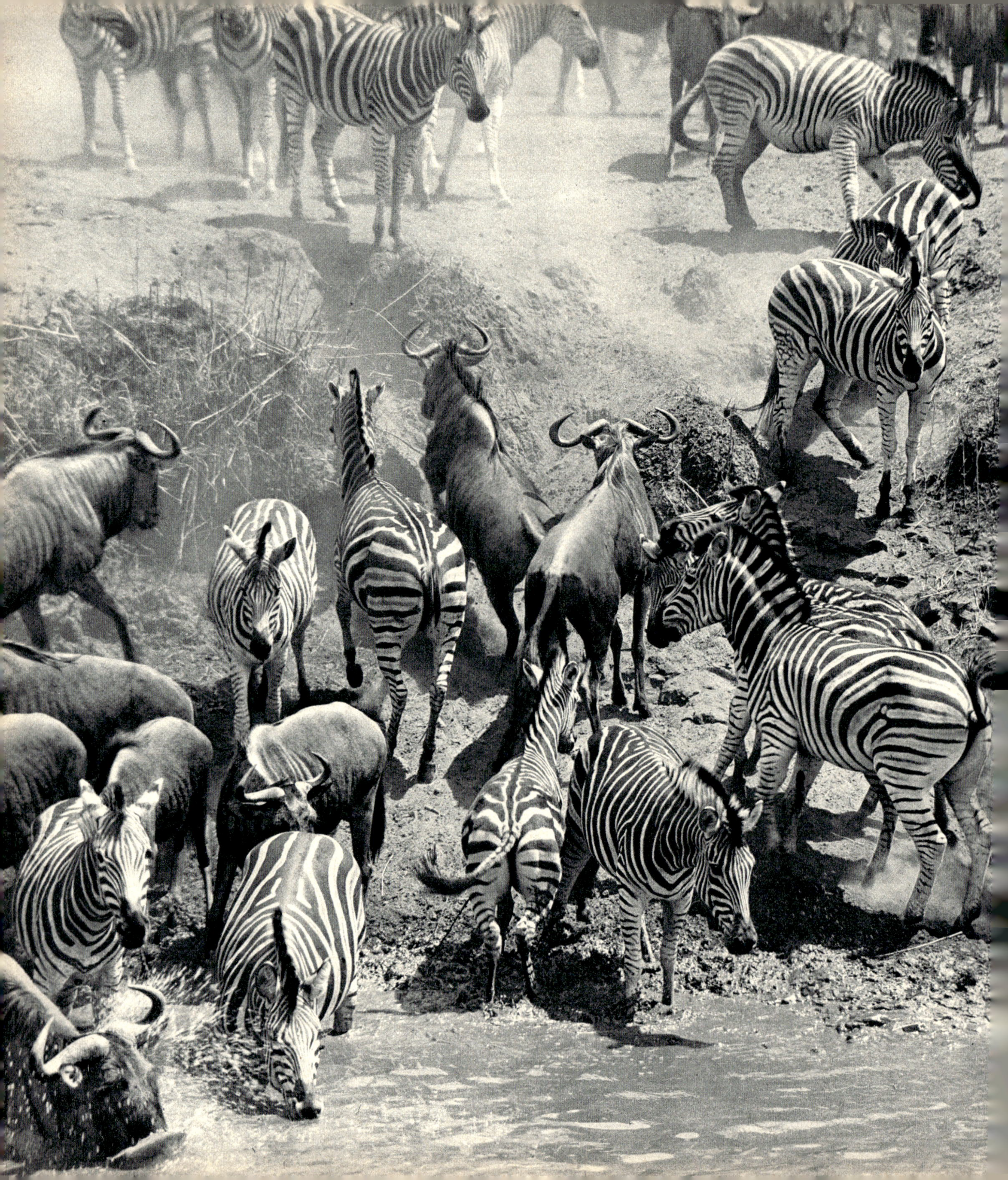

"Herds of wild 'tiger horses' appear suddenly like a cloud of dust over the scorched savannah. In the blinding sunlight they appear first white, then black and finally striped, as they vanish again on thundering hooves." Thus, white hunters in South Africa recorded their impressions of a migration of zebras, but still they took part in the great massacre. It was not enough for the Boers to drive the Burchell's Zebras and Quaggas away from their cultivated fields; they drove both these species, and also the *Blauwbok*, into extinction. The same threat menaced the Mountain Zebras, the Blessbok, the Bontebok and the White-tailed Wildebeest of which only a few hundred still live on farms in small reservations. The Kruger National Park in the Transvaal with its 52,000 acres holds the remnant of this squandered wealth. Here, as of old, Chapman's Zebras and Striped Gnus live together in an ideal grazing partnership. Zebras like to rest at night and Wildebeest doze during the day, so that their close companionship guarantees a twenty-four-hour watch. If Hunting Dogs threaten a calf or a foal of the mixed herd the gnus use their horns and hooves in defence, while the zebras' chief means of counter-attack are their teeth.

A fight between two zebra stallions begins with biting aimed at the neck, front legs, and muzzle of the opponent (1) who rears up (2) and going down again tries to ward off his biting rival (3). Up to now it has been a painful but harmless skirmish, but sometimes a really dangerous kicking battle develops (4) in which the stallions can injure each other so as to cause sterility. The question of which is the stronger will be decided in the circling movement of the fight (5), when each aims at biting the tail and hind legs of the other and both try to avoid being bitten. The continual circling movement, the rearing up and coming down again is so tiring that eventually one contestant, bruised and exhausted, admits defeat. He jumps up and allows the victor to lay its head across his back as a symbol of conquest.

◂ A traffic jam at a water-hole. Chapman's Zebras (*Equus quagga chapmani*) and Striped Gnus or Blue Wildebeest (*Connochaetus taurinus*) in the Kruger National Park, where also a film of fighting zebra stallions was taken. This cinematographic document provided the material for these exact drawings.

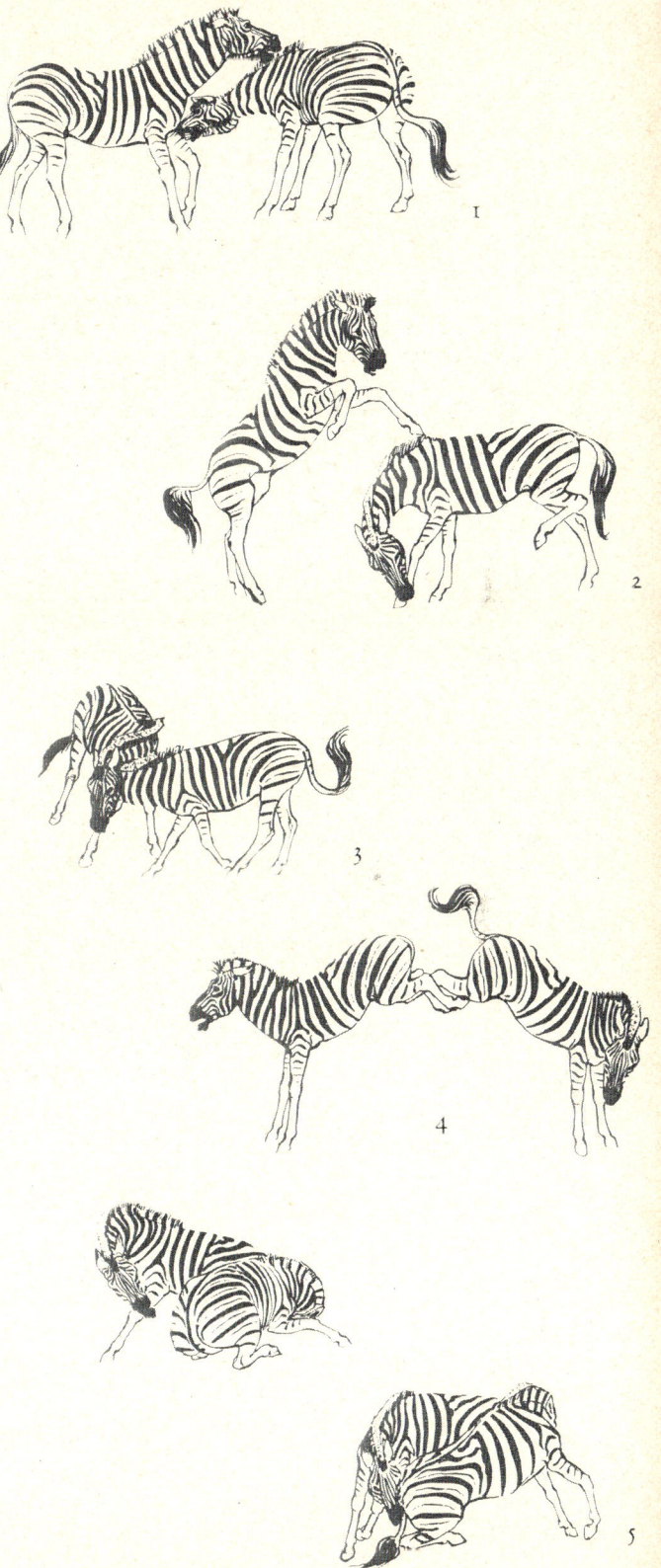

Beauty treatment in the wild: Over 30 starling-sized Oxpeckers meet on the back of a zebra in the Wankie National Park, Southern Rhodesia...

When a layman compares pictures of different zebra species, his eyes begin to swim, but for the expert the pattern of stripes reveals at a glance the origin of the animal. Central Abyssinia and Somaliland are the habitat of the narrow-striped Grevy's Zebras. The five sub-species of the southern steppes are distinguished by a more open pattern. The only pure black-and-white zebras among them are the Grant's, found in Kenya, which have maneless relatives in Uganda. Boehm's Zebra (Tanganyika), Chapman's Zebra (Southern Rhodesia), and the Damara Zebra (South Angola) all have markings of yellowish-white with intermediate brown stripes. The most horse-like were the South African Burchell's which had pure white legs, and the Quaggas which were striped only on the front part of their bodies, both now exterminated. In contrast the sure-footed Cape Mountain Zebras and Hartmann's from South West Africa bear more resemblance to the Wild Ass.

1. Hartmann's Zebra with the typical trellis design on the crupper. 2. Chapman's Zebra showing distinctly the intermediate brown stripes between the black.

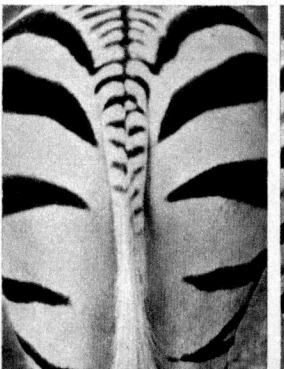

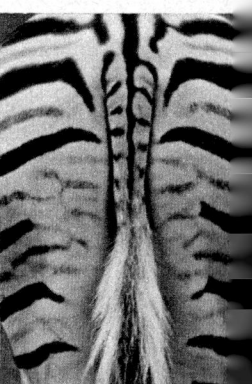

...but he who is forgotten by the small skin conditioners tries to rid himself of ticks by rolling or rubbing against a termite hill.

3. The narrow-striped Grevy's Zebra, and
4. the "roughly painted" Grant's Zebra are those seen most often in zoos.

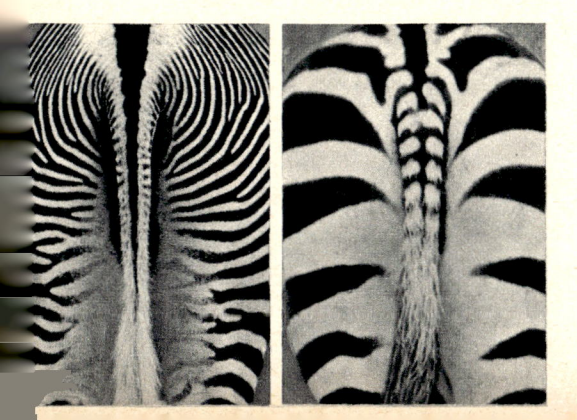

To understand the meaning of the curious striped livery one would have to be able to see alternately with zebra and lion eyes. Some naturalists think the stripes serve as camouflage in the heat-shimmering air, while others believe they serve as a means of identification from a distance... yet every creature would like to be invisible to the enemy and visible to friends! Would ostriches, antelopes and giraffes be so willing as to graze with zebras if they thought their stripes made them conspicuous? In any case, zebras in their striped skins never felt any more unsafe than other animals... until the white hunters arrived. In general, not two zebras are alike, and some even have different stripes on either side. A most sensational oddity is the "speckled zebra of Rukwa", South West Tanganyika. It is black with white d o t s and stripes and trots with the herd through the trackless swampy Lake Reservation, where close-up photography is impossible.

Ten oxpeckers cling to a Sable Antelope *(Hippotragus niger)* ... and twelve more climb about on a Roan Antelope. *(H. equinus)*.

Never a Sable Antelope without tick birds! These vigorous ungulates, inhabitants of the bush, live among thorny shrubs where innumerable ticks fall on their backs. Thus they seem to be the favourite host of the oxpeckers. The most common are the grey-brown Roan Antelopes which live in the south, east and west in the security of the sparsely wooded uplands where, with bizarre faces they snuffle around under the cover of thorn and shrub. Also the proud black Sable-buck does not like to lead his herd of dark brown females across open ground. Because the black silhouette with the yard-long horns strikes the eye too easily, this magnificent specimen of East African bush fauna is now alarmingly rare.

On the coastal hills inland from Mombasa, the Sable Antelopes made themselves very unpopular by eating pine seedlings in the new forest areas of the Shimba Hills. But Nature herself has settled the argument between foresters and animal conservationists, for the seedlings which were imported from Australia do not thrive in Kenya. Bulldozers had already cleared large areas of bush-land for the new forests to grow, but now the antelopes can have back their dispoiled homeland. — Will Angola protect the remaining Giant Sable Antelopes who have found refuge on the high plateau of Cuanza, before the last world-record horns, nearly two yards long, are hung up on someone's wall?

Also this young Niger Giraffe has "visitors"... and the Black Rhino is being treated at the same time by a tick bird and a cattle egret.

Every symbiosis stems from the initiative of the weaker partner, as here for example, from the friendly importunity of the yellow or red-beaked tick birds *(Buphaginae)*. Agile as woodpeckers they creep up and down their "flesh-and-blood trees" and warn the herd of danger by their loud twitterings. With their strong feet and supporting tails they even hold on to their hosts when at full gallop. If the patients sometimes cringe with pain they know full well that the little "medical orderlies" are being helpful when they peck under the skin to get food for themselves and their brood. With precise blows from their beaks the birds puncture the suppurating boils which enclose the pupae of the warble-fly larvae. They pick all the parasites out of the wound and even drink the pus and sanies. Expertly they remove ticks as large as kidney beans which, after a long period of waiting on some tree branch, have gorged themselves with the blood of their host. When the birds extended their attentions to domestic animals, too, the farmers were at first horrified by these "nature şurgeons". They were afraid that healing wounds would be opened up again and re-infested. However, careful investigation has proved that 95% of the ticks found in the stomachs of birds were disease carriers... so the tick-birds are, indeed, guardians of good health.

77

For thousands of years the elegance of moving gazelles has been idealised in art, but no drawing has ever surpassed the natural grace of these animals. When a Waller's Gazelle stands up on its slim hind legs, or a leaping Impala seems to defy gravity, it is like the highlights of a charming ballet; but in fact such movements represent an ability essential to life. The long-necked, long-legged Waller's Gazelles which live in the dry thorny bush round Kilimanjaro and in Somaliland, are often called "giraffe gazelles". They love waterless sun-scorched regions shunned by other antelopes. They are counted among the "animals that never drink" because dew and green food cover their liquid needs. The slim leaf-eaters reach their sustenance — acacias and mimosas — standing up to a height of 6 feet, but in flight they favour the horizontal, slipping away on bent legs, with lowered head. How different from the Impalas in flight, bounding over shrubs, over safari cars and their own kind! In one spring they can lift themselves 10 feet above the ground, but cannot reach to pluck foliage higher than their own head. They, too, are children of the savannah, but as they need their daily drink they never stray far from water.

◄ A female Waller's or Gerenuk Gazelle *(Lithocranius walleri)* in Northern Tanganyika. See also page 82.

► Female Impalas *(Aepyceros melampus)* in the Transvaal whence this species spreads as far as Kordofan in the Sudan. The bucks who stand nearly as high as a Fallow Deer carry lyre-shaped horns up to 27 inches long.

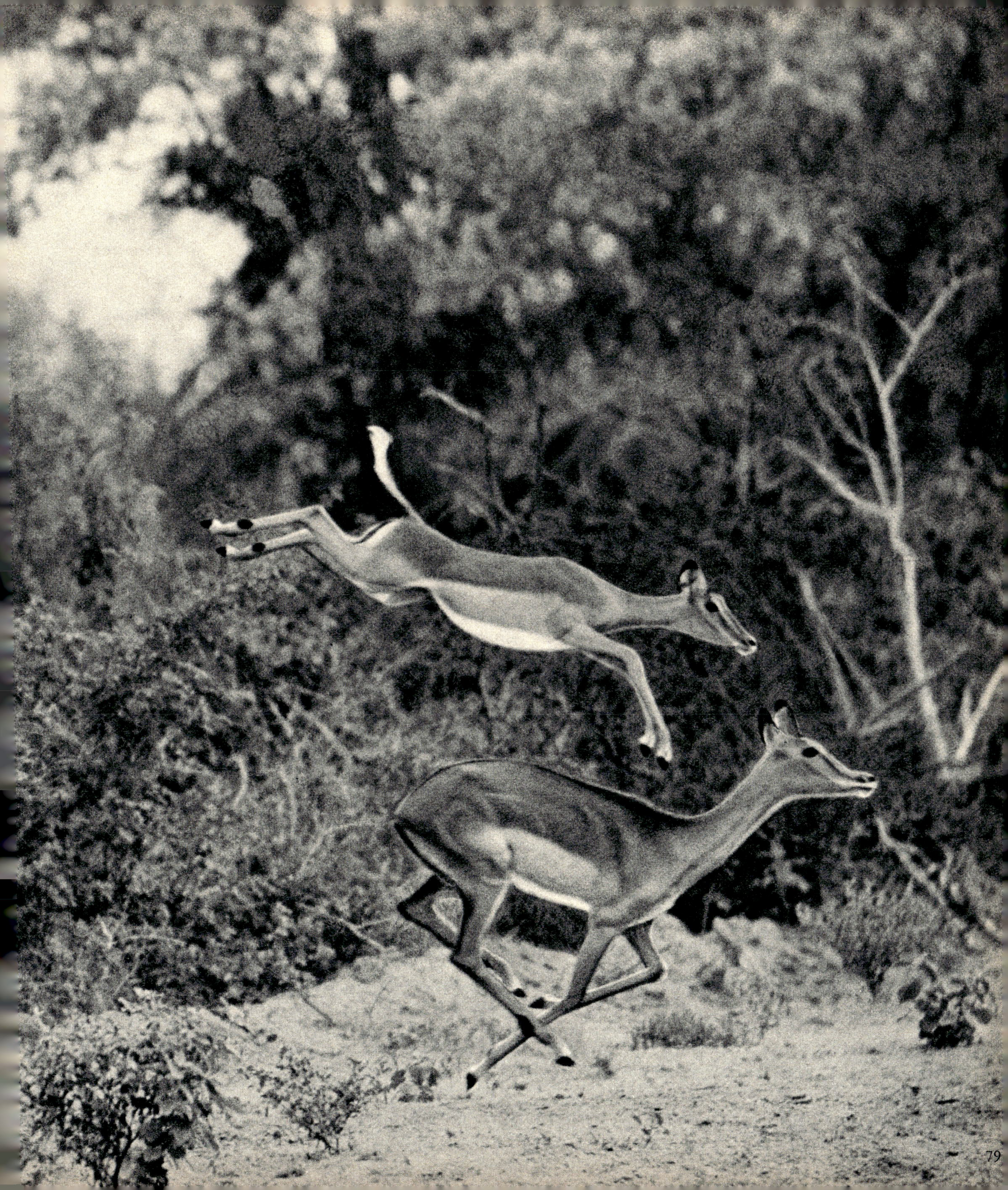

In ancient Egypt the Dorcas Gazelle *(Gazella dorcas)* was dedicated to Isis, the Goddess of Mothers, and since then it has always symbolised maternal joys and sorrows. On the banks of the Nile and in Mesopotamia pregnant women used to touch the limbs, eyes and teeth of their tame gazelles to ensure for their children an equally faultless beauty. The adoration of these sand-coloured animals reached such lengths that the beloved pets were even buried beside their princesses: Dorcas mummies in painted gazelle-shaped coffins have been found in 3000-year-old tombs. In the last 100 years the herds of the graceful 24-inch-high desert gazelles have been decimated by senseless shooting, so that nowadays only small groups wander in the wastelands between Morocco and Syria, Mauretania and the Sudan. Although capture is prohibited by law Dorcas are kept as pets for children in nearly every Tunisian village. The specimen shown here has been settled in the green Taunus Mountains (West Germany) and gave birth in March, after 6 months' gestation, at the same time as her sisters in Africa.

When her time is near the pregnant Dorcas Gazelle goes off alone, in contrast to many antelopes which stay within the security of the herd. *Above left:* She heaves in labour and the new-born is forced out... *Above centre:* ...but hardly has the pain diminished when she turns her head to break open the enveloping membrane. *Below left:* Freed from its covering the fawn crawls forward, led by the maternal tongue-massage, until the umbilical cord is broken... *Below centre:* ...and after half-an-hour it is already struggling to its feet, but it is still as helpless as a deer fawn and too weak to run with the herd like the gnu calf. Instinctively it seeks a place to hide away until lured by its mother's call to the source of milk. The mother never goes near the hiding-place so that her own scent shall not betray the presence of her offspring. Probably for a similar reason, during the first few days, she licks the bowel excretions direct from her baby's bottom before it totters back to its lair.

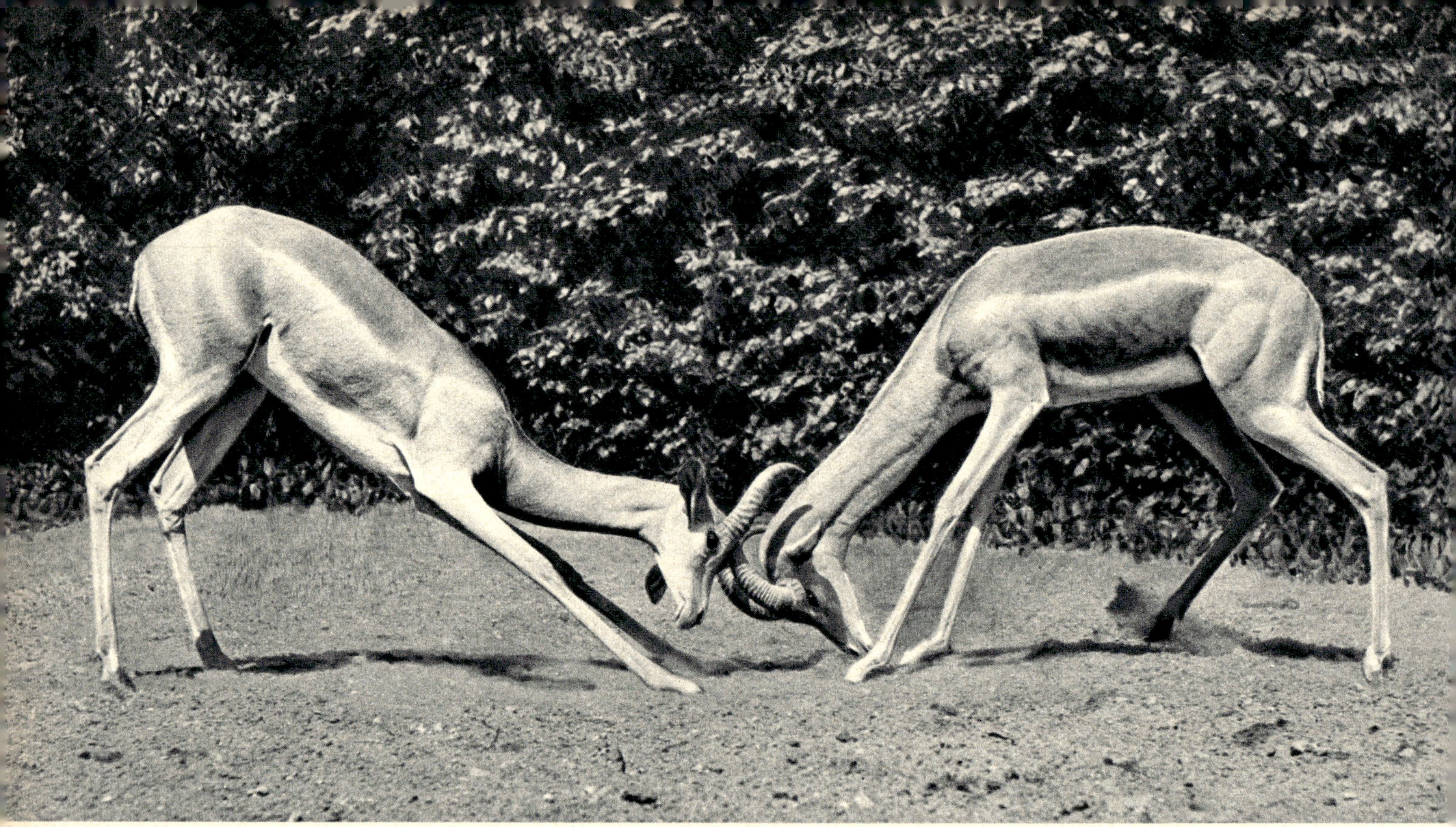

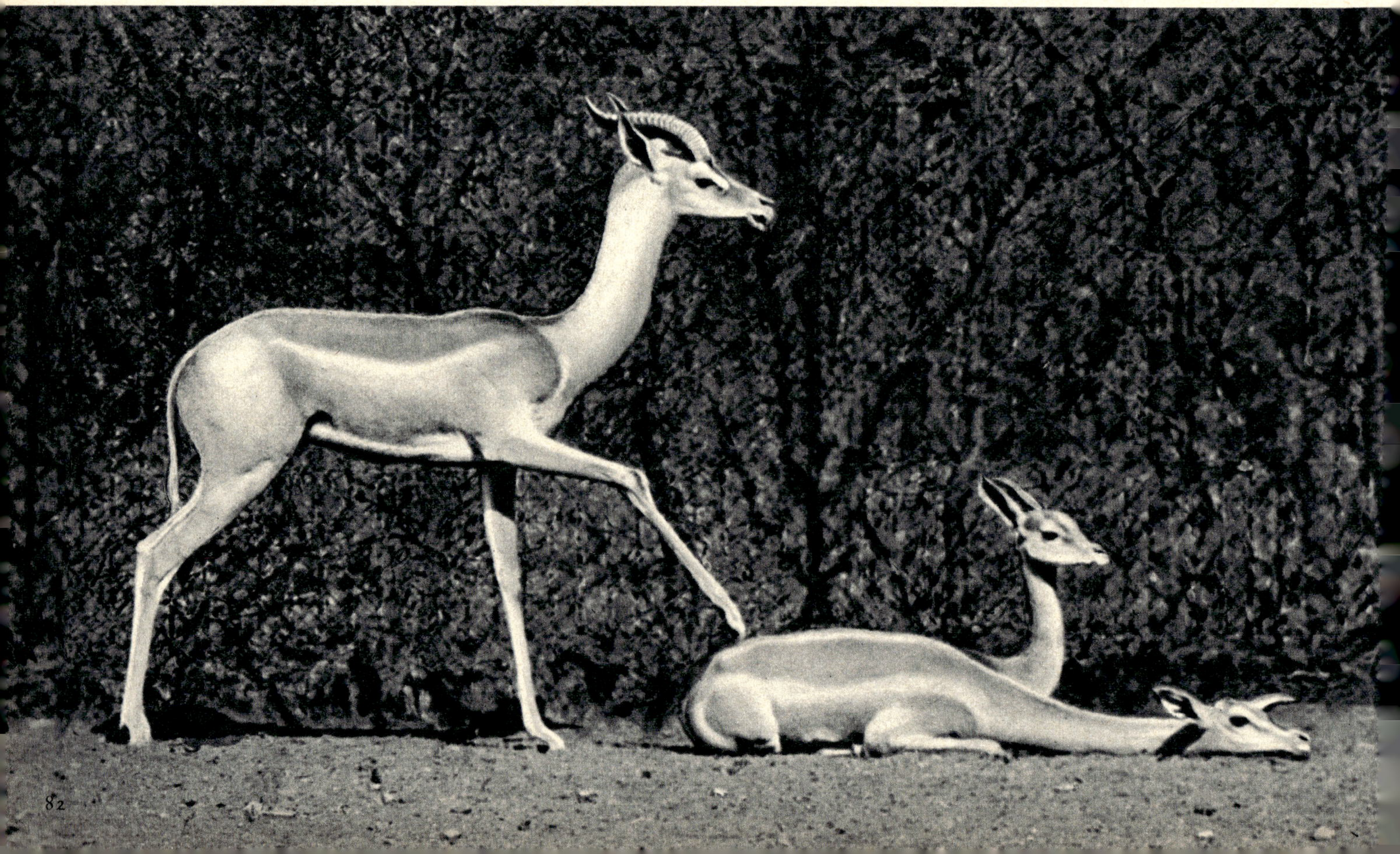

Ten years ago no zoologist had the slightest hope of observing at close quarters the love play of the shy giraffe gazelle. The Gerenuk was discovered in 1878 by an Englishman named Waller and was for a long time thought to be one of the rarest animals in East Africa. The few white hunters who saw these gazelles in the dry bush never came at the right time to watch the elegant love play and fighting between rivals; they were interested only in getting trophies and material for anatomical study. For too long, zoology has confined its interests to the registration of measurements and weights. For too long, menageries were dark prisons in which no animal could live according to its natural habit. Only in the last 50 years have intelligent naturalists been gradually transforming zoological gardens into pleasant nurseries for species capable of adaptation. Recently, the Frankfurt Zoo, for the first time, has successfully bred from the delicate Waller's Gazelle and been able to observe the intimate life of these animals.

Waller's or Gerenuk Gazelles from North Tanganyika in the Frankfurt Zoo. *Above left*: Rival bucks fighting. *Below left*: By tapping her back the buck tries to induce his chosen one to rise from her attitude of humility. *Above right*: When the female allows the buck to lay his head along her back the mating ceremony has reached its culmination point. *Below right*: At Frankfurt, in 1957, the first Waller's Gazelle young was born after a gestation period of 203 days. Since then there are even grandchildren... but none of the small herd has ever shown any interest in water. The moisture-content of their vegetarian diet covers their needs.

A typical representative of steppe fauna; a young Grant's Gazelle buck *(Gazella granti)* in the Nanyuki region of Central Kenya.

If the Grant's Gazelle had shown his back view, the reason why he belongs to the "mirror gazelles" would have become apparent, but he is surely more graceful in profile. His nearest relatives, the Dama or Soemmering's Gazelles, are found only in South Sudan, but in Kenya and Tanganyika the tallest of all the species are the 3-foot-high Grant's Gazelles. Their head ornament which can reach 30 inches in the bucks is less developed in the females, but when both sexes tempt hunters with such trophies the species is doubly threatened. All the more gratifying, therefore, is the report that there are still 40,000 Grant's Gazelles in the Serengeti. As "water savers" they do not join the annual migrations of wild game as they have no need to search for food with great moisture content. They are not only satisfied with sun-scorched grass... they like it, for they have 15 times as many taste buds as man. Nature has developed specialists among the army of herbivores and every animal finds some green food to suit its particular needs without doing any harm to the steppe vegetation. But where the various species have had to give way to herds of grazing cattle, the balance has been upset and dust bowls have appeared between strips of weeds. After a few years, regions which used to support wild game by the thousand have been reduced to hopeless infertility.

A vigorous type of bush fauna, the Nyala bull *(Tragelaphus angasi)* in the Hluhluwe Reserve in Zululand, South Africa.

The marked difference between the horned animals of the steppe and the antelopes of the forest and bush, becomes apparent when the male Grant's Gazelle is compared with the Nyala. In their females the distinction is even greater. As far as head adornment and colouring are concerned "equality of the sexes" is the order of the steppe. However, in the bush, only the bucks are distinguished by horns, mane, size and darker brown colour. To-day, only the photographer can stalk the 5-foot high, 260-pound Nyala, for the nearly extinct species is strictly protected from Zululand to Nyasaland. Hunting for the 32½-inch record trophy has particularly hit the Nyala, for even in their homeland can they exist only in a few places.

They must live close to waterways where they can hide during the day among the moist river-bank vegetation. The Mountain Nyalas in South Ethiopia with their 46-inch-long twisted horns have fared even worse. As leaf-eaters of the middle level both species fulfilled an important function. They pruned the young shoots and prevented vegetation from growing too dense. They even made clearings where the more timid ruminants could browse peacefully in the security of the surrounding trees. Although unaware of the interrelationship, all wildlife is mutually useful and decimation of one species gives rise to a negative biological chain reaction which cannot be reversed.

Greater Kudu ♂, record horns 6 feet; Eland antelope, mother and bull calf ♂♀, record horns 43 inches; Nyala ♂, record horns 33 ½ inches.
♂ = *only the buck has horns.*   ♂♀ = *both sexes carry horns.*

A portrait gallery or a collection of trophies? The traveller whose personal experience does not give him enough satisfaction because he needs visible proof to impress his friends at home, should practice the bloodless sport of hunting with a camera. Out of vanity and folly three generations of Europeans have looted Africa's wealth of horned animals. What remains in new, free Africa must be protected and preserved for posterity. In order to accomplish this, the white man must in future set the native African a better example by replacing the gun with a camera. Stock breeders particularly should seek to maintain the right balance in the competition for food between horned wild game and domesticated herds. Otherwise the day will soon come, when the diversity of antelope silhouettes, with their variously-shaped horns, like sabres, lyres, spears and corkscrews, will have given way to the monotonous picture of ranch cattle. From earliest times Man has fallen back on at least one horned animal for a source of food... in the wild even on whole herds. Our gratitude alone should compel us to protect the most beautiful in this group of mammals.

Red Water Buck ♂, record horns 39 ½ inches; Impala ♂, record horns 36 inches; Uganda Kob ♂, record horns 28 inches.

Addax antelope ♂♀, record horns 43 inches; South African Beisa antelope ♂♀, record horns 47½ inches; Blesbok ♂♀, record horns 19½ inches. *All records measured by tape.*

Among horned animals the adornment and weapon varies from finger-long little prongs to yard-long sabres. Their remote ancestors were attracted sexually by the stimulus of smell alone, but during the process of evolution patches of forehead hair on the male matted together, distinguishing it from the female visually. Thus the hollow horn developed slowly and was probably thrown off periodically. Finally the prongs on the bony base of the forehead excreted more and more horny substance, and the head decoration grew into a permanent ornament. The transition from the horns of young animals to the permanent adornment of the adult is hardly perceptible because of constant peeling: only the number of twists, knots and rings reveals the age of the animal. In some species, the horns, as a male sex status are still dependent on glands, but in the greater number of antelopes, head ornaments have become a characteristic of the species in both sexes and are, therefore, independent of sex hormones. Why nature adorns a female Beisa but not a Kudu is as puzzling as the contemporary existence of the emancipated woman and the odalisque in to-day's world.

Llama gazelle ♂, record horns 12½ inches; Waller's gazelle ♂, record horns 17 inches; Klipspringer ♂, 4 to 6 inches.

Along all the great rivers from the Senegal to the Zambesi the shy Situtunga move through the dense reeds, for these 3-foot-high swamp antelopes love moisture. Once they have chosen a certain region they defend it jealously against all rivals. During the day they stand for hours in the river, singly or in pairs, with only their heads, or even just their muzzles showing above the water. At dusk they begin moving about to feed on the juicy water plants. They are agile and sure-footed on the treacherous swampy ground because of their widely spreading cloven hooves which find a grip on the smallest rootlets without ever sinking. On their nocturnal excursions they always follow the same tracks which wind like tunnels through rushes and papyrus, bamboo and palm forests. Rarely will a Situtunga buck wander out into the savannah, and the moment danger threatens he will give the alarm by violent sneezing and immediately flee back to the river. In the tropical forests the Situtunga share their habitat with the little Chevrotain, a very small, pre-historic deer which has tiny tusks and no antlers and can swim and dive nimbly. Outside the rain forests, the Situtungas' neighbours are the stately Water Bucks, Kobs and Reedbucks, who live mostly among the rushes and reeds and rarely wander out into the savannah.

➤ A young Situtunga or Marsh Buck *(Limnotragus spekei)* looks out from the rich vegetation by the Chari River, Tchad. His horns can grow longer than 32 inches. The "uncrowned" females are deer red in colour.

➤ A Marsh Buck family. The long beak-like hooves can be clearly seen on the female *(left)*.

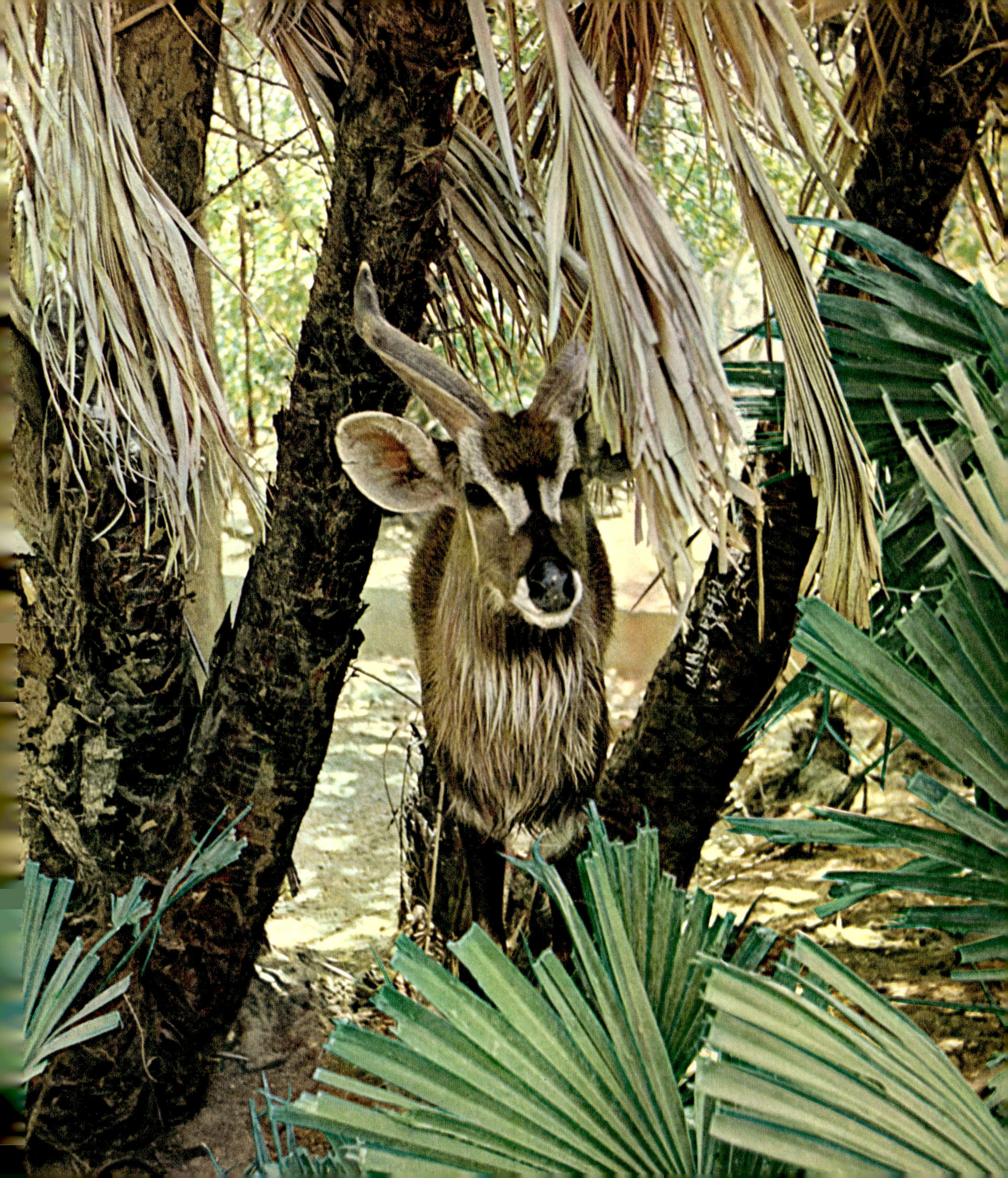

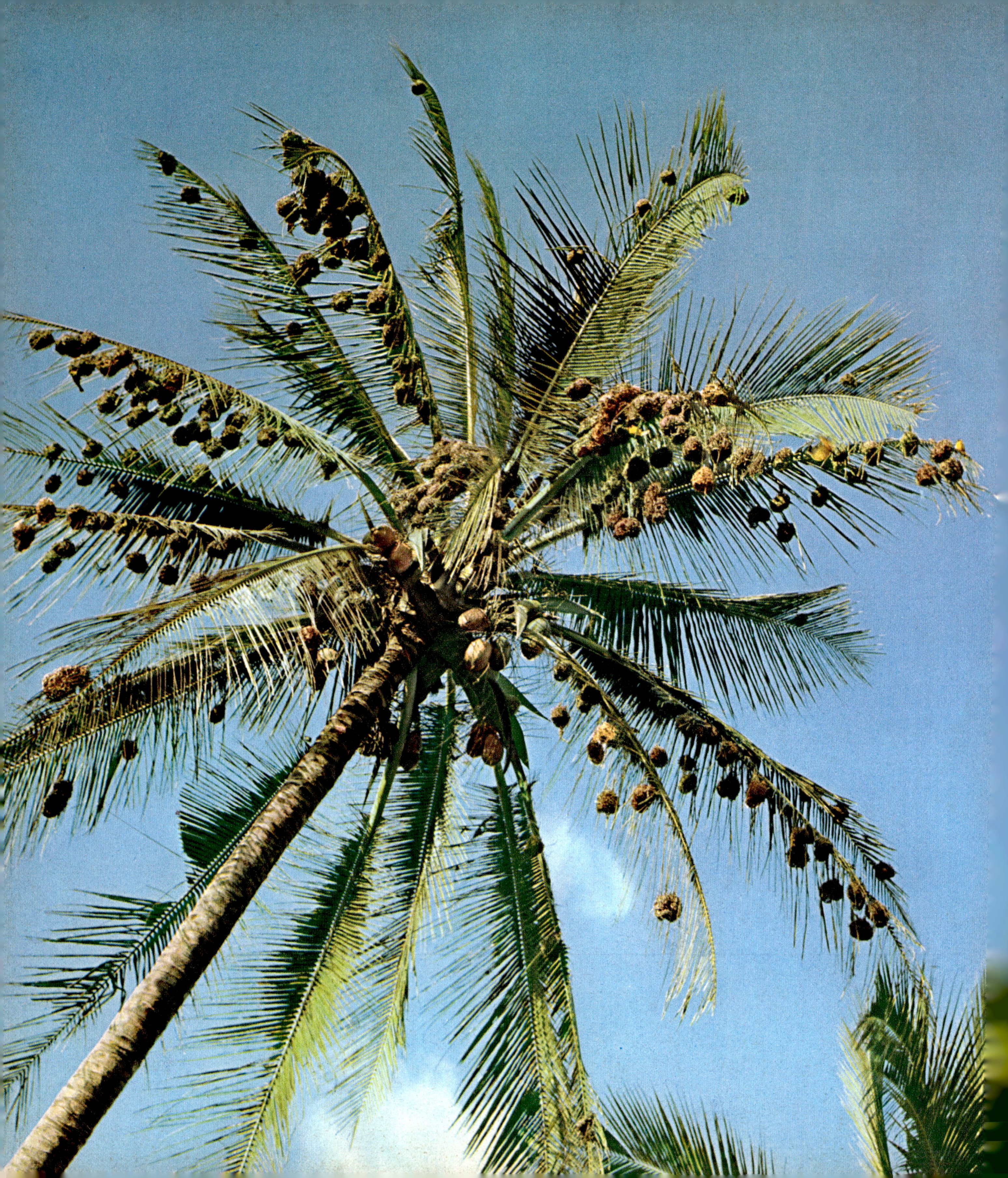

To-day only the birds are as ubiquitous as game once was. One could almost imagine the slender palm trees by the sea bearing two kinds of fruit; while coconuts ripen in the crown, hundreds of pairs of Weaver Birds have hung their globular nests far out along the windswept palm fronds. These gregarious birds need company to feel happy. As long as there is still a hand's breadth of space their progeny will try out the art of weaving on the ancestral nesting tree. Twice yearly, at the beginning of the rainy seasons, the vagrant swarms return and immediately the colourful males begin to weave. Old nests are soon repaired but for a new home the Weavers have to spend two or three days collecting material. When the females are already sitting, the males are still at work on sleeping-nests for themselves. After a day of common activity when they have all sung together, set out in search of food together, and flown together to the watering places, the whole industrious swarm slips into the spherical nests for the night. But even during sleep their community spirit brings about exemplary collective hygiene. Thrice nightly a quiet whispering comes from the tree, and from nearly every nest a white rain falls as by command.

◄ A colony of Weaver Birds *(Ploceidae)* in a Coconut Palm *(Cocos nucifera)* on the coast of Kenya.

➤ The nests farthest away from the trunk are usually the safest from snakes, yet although the Grey-headed Weaver has made its nest at the extreme tip of a twig, the Boomslang *(Dispholidus typus)*, over 5 feet long, has ventured to attack between heaven and earth. Holding on to a stronger branch with the end of its tail the snake has twined round the thorny twig, put its head into the opening, and seized the nesting bird.

A colony of Layard's Weavers *(Ploceus cucullatus)* in an Oil Palm on the Ivory Coast.

Palm trees offer the Weaver Birds a particularly safe home because an egg thief hardly dares to climb out along the swaying fronds. But in the interior where there are no palms the Weavers hang their nests on the outermost and slenderest branches of other trees. Some species of Weaver Birds nest in their hundreds in the high steppe grass where they receive many unwelcome visitors, not only the trampling migrating herds and nest robbers, but especially the lazy females of the Cuckoo Weavers and the Widow Birds, who come and lay their eggs, leaving them to be hatched. — The widely dispersed small Weavers all live in sociable colonies, but no species increases with such frightening rapidity as the Red-billed Quelea *(page 95)*, whose numbers have reached pest proportions from the Sahara's southern fringe to the Cape. In Southern Rhodesia 1,200 nests were counted on a s i n g l e tree, and the whole colony was estimated at eleven million birds, probably the world's biggest one settlement among higher animals. The swarms combine to form tumultuous clouds, and when they settle for the night even strong branches break under their weight.

A community nest of Social Weavers *(Philetairus socius)* in a Camel Thorn tree. Orange Free State, South Africa.

The gregariousness of Weaver Birds culminates in the community nesting of the fabulous Social Weavers. From a distance their nest structure looks like a haystack hung in a tree, but the inset above shows clearly that the sponge-like framework has innumerable entrance holes. When the birds begin their work each pair builds an individual nest, but they weave so close to one another that eventually a whole nest-complex develops under a communal rain-proof shelter. Later generations add more nests; so the structure grows through the decades until it harbours a thousand pairs of birds. If the weight is evenly balanced on strong branches, the nest, which is carefully repaired daily, can survive the tree... However, in spite of all co-operation the right of possession is jealously guarded. Each nest is a little castle on its own. Spiny blades of grass, pointing outwards, protect the entrance tunnel which descends vertically for about a foot to the circular nest chamber, and privacy is assured by strong dividing walls. Of course, such dry refuges are also sought after by others. Snakes and especially Pygmy Falcons move immediately into any vacant apartment.

The locust problem has been one of the main concerns of UN's Food and Agricultural Organization (FAO). No effort was spared to discover the breeding grounds of locusts, scattered in regions of temporary vegetation throughout the deserts from Morocco to Saudi Arabia. To-day, these danger zones are kept under constant observation, so that in case of emergency, eggs and young wingless insects can be exterminated on the ground. For, when locusts have time to feed on the sparse desert vegetation their wings will grow on the 20th day, and, in search of more food, the swarm will rise on the hot air currents and travel with the wind in mile-wide rattling clouds over land, lakes and inlets of the sea. Then the poison sprays from aircraft come too late, for where the "scourge of Allah" settles, no leaf remains.

A swarm of locusts (*Locusta m. migratorioides*). When insecticides were first used against locusts, numbers of migratory storks fell victim as well. Chemicals being used nowadays are alleged to be harmless to birds.

While the scientists of the FAO, the Food and Agriculture Organization, are still working to control the locust plague, a new and potent enemy has risen against the farmers: the enormous host of seed-consuming Weaver Birds, the Red-billed Queleas. From Senegal and the Sudan down to the Republic of South Africa they devour nearly one fifth of the millet and corn harvest on the stalk. Conferences, budgets, and programmes to combat this pest have proved almost useless, and drastic tests such as dynamiting the nesting-trees and spreading infectious epidemics have only called to arms bird lovers the whole world over. However, extermination is not intended, but only a check on the population growth before the Quelea plague reaches the magnitude of former locust catastrophes.

Red-billed Queleas in Southern Rhodesia. When such dense swarms skim the water to drink in flight, many birds are forced down and drowned by the weight of other birds. These losses, though, hardly thin the flights.

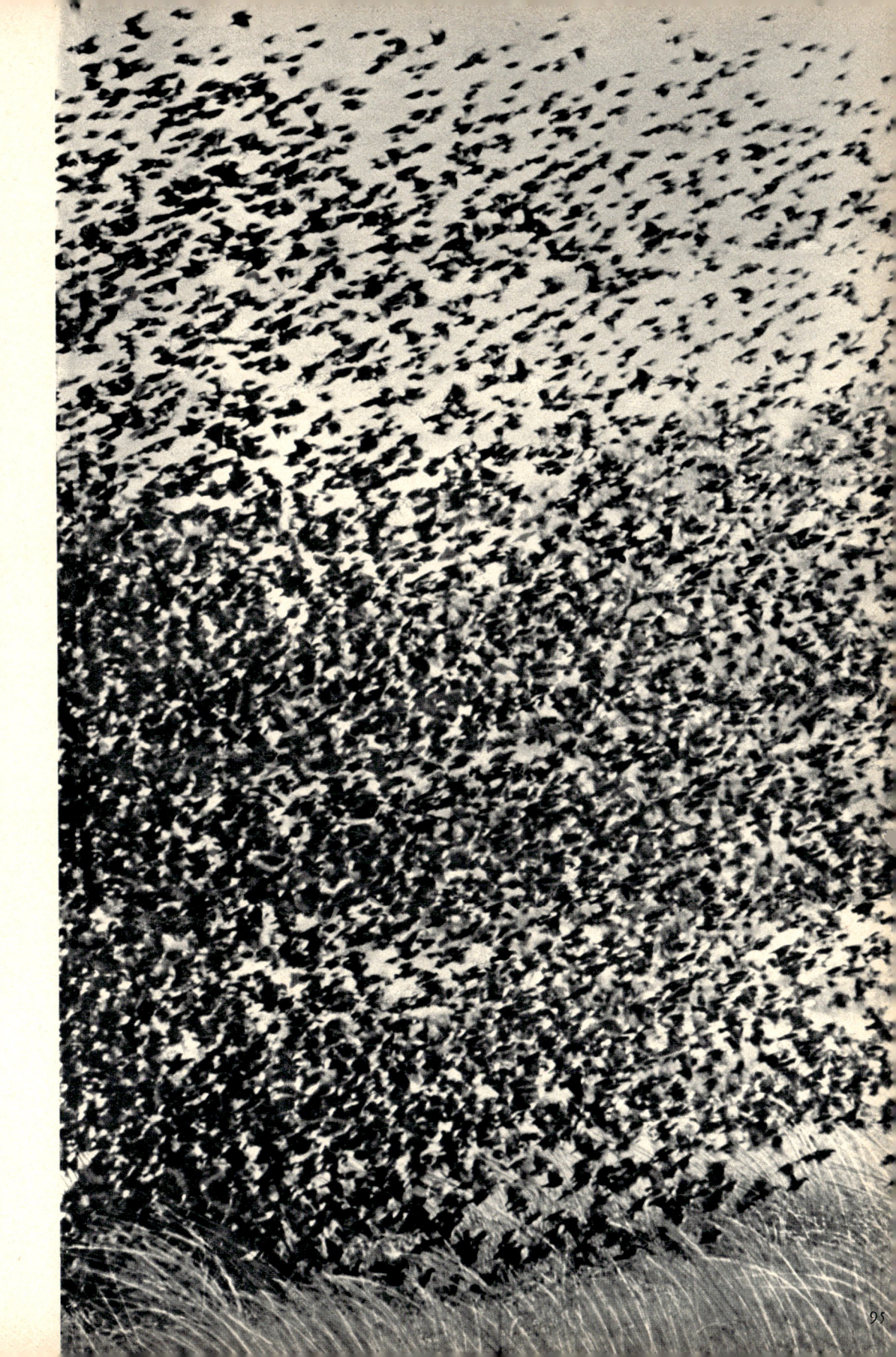

European Spoonbills *(Platalea leucorodia)* arriving at their winter quarters in Banc d'Arguin, coast of Mauretania.

Africa's wealth of water-fowl is one of the undiminished charms of the Continent. When winter migrants from Europe join the swarming indigenous birds, a period of bustling activity begins on coasts and lakes. The newcomers — Spoonbills, Ruffs, Greenshanks, Terns, Snipe, and Sandpipers — all seek vacant places on the shores where they can rest after their long journey. The new generation which has grown up in the north has to get used to its unfamiliar winter home, while the "genuine Africans", disturbed by the noisy invasion, guard their own sites defensively. Some migratory birds such as the European Spoonbills hardly fly beyond the Tropic of Cancer where the sub-tropics begin. Spoonbills which were hatched on Neusiedler Lake in Austria or on the Danube Delta, fly to the Nile by way of the Bosphorus, while Dutch and Spanish Spoonbills winter in Mauretania. Thus, they will never meet their tropical cousins which have red facial masks and red-rimmed blue bills. These birds live on the lakes of Central Africa... in a true paradise for water-fowl, where the ornithologist can find assembled over 360 different species.

Crowned Cranes *(Balearica pavonia)* in the Waza Reservation, North Cameroons. See also pages 108–109.

Such birds as spoonbills, ibises, avocets and flamingoes which live on plankton, filtering tiny creatures from the water, are free to increase at will; so, too, are the great fish-eaters, the herons and pelicans who are not yet hunted down as competitors by the fishermen of Africa. But quite a number of wild ducks and geese are on the FAO list of harmful plant-devouring pests. Thanks to their beautiful appearance the Crowned Cranes are not penalised for looting rice paddies and millet fields. Around Lake Tchad and in the region of the Niger they are still plentiful, and when 50 to 100 of these big birds, with blaring trumpet calls, settle on a paddy field, all the young seedlings are soon finished off, green stuff being their favourite food. However, during the breeding season, the Crowned Cranes hunt for insects and frogs in the vicinity of their marsh nests, but as soon as there are seeds to harvest they return to the fields. Unlike those in the Niger and Congo regions the Crowned Cranes in the south and east strut about only in small family groups, as many are caught to be kept as ornamental garden pets. Also Blue Paradise or Stanley Cranes of the African veldt with their long feather trains are rarely met in the wild to-day.

Startled swarms on wing and water:

Flamingoes *(Phoeniconais minor* and *Phoenicopterus antiquorum)* along the shore of Lake Nakuru (South West Kenya) which was proclaimed a bird sanctuary in 1961. This soda-saturated lake of 26 sq. miles is not a nesting place but is used as a feeding-ground outside the breeding season. Half a million to a million birds may congregate here annually.

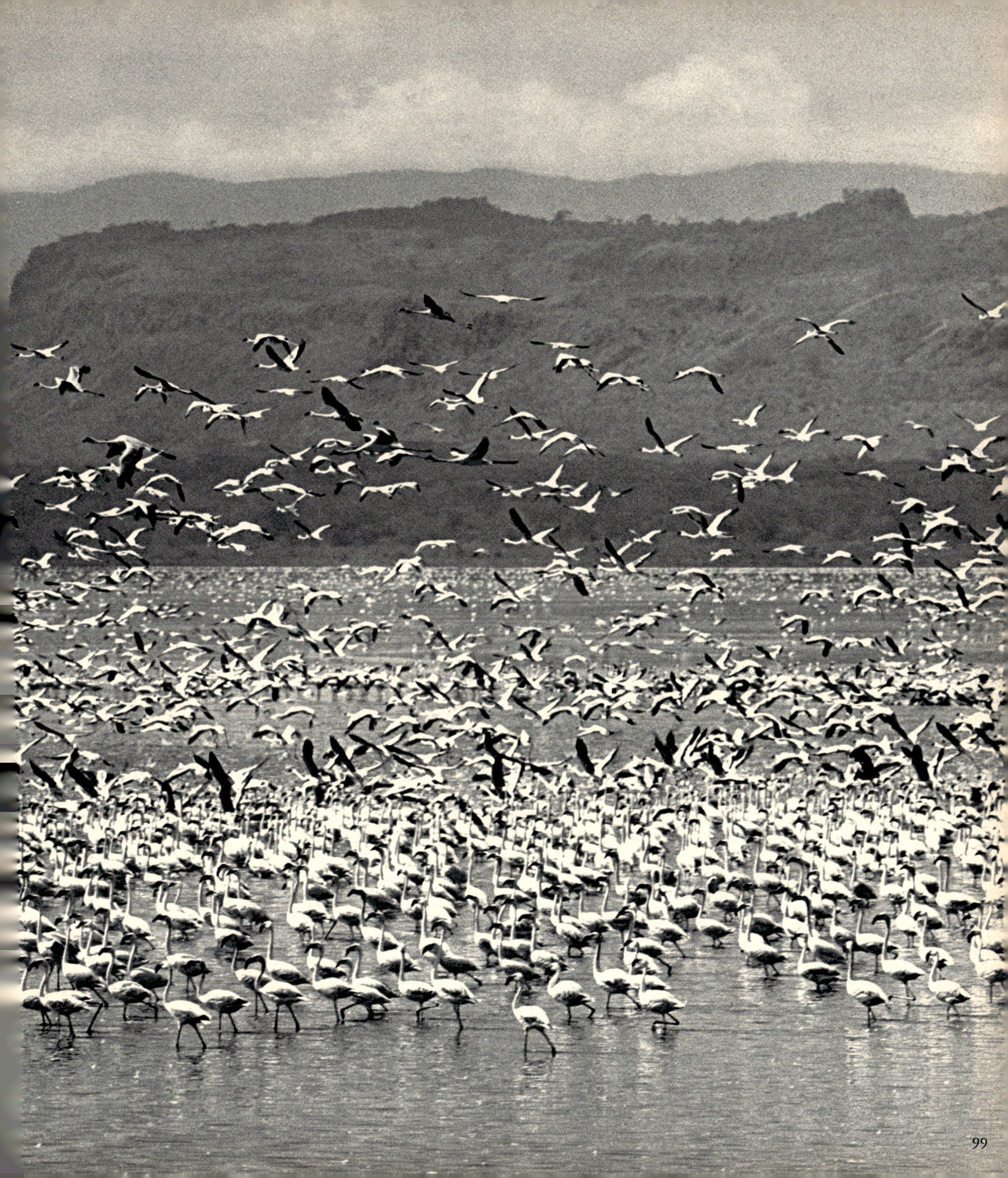

Two paradisaical scenes in the Queen Elizabeth Park in Uganda. Cattle Egrets *(Bubulcus ibis)* rest near the Weaver Birds' nests...

Nature demands that its creatures live next to one another, over one another, and with one another... but how rare are such moments of quiet harmony! The white Cattle Egrets have withdrawn to the branches, thereby leaving in peace the insects on the hippopotami's backs. Like all specialists these birds are so successful in their profession that their services are welcome wherever they go. They are allowed to rest on elephants, to climb all over hippos, and even to slip between the legs of rhinos and buffaloes to search their bellies for parasites. If the white swarm flies up in alarm the herds take warning and rush off, but keen hunters would judge by the egrets' flight the direction a herd was taking... When the great mammals began to decrease in numbers the little white egrets found new "customers" in the increasing herds of domestic cattle. Protected as benefactors they have grown to such numbers that the vast continent has become too small for them. The Iberian Peninsula was the nearest expansion area, but they migrated about 30 years ago to South America where they bred successfully. Scores of Cattle Egrets have also made their home on the larger islands of the Caribbean and more and more settle in the South of the USA without going through "Immigration". Even Australia reports an invasion since 1948!

...while comic Hammerheads or Umbrettes *(Scopus umbretta)* use the good-natured Hippotami as floating islands.

Ornithology accepts the Cattle Egrets and Tickbirds as the skin conditioners of the big mammals, but photographs prove that other birds, too, take advantage of the floating colossi. Who could have believed that even the small Jacanas, also known as Lily-Trotters because they walk on rafts of water-lilies, are permitted to peck about on the skin of the hippopotami, and that many other water-birds like to use these floating islands of flesh as their meeting ground? Here five Umbrettes have made a safe landing. The Boers called these dusky chaps "*Hammerkops*". In all African waters, from the mangrove bays to the paddy fields, four species of Hammerheads are to be found. All are highly skilled builders; their enormous, very durable tree-nests have a circumference of six feet, are three feet in height, and weigh two hundredweight. After a building period of six months the reed house, in which clay is used as mortar, is closed in all round and has only one small opening. Amazingly, the interior is divided by reed-walls into a kind of a guard's "lobby", a central room, and, at a slightly higher level, sleeping quarters and a hatchery. Legend relates that other birds help to build the home of the pampered "Sultan Birds" and even decorate the wall with fragments of bone.

Giant and dwarf hunting for frogs. A Whale-headed Stork or Shoebill *(Balaeniceps rex)* and a Cattle Egret in the Queen Elizabeth Park, Uganda.

For a long time stories of Abu Markub, the "Father of the Shoe", were dismissed as Arab fairy tales. It is only a hundred years since the Shoebill moved from legend to zoology books. Its home is in the papyrus swamps along the White Nile, where it builds yard-high nests, but a vagrant bird will fly southward now and then to the lakes of Uganda. To watch the giant Abu Markub strutting about is a surprising enough experience, but it is even more astonishing to see the heavy grey stork spread its wings and rise into the air. The strangest thing of all is the mighty beak which really does resemble a clumsy wooden shoe and yet can thrust with lightning speed. When this cautious hunter has spotted his prey in the marshes or in shallow water, he jabs with the hooked point of the upper maxilla, and the hapless victim has vanished in a flash; shad, lung fish, lizards, turtles and tortoises... even crocodile babies perish between the sharp horny cutting edges of this incredible beak. And the Shoebill can use this monstrous structure during the mating season to clatter merrily.

A companion of the wild flocks in the Serengeti, Tanganyika: a Giant Bustard *(Otis kori)* displaying, unworried by the Gnus.

Among the many animal societies living in co-existence in the steppes, the Bustard struts around as the odd man out. Some species are no larger than fowl, others are the size of sheep. Like the Herons and the Tickbirds, they profit from the insects teeming around grazing animals. When the tramping hooves startle swarms of insects out of hiding, the Bustards consume vast numbers of these pests. They slake their thirst by pecking into wild water-melons, but have become so accustomed to drought that during the rainy season they often move away to drier regions. When there are no insects, Bustards hunt for small reptiles and mammals or pick seeds and the resin from acacia trees. If danger threatens they seek flight by running and jumping high into the air with extended wings. During the mating season the male Bustard entices the female with an impressive ritual. First he raises his tail vertically, displaying the white under-feathers, then he turns in a circle, stamping on the ground, inflating his throat and emitting an eerie "woom-woom". Ecstasy ruffles each individual feather until the male looks like a huge quivering ball of plumage.

Openbills *(Anastomus lamelligerus)* and Baboons on the look-out for fish in a drying-out pond. Tsavo National Park, Kenya.

In times of mass death the strongest survivors grow fat. During the great drought in the Tsavo National Park in South Kenya the first to be threatened were creatures living in shallow waters; crayfish, snails, mussels and fish lay exposed in the mud of drying ponds. Thus fanciers of such food found a rich feast; but, as soon as the last drops of water had evaporated, all who were able left the desolate place. Troops of Baboons would go in search of other watering-places; Openbill Storks and other wading-birds moved off to the Shiré marshes, Nyasaland, to Lake Victoria, or even as far as the Zambesi. The bigger animals had to stay and sweat it out because to leave the protected zone would have exposed them to other dangers. So the dry hills west of the Tsavo Park were deserted, while in the east the game crowded in their thousands on river banks and at water-holes, trampling down the sparse vegetation and thereby favouring future erosion. At its inauguration in 1948, this huge reserve seemed large enough, but when rainy seasons failed, it proved too small. Meanwhile rains have come again, but in future the pumping station on Tsavo River, set up during the emergency, will secure an adequate supply of water in periods of drought.

A flock of wild Ostriches (Struthio camelus) at a water-hole in the Waza Reserve (56,000 acres), North Cameroons.

Ostriches are exceptionally well-equipped for life in the heat-shimmering semi-desert; if they can find enough succulent plants they hardly need to drink for six months or more. Their long eyelashes and triple eyelids form a protection against sandstorms and glaring sunshine. Thick-cushioned soles under their twin-toed feet insulate them against the burning ground, and when they are escaping at 25 to 30 m.p.h., predators soon give up the chase. These earth-bound birds are immune to every threat except the guile of man. The Bedouins knew that the Sudan Ostriches always used to run to the leeward, so they rode against the wind to cut them off. Bushmen used to deceive Ostriches by disguising themselves in an array of feathers and then closing in on the flock. Had settlers in South Africa not had the idea to create Ostrich farms the world's biggest bird would have been exterminated long ago, and we would see it only in museums, along with the ten-foot high *Aepyornys* of Madagascar. This huge flightless bird became extinct in early historical times. As "Roc" it still flies through Arabian fairy tales, because Sheherezade did not know that the flight of birds was limited to those under 40 pounds in weight. But to compensate the feathered giants for the loss of the freedom of the air Nature has endowed them with other aptitudes.

Farm ostriches cannot indulge in cockfights or in the free nomadic life of their wild cousins; but the old excitement flares up in the mating season. Although the female is "allotted" by the farmer and not fought for, the ritual is still performed. The cock kneels before the hen with legs bent forward, spreads his wings, waves the feather fans and sinuously bends his neck like a snake. He turns and twists his body until he has scooped out a nest-like hollow in the ground, or, grunting from his distended throat, he scrapes it out with his feet. During the following month the brown female fills the nest cavity with 17 to 20 eggs weighing 3 pounds each, the equivalent of two dozen hen's eggs; but the egg of the giant Madagascar "ostrich" was six times larger. The hen often shirks her maternal duties, but usually both parents incubate the eggs, she during the day and he at night. If they are disturbed in the wild they "turn invisible" by stretching flat in the sand, neck and head extended — a well-known "ostrich attitude". Should the attacker not be deceived they jump up to divert attention from the nest and threaten the enemy with murderous kicks which can be fatal even to man or lion.

However, during the 6 weeks of incubation on the farm no danger threatens. In the last fortnight before the chicks are hatched the body temperature of the incubating parents rises to such a degree that the metabolism of the embryo is strongly activated. By absorbing the remaining albumin the chick grows rapidly until the thick dried-out shell bursts with a sharp crack... but it is still some hours before the chick can free itself. For the first five days it subsists on the jelly accumulated under its skin. Then it begins to peck cheerfully. At 18 months the new generation has grown up, but the young birds do not become sexually mature before their 3rd or 4th year.

➤ An ostrich family on a farm in the Oudtshoorn region, Cape Province. From 1903 to 1930, when the fashion for ostrich feathers was at its peak, farms grew extensively. The export of feathers taken from 750,000 birds ranked fourth in value after gold, diamonds and wool. To-day, only about 50,000 ostriches are kept, each yielding an income of £1,000 / $ 3,000. From the age of six months, soft "plumeau" feathers can be cut, and from then on until the 15th year feathers can be "harvested" from cocks and castrated females. In the wild an ostrich will reach an age of 45 years but on farms they are culled long before that. Everything is usable; the skin is material for fine leather goods, the flesh from the thighs is made into "biltong", and milled bones are used as fertilizer and cattle food. In addition to all this, one may find in an ostrich stomach about 12 pounds of such digestive aids as sand, stones, and many items lost by visitors.

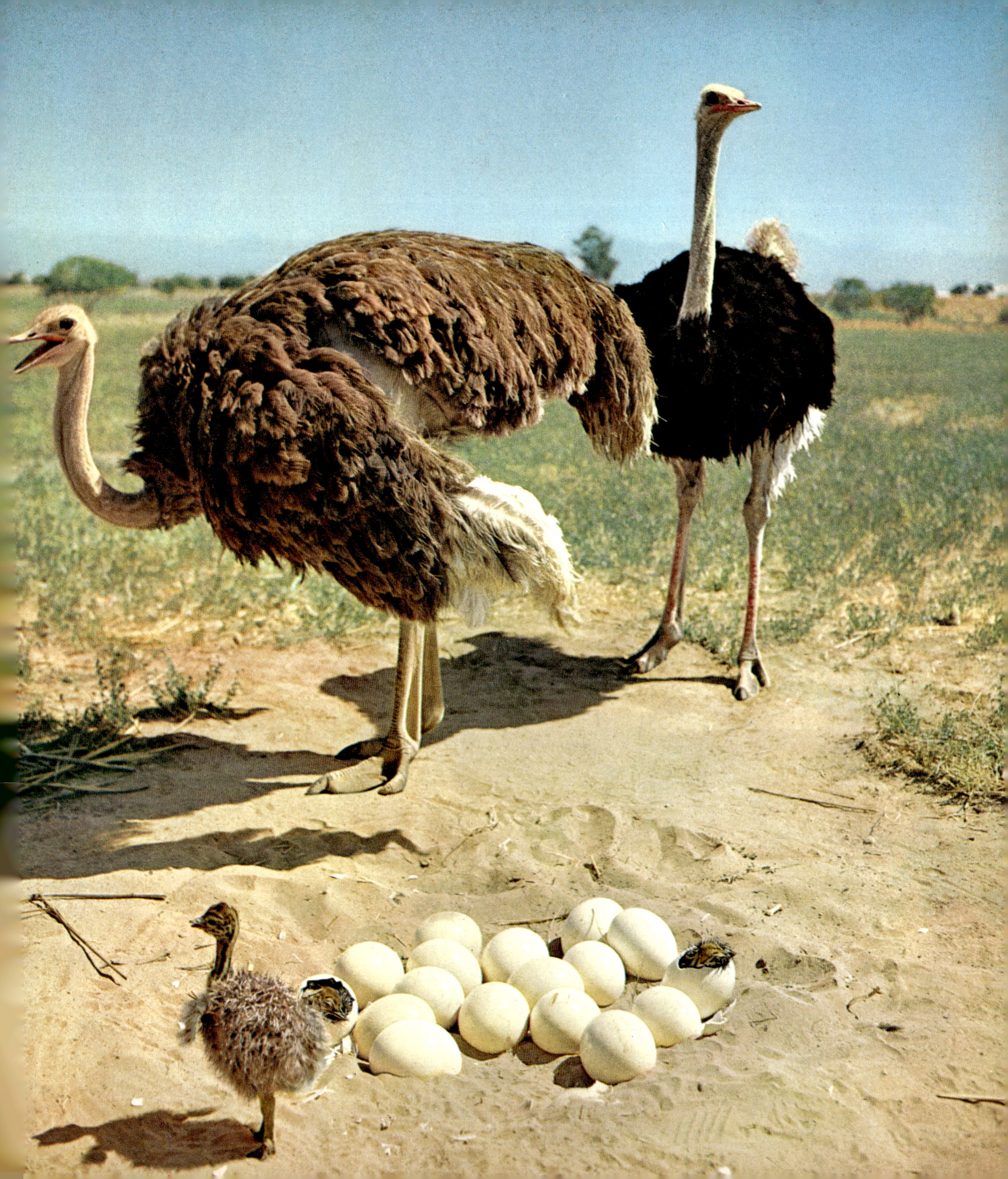

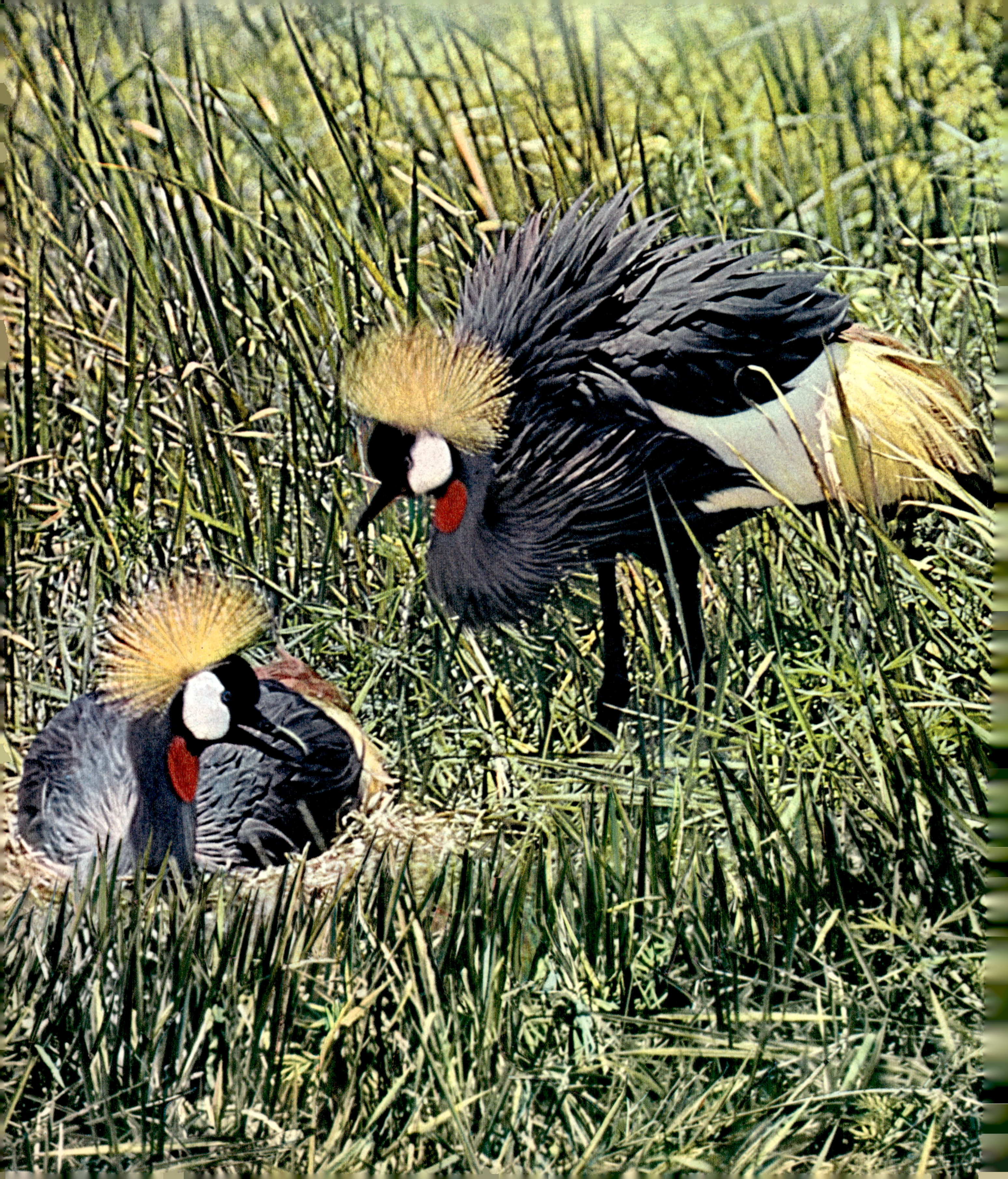

The mating dance of the Crowned Cranes is one of the most beautiful spectacles in the bird kingdom. No wonder that the natives, still living close to Nature, have imitated this choreography of love. By ritual magic, Negroes have always tried to acquire the most admirable characteristics of their fellow creatures. Birds and animals have had to give their lives to lend courage, speed and strength to warriors; to decorate their bodies with furs, feathers, teeth, claws, horns and beaks. But the maidens of the Watusi tribe in the Congo do not adorn themselves with borrowed plumage; they are far more subtle in their adoption of the graces of the Crowned Cranes. They study every movement, every dance-step of these elegant birds, and then create the most enchanting pantomime of all African folklore. The mating ceremony of the Cranes goes through many phases of advance and apparent withdrawal. For seconds male and female stand facing each other with staring eyes, then jump back and come forward again, wings outspread. Mute bowing changes to high leaping into the air with blaring trumpet calls, and finally the birds dance round and round each other with spritely steps until the excitement dies down and a caressing entwining of necks seals the union.

◀ A pair of Crowned Cranes *(Balearica p. regulorum)* change shift while nesting in a swampy meadow (Rhodesia).

▸ Two phases in the mating dance of *Balearica pavonia*. – *Below:* Nursing the tiny chicks. (North Cameroons.)

Bird photography in Africa is a fascinating hobby which easily diverts one from lions and elephants. The more patient among ornithologists observe family life from a camouflaged hiding place, while those more interested in movement point their cameras towards the sky. The rapid beat of tiny wings is too fast for "Man's third eye", but the large water birds are far more satisfactory subjects, especially the web-footed varieties, some of which show amazing aerial prowess. The Pelican, weighing 20 to 40 pounds, is the heaviest flying bird. The additional weight of only 4 to 10 pounds denied the Dodo of Mauritius the freedom of the air, with the result that this stocky bird of the Mascarene Islands (east of Madagascar) was exterminated as early as the 17th century by meat-hungry seafarers. The fastest in flight over the oceans are the magnificent Frigate Birds — the Man O' War and the Ascension Frigate Bird — with a wing span of over 7 feet, both still masters of the South Atlantic. They visit the coasts of West Africa before gathering at their rookeries on Cape Verde Islands and Ascension. In the air they are daring pirates and snatch fish booty, hard won in a dive, from their relatives the gannets and cormorants, or seize the flying fish escaping from the dolphins. By contrast, the Tropic Birds or Boatswains are skilful divers and the most graceful of the web-footed tribe. They breed on remote cliffs along the Red Sea and the Indian Ocean, but even there they are disturbed by man robbing them of their long tail feathers.

Above: Pelican *(Pelecanus rufescens)*, wingspan 8 feet. *Centre:* Darter or Snake Bird *(Anhinga rufa)*, wingspan 41 ins. *Below:* White-tailed Tropic Bird *(Phaeton aethereus)*, wingspan 40 inches. Tail feather 20 to 29½ inches.

Large and small Herons, brown and white Ibis, odd storks like the Marabous, the Openbills and the Wood Ibis can all be seen over the inland waters of Africa. One of the most imposing silhouettes is that of the enormous *Jabiru* or Saddlebill Stork, who loves to glide at great heights. When hungry this stork comes in to land and hunts with graceful dancing steps, swallowing frogs, crayfish, and even 3-lb. lung fish. By contrast, the Ibis with their sickle-bills filter only the smallest creatures from the mud of swampy river banks. Because the flight of these birds in advance of the rising Nile announced the coming of floods, the ancient Egyptians regarded the Sacred Ibises as harbingers of fertility who knew more of the secrets of the life-giving river than did the wisest of men. — The tropical Snake Birds or Anhingas prefer flooded regions, swimming submerged with only their snake-like necks showing. These birds are surface divers, going faster and deeper than cormorants. A curious anatomical adjustment makes fishing easy for them. The 8th and 9th cervical vertebrae form a Z-like kink in the neck, enabling the head and bill to be used like a spear on a spring, to give more force when thrusting at a fish. Similar anatomical structure also helps herons to fish, but prevents the usual preening and oiling. In compensation, so-called powder down feathers spreads a kind of talc which keeps the plumage waterproof. Cormorants and Anhingas however get so wet that, after fishing, they have to spread out their wings to help them dry.

Above: Black-headed Heron *(Ardea melanocephala)*, wingspan 4 feet 6 inches. *Centre: Jabiru* or Saddlebill Stork *(Ephippiorhynchus senegalensis)*, wingspan 7 feet 8 inches. *Below:* Sacred Ibis *(Threskiornis aethiopica)*; wingspan 5 feet.

Many of Africa's birds of prey are similar to those of other regions, but the Secretary Bird *(Sagittarius serpentarius)* is unique. When it struts across the plains on its cranelike legs and raises its crest in excitement it actually does resemble an 18th century secretary with quill pens stuck behind his ears. However, this secretary has no interest in calligraphy but rather in the "signatures" of snakes and lizards traced in the sand. With a bound it closes in on its prey, spreads its wings like a shield, and crushes even tortoises with its powerful talons. When threatened it flees at a run as it prefers not to fly. But when the hungry fledglings cry from the nest high in a tree, the striking silhouettes of the parent Secretary Birds are often seen against the sky.

The Cape Sea-Eagle *(Haliaëtus vocifer)* has been called "The Voice of Africa" for its loud cry resounding over inland waters. Even when gliding the proud bird throws back its head to utter its challenging "cow-cow-cowcowcow", for surely it deems itself "Lord of the Lakes". Each couple occupies a wide territory where there is abundance of food. Dead fish scooped up on the surface are easy loot, and should Their Majesties feel it to be too much trouble to fish for themselves, they force other water fowl to sacrifice their catch. Some birds save their own skins by such a tribute, for should the Sea-Eagle's hunger not be satisfied, it would attack the reed-nests of its neighbours.

The Crowned Eagle *(Stephanoaëtus coronatus)* is the fiercest of African eagles. It inhabits the rain forests between Sierra Leone and Uganda, is common in the Congo, but becomes rarer to the south. In appearance and in its way of hunting it combines all the best features of eagles, hawks, and owls. Observers can see the Crowned Eagle only when it rises occasionally from a high look-out, because this fierce bird of prey prefers to hunt by gliding down into the green twilight of the foliage to hover silently like an Eagle Owl over the cautious guenons or duiker antelopes. Hardly has its prey been chosen when the eagle plunges screaming, with a hawk's swiftness, onto the petrified victim. Because of its outstanding skill as a hunter, the magnificent Crowned Eagle, with its 6-foot wing span, is revered by the Pygmies as the royal bird whose plumage may be worn by none but the tribal chief.

The Long-crested Eagle *(Lophoaëtus occipitalis)*, too, haunts the forests while the Black Eagle and the Martial Eagle circle over the mountains and plains. The Long-crested Eagle prefers the humidity of the forest and loves to perch on the highest tree, waggling its crest. In Kenya it will come quite close to villages, where it makes itself useful catching rats and mice, but its favourite prey is the brightly coloured pigeons. This feathered booty is not easy to catch, for when startled by the warning cries of other animals, it vanishes into the thicket. Thus Nature has her own code of fair play, and everyone has a chance; so the Long-crested Eagle must sometimes go without food for an astoundingly long time and shows its displeasure only by its drooping crest.

A Palmnut Vulture *(Gypohierax angolensis)* collecting its favourite food from an Oil Palm in the Congo Forest.

When European ornithologists first studied this predatory bird they thought it was an exceptionally light-coloured species of eagle, but later its anatomy revealed its relationship with the vultures, and it was called Vulturine Fishing Eagle. However, its other name, *Palmnut Vulture,* is far more apt. This eccentric creature begins life as a vegetarian. When the single young is hatched it is fed on nothing but the husks of the palm seed so that the airy nursery, at a height of 30 to 180 feet, never becomes a fly-ridden charnel-house. Even after 47 days, when the fledgling leaves the eyrie it will still be fed for another month on palm fruit and because of this diet it has to keep to the tops of the tropical palm trees *(Elaeis guineensis* and *Raphia vinifera).* Later on, when fishing for crabs on the shores of the lakes, it will sometimes eat a dead fish, but it always comes back to the palms for its dessert. With maturity the bird's hunger for flesh grows, and it becomes a true predator hunting lizards and young monkeys. But as if to deny its relationship with the bare-necked scavengers, it rarely feeds on carrion. Should its hunting skill decline it can always return to the vegetarian diet of its youth.

The Bateleur *(Terathopius ecaudatus)* has caught a Guinea Fowl. Was it a wild one or the treasured possession of some native woman?

"Bateleur" is a French word meaning juggler or buffoon, but what a name for an eagle! Towards the end of the 18th century, the French naturalist François Levaillant was travelling in Africa when he noticed an unfamiliar bird of prey giving an aerial display of the drollest kind. He called the bird *bateleur* — the word for the roving jugglers giving open-air performances. The name fits well, for this jester does not possess the dignity of other eagles. With its reddish talons and red beak with a blue hook it even looks like a made-up clown. When perching it can never sit still, but is constantly flapping its wings and turning its head inquisitively in all directions. When it takes to the air it ornaments its line of flight with elegant loops, then starts diving, surges up afresh, and soars upward to begin the fun all over again. Perhaps the males of the species once invented these capers as a mating display to impress the female, and enjoyed them so much that it could not stop the habit. Because of these aerobatics the Bateleur is the best-known eagle between Lake Tchad and the Orange River. It hunts mostly for reptiles and rodents but a Guinea Fowl is far better catch. These ornamental fowl, known the world over, still run wild in their homeland and continue to increase in spite of their many enemies.

A banquet of scavengers: Marabou Storks *(Leptoptilos crumeniferus)* and Vultures besiege an elephant carcass. Uganda.

Vultures are always the first to discover the death of big game, but as they cannot penetrate the thick skin of the carcass they must wait until the smell of putrefaction attracts the clawed scavengers, who then get the greatest share, while only the left overs remain for the vultures. It is to the latters' advantage if the Marabous arrive first, for these hack open the skin with their enormous beaks, so that the vultures can drag out the flesh and intestines, an impossible task for the Marabous. Hardly has a vulture torn a scrap for itself when a Marabou demands its tribute, becoming violently aggressive at the least denial. It is an unwilling co-operation, where one helps to satisfy another's hunger, but without this feeding partnership all would go empty-bellied. — Often the Marabous will fly behind a bush fire and gorge themselves on the resulting "mixed grill", but during the breeding season they prefer to hunt fish and water rats in the close vicinity of their nesting trees. Many pairs nest close to villages where they are popular as street cleaners. They consume every kind of refuse, even the legs of cattle complete with hooves, and then, after gorging themselves, stand about like peevish adjutants while their digestive juices are at work. Another name for the Marabou is crop stork — in Arabic *Abu Sein*: "The Father of the Leather Bottle"— but the long, sometimes red neck sac is not a food storage crop but probably, as with Turkeys, an organ of display.

The Spotted Hyaena *(Crocuta crocuta)*, rarely seen after dawn, is shown here among vultures in the Amboseli Reserve, South Kenya.

All through the ages hyaenas —"cowardly and stinking"— have imbued man with as much horror as nausea. That they are considered to be the ultimate in ugliness is due only to the comparison with noble dogs to whom they are in no way related. They represent a distinctive family of their own which got detached during the tertiary period from the cat tribe. Every "hideous" characteristic of their bodies has some purpose; the long front legs with the clumsy paws can nail cadavers vice-like to the ground, the thick neck-muscles and ugly arched jaws give the teeth the power of bone crushers, and the fur is so rough that it is not easily matted by constant contact with blood and decay. — During the last glacial period huge Cave Hyaenas howled and hunted throughout Europe, but today the Spotted Hyaena, or *fisi*, is the largest and most common south of the Sahara. It shuns the sun, lurking underground or in caves where the black offspring are born with eyes already open and jaws lined with sharp little teeth. It was once believed that hyaenas were hermaphrodites because the females have a functionless scrotum, but this superstition proved to be as groundless as the belief that all hyaenas were possessed of the "evil eye". Nor is their "satanic laughter" a devil's message but just their way of calling the group together. Only when unable to find carrion will hyaenas slink around herds of goats. They never dig up cadavers as is often maintained, but the Masai ceremoniously offer their dead to hyaenas, seeing in them messengers of their God *En Gai*.

Young Cape Hunting Dogs (*Lycaon pictus*) are unpleasant play-mates. Only the strongest of the litter survive the rough life in the pack.

The most ferocious carnivores of the Dark continent are the Cape Hunting Dogs. Thanks to their ability to hunt down living prey in broad daylight these skewbald Wild Dogs have no need to prowl at night in search of carrion. The first settlers in South Africa met packs of hundreds which attacked their cattle once the wild herds had been exterminated. In retaliation high premiums were paid for shooting Wild Dogs, and the packs in their turn were hunted down. To-day, only small groups of 6, 10 or 25 at the most, roam about in deserted regions. Wild Dogs emerge from their earth holes at daybreak and begin hunting on a wide front. As soon as the pack sights an antelope herd it closes in silently until the leading dog gives tongue. This is the command to attack a chosen victim. Instantly the pack divides. One half drives the fleeing game in a wide circle while the other cuts through at the right moment to head it off. When the quarry begins to show signs of exhaustion the dogs leap at it and tear hunks of flesh from its hind quarters until loss of blood saps the antelope's strength. It is cruel hunting but nevertheless it has its purpose in the economy of the wild. A large pack can fell lions weakened by old age, and when the dogs have sated themselves on the King of Beasts they devour their own kind fallen in the deadly struggle.

A Wolf-like Jackal *(Canis lupaster)* shows its teeth to a rival Vulture disputing its right to carrion.

Master Jackal stands somewhere between Reynard the Fox and Isengrin the Wolf, not only anatomically but in the psychological sense, too. The ancient Egyptians bestowed on their God *Anubis* the snout of a jackal and the tail of a lion, and in innumerable Arabian and Negro fairy tales it is the intelligent and wily jackal who triumphs over the rather simple-minded hyaena. The four African species of jackals are impudent rascals, raiding chicken runs and hutches by night, plundering vineyards, and stealing everything edible from houses and tents. In the wild they hunt rodents and dwarf antelopes or, with caution, thieve from feasting lions. They do not live in disciplined packs like Hunting Dogs, but howl themselves together one might say, into loose bands in which each one seeks its own advantage, leaving the others in the lurch when in danger. Young jackals begin to follow their mothers at the age of two months, by which time they are already competent thieves and howlers. By contrast, their cousins, the Abyssinian Wolves or *Kaberu*, are skilled and dreaded hunters, while in the south and east Bat-eared Foxes roam, contenting themselves with a diet of insects, eggs, and fruit. Compared with the unpalatable flesh of the carrion-eaters, the meat of these foxes is such a delicacy for man that often they have to pay with their lives for their non-predatory habits.

The Desert Lynx or Caracal (*Lynx caracal*) represents the long-legged type of cat. The facial mask is especially comic in the kittens.

Like the jackal the caracal gets its name from the Turkish. Its domain extends from Africa to Transcaspia and Western India. In Central Africa the Banda tribe call it, with some exaggeration, *Bakanga* — "maneless lion" — but all natives have reason to fear the wild caracal. When man surprises a lion or a leopard at a kill it usually keeps on eating or vanishes, leaving its prey behind. By contrast, the caracal becomes savage and attacks instantly. Unlike the northern lynx it avoids the forest and slinks by night across the desert or savannah seeking its favourite prey — hyrax, dik-diks, baby antelopes and wildfowl. It possibly also hunts ostrich chicks, but reports of a caracal attacking a full-grown sitting ostrich sound like hunters' talltales. The other African wild cats are just as ferocious and irritable as the caracal or Desert Lynx: the Golden Cat of the rain forests and the Jungle Cat of the Egyptian reedbeds — but it is the Nubian Fallow Cat — bred, tamed and made sacred by the ancient Egyptians — which has become familiar to man, subsequently beloved as a pet throughout the world.

The Feline or Small-spotted Genet *(Genetta genetta)* exhibits the totally different anatomy of the short-legged cat-like viverrines.

Black spots and stripes are the camouflage of many small hunters in Africa. The biggest of these is the Civet *(see p. 135)* which, when angry, lets off a quantity of a substance known as "civet", and used in the manufacture of perfumes. This musk-like secretion of the anal gland serves to mark out their hunting territory, to attract the opposite sex, or as a defence. The slimmer, long-tailed Genet gives off less of the secretion than does the Civet itself — which is the greatest producer — while the even smaller Linsang is completely odourless. Both are so light as to be able to climb trees to rob nests. Perhaps for as long as the Nubian Fallow Cat has been domesticated, Arabs and Negroes have kept these small creatures in their huts to catch mice. The Water Genet of the Congo forests is a skilled catcher of fish and so shy that it has only once been captured alive. — In Africa even the weasels are striped black and white. The family of martens and polecats is represented by the Zorilles who resemble the American skunks with their black and white markings, being just as great "stinkers". They eject their nauseating liquid into the eyes of their adversaries. Thus, Zorilles are wisely ignored by the bigger cats. Their harlequin tunic is no mere camouflage but serves as a warning. Any animal coming too close will be unable for days to scent prey or danger because of the clinging stench that blunts its sense organs.

Curiosity or prudence? These twin Cheetahs (*Acinonyx jubatus*) were uncertain whether to be friendly or to retreat.

Cheetah young bear little resemblance to their parents. Only the black "tear marks" indicate that one day the near white fluffy kittens will grow into elegant hunting leopards with sleek spotted fur. The typical spots are already visible on their legs but until the fourth month they will still wear the baby mane covering their backs, and they will still be able to retract their claws to slap one another with velvet paws; later on, these will become blunt, protruding "dog's claws". Anyone wanting an exotic pet, amusing at first and eventually growing into a noble house companion, able to purr like a cat and to run like a greyhound, is well advised to get a cheetah kitten as young as possible. However, huntsmen of the Orient know that a cheetah caught too young will never be good for chasing, for it was separated from its mother too soon for her to teach it the art of hunting. To capture half-grown animals usually involves some losses because the frightened creatures injure themselves struggling against ropes or in cages. It was in this way that the Indians exterminated their cheetahs; and they have, since 1940, sought to replace them with African cheetahs. But these magnificent animals are now reduced to the danger limit in Africa and it is hoped that the newly independent countries will not allow their export.

Childish aggressiveness. The young Serval *(Leptailurus serval)* shows its teeth without being otherwise disturbed.

Can it be that the small predatory cats owe their characteristic nervous tension to their slender body structure? Compared with Wild Cats, Lynx and Servals, Lions and Leopards appear to be phlegmatic in the awareness of their size and strength. The permanent aggressiveness of the smaller cats stems perhaps from the fact that they have to capture small prey ten to twenty times a day, while the big fellows can live for days on a single kill. The long-legged Serval rather reminds one of a miniature Cheetah with big ears. Its hunting grounds range over savannahs, bushland, and wooded mountains, where, at dusk, it preys on rodents, lizards, and ground fowl and, being a fine climber, it can go after birds roosting on trees. A full-grown male Serval will bring down even dwarf antelopes. Its ears act like parabolic reflectors when hunting small animals at night. Servals are extremely cunning and avoid the most craftily hidden traps. Black-coated furs occur, especially on high ground in Kenya and Abyssinia; the geographical limits of such hereditary melanism have yet to be explained.

It looks as if the Suricate *(Suricate suricate)* is trying to undermine the prickly hedgehog fortress.

The clowns among the small predators of South West Africa are the Suricates. Always busy, always cheerful, bustling about in the vicinity of their cave colonies, these cousins of the mongoose show astonishing zeal when excavating tunnels with their powerful digging claws. They like to show off, too, standing up on a rock and letting their long "stick tails" hang straight down. When a "watchman" stands like this, to his full height of fourteen inches, turning his head in all directions, he can detect every dark spot in the sky. Before the Crowned Eagles and Bateleurs have even started to dive, the colony has been warned and not a single Suricate is to be seen. Once the danger is over they are busily running about again scratching for insect larvae and hunting for all kinds of small prey. In true mongoose fashion they do not fear snakes although they can handle only younger ones. It is doubtful whether this Suricate will succeed in turning the hedgehog over and forcing it with a "stink douche" to unroll itself *(see above)*. Nevertheless, the spiny one must have been greatly alarmed to roll up in so tight a defensive ball, for the long-legged, big-eared African hedgehogs are usually not in a hurry to do so.

The Ratel or Honey Badger *(Mellivora capensis)* loves honey and fruit but hunts rodents, birds and tortoises too.

No larger than our own badger, but what a dangerous neighbour! Man and beast alike make a wide detour round the irascible Ratel or Honey Badger who attacks every intruder without warning. According to eye-witnesses a Ratel even made an onslaught on Elsa, the famous lioness, and has left its claw marks on a buffalo. These outbursts of temper have little to do with self-defence but stem from excessive energy, probably induced by honey, which spurs the ferocious little creature to high peaks of sporting performance. In the search for its favourite food the Honey Badger has a capable helper — the Honey Guide. This partnership of bird and badger is one of the most interesting phenomena of communication between animals. The Ratel will stand up where it is in is full view and whistle for a honey bird. The bird then leads the badger, calling continuously, and guides it to a beehive hidden in the trunk of a tree or in a hole in the ground. On the spot the Ratel breaks open the beehive with its strong claws to get at the sweet honey, while its feathered partner picks out the bee larvae which it could not have reached without the badger's help. Both robbers are well protected against the stings of the infuriated bees, the one by its thick fur and the other by a dense coat of feathers.

A Wart-Hog sow *(Phacochoerus aethiopicus)* with one of her young. Usually the deserted lair of an Aardvark serves as a home. *Above:* Boar.

Among all the graceful animal figures of the steppe the grotesque Wart-Hogs stand out like unwitting comedians. They choose to roam about in the company of grazing zebras and gazelles, crouching on their calloused "knees" and using their tusks to plough up the earth for tubers and maggots. Should their more noble browsing partners take flight the Wart-Hogs follow holding their "paint brush" tails stiffly erect. As there is hardly any cover in the steppe they invariably run to their earths into which they proceed backwards, never to loose sight of their pursuers. Even the piglets know this drill although often they are not quick enough to escape an eagle. A full-grown boar, whose four tusks eventually grow to twice the length of its eye warts, can defend itself even against a pack of Hunting Dogs. — The grey variety are beasts of the plains, but the Bushpigs *(Potamochoerus porcus)* live in the forests of West Africa. Whenever they come out to plunder manioc and yam fields the natives make up for the loss by a good meal of pork, but the Giant Forest Hog is never seen outside the rain forest. The Whites "discovered" it only in 1904, but it has always been looked upon by Negroes as a symbol of physical strength, being the emblem of some of their secret societies.

An orphaned "warthoglet" seeks protection beside an East African Oryx or Beisa *(Oryx beisa)*.

It used to be fashionable among big game hunters to bring home at least one oryx trophy, and, as a curiosity, the head of a Wart-Hog. They still hang together, glass-eyed, on the walls of many gun rooms, but here, living together, they demonstrate far more impressively the visual characteristics of the species, and — whether warts or horns — they neither beautify nor disfigure, but serve only to distinguish. Experts pronounce the Oryx the most beautiful antelopes of their size in Africa and award the palm to the South African Beisa, the Gemsbok of the Boers *(Oryx Gazella)* which, with its 5-foot long spearlike horns, can brave even lions. Some ten thousand of these creatures, unique in the harmony of form and markings, still live in the desert reservations of Angola, South West and South Africa. The East African Beisa *(see picture)*, too, is at last under protection and lives in the savannahs of Eritrea, Somaliland and North Kenya, but the related fringe-eared Beisa is seen only south of the Equator. — The rarest of all oryx, the White Oryx *(page 63)*, living along the edge of the Sahara, is in greatest peril, having been terribly decimated by desert troops hunting with cars. How much wiser were the ancient Egyptians and Nubians; they tamed the northern Oryx and used them as domestic animals, as we know from many bas-reliefs on such buildings as the Pyramids of Gizeh.

The neat Dik-Dik *(Rhychotragus guentheri)* from the steppes of East Africa is only 14 inches high when fully grown.

"Antelope" means "flower-eyed" and the smaller and daintier the head the larger seem the almond eyes. The graceful Dwarf Antelopes, Oribi and Dik-Diks are like miniature models of the long-legged gazelles, and studying them closely is like looking back to the beginnings of the evolution of ungulates. All hooved animals, from the primeval horse to the ancestors of the elephant, were creatures not more than a yard high creeping about in the undergrowth. At that time, no slender-boned animals existed but only thick-set dwarf forms like the present-day Duikers, the size of a hare, and the Chevrotains which inhabit the thickets. Among the smallest of present-day species are the 9½-inch high Blauwboks which slip between the entangling maze of forest lianas. The most mercurial of these creatures are the Disneyesque Dik-Diks. When a troupe is in flight their little bodies bounce up and down in the long grass like rubber balls. Leaping yard-high they glance quickly backwards, change direction in mid-air, and never seem to touch the ground. The Dik-Dik and Oribi are geographically creatures of the steppe but psychologically they are "forest-dwellers" in the tall grass and have to decide at any given moment if it is safer to hide or to jump up high to get a better view. Their mountain-dwelling relatives, the 2-foot high Klipspringers or Klipbokkes, know no such dilemma. Sure-footed as the chamois they leap expertly from ledge to ledge along the steepest rock face.

A Bongo fawn *(Taurotragus euryceros)* at rest. The camouflaging white stripes on its chestnut-red coat will not disappear with age, but are the species' permanent markings.

When Dik-Dik mothers lead their young about it looks as though fawns were playing with plush toy animals. Compared to such tiny offspring, the new-born Bongo calf is a giant. Its deer-sized parents, who weigh 450 lbs. and carry lyre-shaped horns a yard long, are among the most majestic of antelopes. They are as elusive as the okapis, and live in the humid virgin forests along the equatorial belt where, in the bewildering play of light and shade, they are almost invisible — so effective is their camouflage. As with all forest antelopes, the temperament of the Bongo is held in check, for flight among the obstacles and tangled undergrowth of the forest requires far more care and attention than does the headlong flight of animals of the steppes. Very few hunters can boast of Bongo trophies, for these shy animals feed only between dusk and dawn and their spoor is usually lost in the shallow brooks which they love to follow. During their nocturnal excursions these discreet creatures feed on certain leaves, ripe fruit, rotting wood fibres and pungent bark from fallen trees, which are a delicacy for them. In the rain forests filled with the din of croaking frogs and screeching monkeys, where vision is confined, it is a matter of life and death to be able to distinguish friendly sounds from those signifying danger; hence the Bongo has enormous ears, more important to its survival than good sight.

An Eland *(Taurotragus oryx)*, having just freed her young from the embryonal envelope, quickly consumes the placenta before jackals, scenting the blood, discover the new-born.

60 million years ago Nature perfected one of her highest achievements with the development of the placenta: the transference of the breeding-place into the abdomen of the mother where the embryo would be safe and protected against outside interference to ripen to full vitality. The civilised human mother has learned to understand what is happening inside her, but has lost the primeval knowledge of instinctive behaviour during birth. On the other hand, there are still primitive people who, like animals, do not understand the connection between fertilisation and birth and try to explain the miracle of new life by magic. How much more surprising must be the unexpected event for a three-year-old eland when she throws a calf for the first time. In that decisive moment, when her supple body, trained by constant movement, is relieved quickly and relatively painlessly of its living burden, she acts instinctively as her own midwife. She does what any cow or mare in a stable would do if not hindered by man; she tears open the enveloping membrane which enfolds the lanky limbs of all hooved animals, severs the umbilical cord and massages the new-born with her tongue to stimulate circulation. Finally she consumes the vitamin and hormone-rich placenta, as if she knew that this unusual food would encourage the supply of milk and help to restore her own organs.

In the nursery of the Kongonis or Coke's Hartebeeste (*Alcelaphus cokei*), one of the calves has grown so much that it has to kneel to suckle.

The magnificent eland and the *Hartebeeste* seem to be a hybrid mixture of cattle, horse and stag, and among these is the largest of all the antelopes, the Giant Eland. The bull stands 6 ft. at the shoulder and weighs 2,000 lbs. It has been tried often, unsuccessfully, to cross the smaller eland with domestic cattle to obtain a breed resistent to the tsetse fly. Instead of artificial crossing experiments it would seem far more promising for the future to keep herds of eland in a semi-wild state, as has been done on a few farms in South Africa and Rhodesia. Later on elands would replace imported cattle and, it is hoped, would get used to being milked.

Zoologists once divided the *Hartebeeste* into 90 sub-species because of the bizarre forms of their horns. These animals appear ungainly and ill-proportioned until one sees them in movement. In play or in flight they demonstrate the whole gamut of their running technique, from an elegant pace to a swinging trot and then a high-spirited gallop. Whether Kaamas from the Transvaal, Toras from the Sudan or Kongonis from the Masai steppes, the *Hartebeeste* always congregate in the same habitats as zebras, gnus and gazelles. Even among herds of these other species the Hartebeeste fight their curious duels in which the opponents kneel down and clash their heads together with resounding cracks.

"Forbidden" hunting: hidden in a tree to watch for the passage of game, a black archer has killed a Lesser Kudu.

In this nuclear century with its weapons capable of destroying the "civilised" World, the poison arrow is still looked upon as the most treacherous means of killing. But where would the human race stand to-day if our ancestors had not made use of poisonous plant juices in their fight for life? Biochemists and toxicologists who study these primitive sorcerers' brews are finding interesting connections with modern pharmaceutical products. For example, it is quite possible that the shrub *Acocanthera schimperi*, which blossoms from Eritrea to the Transvaal, will provide humanity with a new remedial agent against certain cardiac disorders. Among East African tribes this plant has always been used for making arrow-poison. The dark-green leaves, the red fruit, and the bark are boiled together into a thick black porridge for 9 hours, during which time warriors and musicians dance round the magic pot. Every tribe, Giriama, Ndorobo, Wasanya, Wakamba or Wanduruma, adds its own specific ingredient according to secret recipes, e. g. the poisonous bud of *Discorea*. The Giriamas even throw a few Elephant Shrews into the potion for good measure, to ensure that their quarry will not flee in zig-zags but in a straight-ahead manner as the little shrews run. — Before he draws his bow the archer removes a cap from the arrowhead used to prevent evaporation of the poison. For a bowman hunting to feed himself and his family, to be a good shot was no crime; but too many natives, having been corrupted by the profit motive of the white man, have disgraced themselves by becoming poachers.

"Authorised" slaughter: by order of the Tsetse Control Commission approximately 60,000 hooved animals were shot in Uganda.

When a government proclaims a massacre of game there are always so many volunteers that protests of good sense come too late. There are many gaps in the appalling statistics of the officially organised extermination of animals, but it may suffice to note that in Natal alone, during the Twenties, half a million hooved animals were killed; later, just as many in Southern Rhodesia were exterminated, and between 1952 and 1962 in Uganda another 60,000 antelopes were destroyed — all without any economic use being made of the meat or hides. Their death was a tragic error of judgment. The pernicious circle begins with the trypanosomes, 13–33 micro-millimeter-long flagellates which multiply in the intestines of the tsetse fly and are transmitted by the bite of the insect. The parasites invade the lymph, blood and brain fluid of the victim and cause sleeping sickness in humans and *nagana* in imported cattle. The wild game acting as carriers are immune, a significant fact which the European settlers have failed to comprehend. Nor were they able to understand that a quarter of the land area of Africa is unsuitable for cattle raising. They cleared the bush to deprive the tsetse fly of shade and butchered the antelopes to get rid of the bacteria they carried in their blood, but the rats — the true carriers — survived... so the massacre did nothing to stop the epidemic. Regions now empty of game have to be sprayed with insecticides and the imported domestic cattle must be innoculated with anthrycides as a protection against *nagana*, but it has long been proved that with sensible management the indigenous, immune game could produce three times more meat.

The Zambesi deluge in 1959. A Steinbok *(Raphiceros campestris)* tries to swim to safety...

Natural catastrophes have always been disastrous for living creatures with all the calamitous changes of environment and the consequent doom of whole communities; but since 1959, man can boast of having provoked a flood comparable to the Deluge. The head waters of the Zambesi are on the borders of Katanga, Angola and Northern Rhodesia. The river flows through the eastern part of Angola, over numerous rapids and cataracts in Northern Rhodesia and, broadening to 3,000 yds. in width, it crashes 350 feet down the Victoria Falls and thrusts with tremendous force through a narrow chasm. To contain this great rush of water, and turn it into useful energy for the most industrialised region of Africa — before it drains away towards Mozambique and into the Indian Ocean — the former Federation of Rhodesia and Nyasaland erected at Kariba one of the largest dams in the world. Fifty-one thousand Negroes were evacuated from the area doomed to be flooded... but the hundreds of thousands of wild animals living on the banks of the river, suspected nothing of the impending disaster.

...and a Civet *(Civettictis civetta)* in deadly peril swims past the nests she used to plunder.

When the flooding began whole herds of antelopes, giraffes and elephants sought refuge on the hill tops, and monkeys, civets, genets and snakes moved up into the trees. But over an area of more than 2,000 sq. miles the floods went on rising. In the end, every creature took to the water in despair and swam as long as its strength lasted. It was then that "Operation Noah's Ark" began. A number of volunteers, black and white, set out to rescue all that was left to save, but they were so badly scratched and bitten by the terrified animals that, in spite of their brave effort, they could not carry to safety more than 6,000. Only the strongest escaped on their own and to-day, Kariba Lake, about the size of Wales, is the biggest animal cemetery in our modern world. The north shore is bordered by cultivated land, but on the Rhodesian side to the south, new reservations have been created which UNESCO has strongly recommended should be enlarged into a National Park and become a sanctuary. Thus the victims will not have been sacrificed in vain to the march of progress, and the survivors will be able to thrive and multiply.

This picture proves what no one suspected: the East African Porcupine *(Hystrix galeata)* can swim.

No matter how diligently the behaviour of animals is studied to discover inherited or acquired abilities... surprises always crop up. During the Kariba "Operation Noah's Ark", porcupines were often seen from the rescue boats, not drowning but swimming with vigour and determination. It has since been observed that porcupines willingly enter the water for no other apparent purpose than to rid themselves of the parasites in their spiny coats. Usually these two-foot high primeval rodents trot about unhurried in the steppe and savannah, but in the face of an enemy they know how to defend themselves. They stamp their feet, ruffle their spiny armour and rattle their hollow tail needles. Few predators realise that a quick bite in the snout would render the porcupine helpless, but long before such a thing can happen it has rolled itself into a prickly ball. Many a young lion who would not leave it alone has suffered from lingering suppurating wounds, caused by the barbed needles of a porcupine, and for many painful years has been prevented from normal hunting. Only after such a predator has been shot as a cattle thief or as a man-eater, is the true reason for its behaviour disclosed — a few porcupine spines deeply embedded in a front paw.

A Clawless Otter *(Aonyx maculicollis)* in the Congo River differs from the European otter in not having webbed feet or claws.

Where the Congo stretches wide, hippopotami and crocodiles lazily lie at ease, but on the clear upper reaches of the river and its tributaries whole families of Clawless Otters bustle about, screaming and whistling. Unlike their much-hunted European cousins they need not hide during the day... and since the abundance of fish is not reduced by industrial pollution, they are free to catch the fattest fish and eat nothing but the brains rich in lecithin. Only when diving must they be careful not to enter the realm of the yard-long Electric Catfish which defends its hunting grounds with 400-volt shocks.

But one creature the Congo otter will never meet is the legendary *"Chenuzi"* which the native tribes claim sometimes to see. This bewitching water sprite is supposed to have childlike hands like the Clawless Otter, to be tinted metallic-red like the Giant Otter Shrew *(Potamogale velox)* and to carry its head high out of the water like the big manatees which occasionally come up the Congo from the West African coast; further, the *"Chenuzi"*, like the Electric Catfish, can paralyse human beings. Small wonder that in the minds of the natives the varied river fauna has combined to produce this creature of fantasy.

In "flight" the Springhare *(Pedetes surdaster)* looks like a dwarf kangaroo. With the balancing tail it measures 33 inches.

Hares, similar to our own, are found more or less everywhere in the Dark Continent, but the curious Springhares leap about in the steppes and semi-deserts from the Cape to Kenya. They hide behind the blocked entrances of their earths during the day and come out to feed at dusk. When nibbling or digging for tubers they squat rather clumsily on their long hind legs or sit up like squirrels, looking round with big night-eyes. The family groups communicate by low grunting and bleating, but when specially juicy grazing has been discovered the call goes out, and with 2 or 3 yard-long leaps they gather together quickly. When the need is urgent they "fly", using the kangaroo technique, with bounds of 6 to 10 yards, vanishing into their burrows long before their dumbfounded pursuer has picked up the broken scent spoor. The North African Jerboas boast of a similar performance in miniature. They, too, awake at night and hop through the desolate wastes in such numbers that it is hard to see how all can find enough to feed on. However, in turn these frugal eaters are themselves the chief food of the sly little desert foxes which Arabs call fennecs.

Four curious inhabitants of inhospitable landscapes: a Fennec with young *(Vulpes zerda)* — a Hyrax or "Rock rabbit" *(Procavia)* — an Elephant Shrew *(Elephantulus)* and a Crested Rat *(Lophiomys)*.

On the rocky terraces of the African mountains and the high scorched plateaux of the Sahara, hundreds of hare-sized creatures sun themselves — the Hyrax or "rock rabbits". Superb acrobats, they run up and down the sheer rock face and even dare to leap from 10 to 15 feet when it is necessary to escape from an eagle, caracal or leopard. Because of their appearance these small vegetarian cave-dwellers were originally counted among the rodents, but anatomists later found that the insignificant-looking Hyrax was a close relative to... the elephant! First of all the horny toes, without nails or claws, show how a hoof may have developed; then there are the elongated incisors and the ruminant's double stomach. Finally, the new-born of these astonishing animals are as fully developed as a foal. — The Elephant Rats and Elephant Shrews, too, are outsiders in their animal family, for alone among insectivores they do not shun the light, but hunt in semi-deserts and savannahs during day-time, using their long tongues to fish larvae and beetles out of their hiding places. — Lastly, illustrated above, is a unique East Africa rodent, the Crested Rat; a master at climbing who, when angry, so ruffles up its mane that it looks like a hedgehog in war paint.

139

The comic Spiny Ground-Squirrels *(Xerus erythropus)*, barely 11 inches long, are the marmots of Africa.

In the semi-deserts, steppes and savannahs between East and West Africa the Spiny Ground-Squirrels burrow their deep earths. These animals got their name from the thin and bristly hair of their red-brown coats, but if they lack the silky fur of their cousins, their "language" is richer than the "voice" of other squirrels. With its four notes and a variety of modulations they seem capable of expressing every mood. Like the marmots they are active during the day and in spite of the creeping, slithering and flying creatures which prey upon them, they venture much farther from their earths than do their cautious Alpine cousins. Nor are they totally vegetarian, for they like to vary their diet with snacks of insects and birds' eggs. But because of the nature of their environment, these delicacies can be enjoyed only at the beginning of the rainy season, when the dry grass sprouts again and the birds are nesting. After the last downpour the insects hatch out and there are full stomachs until the new drought brings hunger once again to animals of the semi-desert. Although the Spiny Squirrels can do without water for a surprisingly long time they are eventually forced to retire to their earths in a state of coma and live, like the hibernating marmots, on their own fat.

A family of East African Dwarf Mongooses *(Helogale undulata)* surprised at their sunbath.

The reflected glory of Rikki-Tikki-Tavi, the Indian Mongoose, and the Ichneumons, the Pharaoh's Rat, sacred to the Egyptians as snake killers, falls on the whole mongoose family. But the story told by Herodotus, of the Ichneumon slipping between the jaws of the crocodile to eat its heart, is just as fanciful as the belief that the mongoose is immune from snake bite. This apparent immunity can be simply explained by the fact that the poison fangs of the reptile cannot penetrate a thick fur. But in fact, all mongooses, small or large, are as wild and snappy, clever and sly, as innumerable folk tales would have them be. Whether attacking or defending themselves they are peerless in skill and endurance. They hunt not only reptiles, small mammals and birds, but they know also how to suck out birds' eggs, to extract snails from their shells and to open hard-skinned fruit. They hold the loot between their hind legs and, to break it open, catapult it backwards with their forepaws against a tree or a rock. Their homes are mostly under termite hills, and when a whole family emerges they frisk madly about, trilling and chattering in the sun, until mother gives the signal to move off. Then the whole party follows head to tail, resembling a huge snake gliding through the savannah.

A young Aardvark *(Orycteropus afer)* beside a termite hill.

Unrelated to any present-day animal, the Aardvark, the last survivor of a 60 million year old family of mammals, is an outsider in the zoological system. Not only are the donkey ears curious on an ant-eater, not only are the camel's hump and the Kangaroo tail remarkable, but the primeval tubular teeth, 18 in number, which resemble those of a shark, are almost useless to this eater of termites. The Aardvark owes its survival to its claws which are hard as steel. When in danger it can dig itself in with such a speed that stones and clods of earth bombard its surroundings. Its home is a complicated labyrinth 9 to 18 feet deep, where many a native boy, with an intensive desire for aardvark meat and skins, has been asphyxiated in the maze of underground corridors. The Aardvark spends its day in the safety of inaccessible burrows and appears at dusk to look for termite hills. Without much trouble it breaks open these structures, hard as concrete, and with tongue and lips licks the galleries and breeding places empty. If the hill is big enough, it sleeps there after its meal, so as to wake up next evening near a well-spread table.

Who would have thought that the nearest relative of the hyaena was a harmless insectivorous wolf which has lost its ability to kill? No one knows if this change was caused by outside influences or derived from inside the body itself. Was it unfamiliar food which induced the deterioration of the less and less used teeth, as in *Homo sapiens* to-day, or was it lack of calcium which caused the teeth to degenerate and forced the Aardwolf to adapt itself to a soft diet? This debasement has now become part of the animal's heredity, and between the barely visible molars are great gaps, because even these rudimentary teeth fall out as the wolf matures. Consequently, not only has the lower jaw grown weaker, causing a modification of physiognomy, but, with the loss of a carnivore's power to attack, there is a change of character. Shy and lacking in vitality the Aardwolves rest during the day in their earths, or in abandoned aardvark warrens, and venture out in small groups only at night. As termite hills are much too hard for them to break open, they dig up colonies of earth termites.

An Aardwolf *(Proteles cristatus)* female with whelps in her cave.

This photograph evokes the atmosphere of a virgin forest except for the sounds, the screeching of tree-frogs, birds and monkeys. In the tangled growth of the lianas a mammal creeps about disguised as a saurian, the Giant Pangolin. For this spiny anteater, a toothless knight in armour, the pagoda of the termites presents a well-stocked larder, as indeed it is for all these walking "pine cones". There is the Pangolin of the steppe, revered by the natives as the "Father of the Tree Bark", which walks upright on its hind legs and feeds on the termite hills of the plains. In the forests the long-tailed Pangolin climbs through the branches in search of the spherical nests of the tree termites. In size the greatest enemies of termites are the Aardvark, the Aardwolf, and the Pangolins, but there are countless smaller fry, too, which enjoy the delicacy of a meal of termites, e. g. the Elephant shrews, certain frogs, reptiles and warrior ants. Even within the termite stronghold there exist parasites: many insects give their larvae to the termites for board and lodging, so that a whole host of retainers lives on the substance of the termite state.

◄ A Giant Pangolin *(Manis gigantea)* about 6 feet long investigates a pagoda of *Cubitermes* in the virgin forests of the Congo.

The biggest termite buildings of the African *Bellicositermes* are 22 feet high with a circumference at the base of 45 feet. These colossal achievements are possible only if the royal parents of the state will live for decades to guarantee (by the production of 10 to 30 thousand eggs daily), the necessary reinforcements of soldiers and workers. The giant termite castle is the visible centre of subterranean ramifications of corridors leading to feeding places, such as trees chosen for the most appetising meals of cellulose. The central skyscraper is the work of many generations, built of layers of chewed earth mixed with saliva and the secretion of the frontal gland, and hardened during the heat of the day. The interior is quite cool, for the termites invented air conditioning long ago. From the "cellars" and "well shafts", which, with one species, reach down to underground water, humid air circulates through the ventilation channels which honeycomb the outer walls. Because the pale wingless inhabitants spend their life in the dark, every room, every corridor, has its purpose in the social life of the termite state. Only the winged, sexed individuals swarm into the light at the beginning of the rainy season. On such days, the air above the termite hill teems with flocks of hungry birds.

➤ A pyramidal building of the *Bellicositermes* near Maridi, Sudan. For a picture of a termite queen see page 184.

For a Tree Pangolin with a bellyful of termites, this is the most relaxing pose. Thanks to the naked underside of the armoured tail it can grip firmly on the branch. When some danger threatens, strong contracting muscles serve effectively to roll the body into a tight ball which no enemy can break open to attack the vulnerable belly. Hence, this mammal in the armour of a saurian feels perfectly safe, particularly as the horny scales are continually being renewed from leathery skin papillaries. Some superstition surrounds the "invulnerable creature", and natives of the Congo believe that to burn a pangolin scale will keep predatory animals at bay. If the tribe is successful in killing a Pangolin, the bigger and smaller scales are bestowed upon members of the community according to rank, and the claws are given to the hunter as a lucky charm.

← The Long-tailed Tree Pangolin *(Manis tetradactyla)* reaches 4 feet in length, of which the tail alone is two thirds.

Pangolin babies arrive in this world in a roomy basin-shaped hole 9 feet underground and are suckled for a long time. The young of the ground-living species ride comfortably on the tails of their parents, but the little Tree Pangolins have to train early as climbers. Once they are weaned they soon get accustomed to their proper diet of termites. The long tongue, set in a sheath reaching to the sternum, secrets a sticky saliva. After glueing hundreds of termites...and sand particles, the tongue is withdrawn through the tiny mouth opening. Although the Pangolin has no teeth it can deal easily with the unchewed meal. The coarse linings of its stomach act as a mill and, at the exit, horny grooves "chew up" the last remains of chitin, the hard outer covering of insects.

➤ Young Small-scaled Tree Pangolins *(Manis tricuspis)*. All Pangolins are strictly protected.

A Vervet or Green Monkey rests to suckle her young
(*Cercopithecus aethiops*).

Tiny hands and even a curious little head ca
(*Erythrocebus*

Often the love of human mothers who over-pamper their children is compared with the attitude of the monkey mother to her young, but as in all comparisons between *Homo sapiens* and the primates, the parallel is false. The mother love of the monkey is limited to the period when the young is helpless and, unlike the mother love in Man, ceases with adolescence. What we find so very "human" in monkey mothers is their pride in the miniature image of themselves, the way they hold it up, full of enchantment, to show it off to their friends. Such demonstrations of affection seem to indicate more feeling than is shown by other mammals. When the monkey mother carefully parts the hair of her young with a moist finger to pick out parasites and thorns, we attribute greater tenderness to her than to the hooved animals and predatory cats licking their young. All mammals certainly grieve when their offspring has been taken away or dies. They search for days and cannot believe that the motionless baby no longer needs their over-full milk glands. But monkeys, because of the more intimate relationship, meet the sudden biological change with far more extreme behaviour, carrying even a decomposing baby around, or substituting a dead mouse for their dead infant, and in captivity, when the corpse is taken away from them, they pine in despair.

in the fur of the thirsty Patas Monkeys
...eroons.

A proud White-tailed Guereza mother with her woolly white baby *(Colobus caudatus)*.

From the point of view of behaviour, new-born monkeys stand midway between the baby mammals which need a nest and those which trot along with their mothers shortly after birth. Even before the umbilical cord is broken they are clinging to their mother's body and their need for warmth and protection sometimes lasts as long as the gestation period in the womb. Even if during these months the monkey mothers curb the urge for rapid movement, the active life of Guenons, Mangabeys and Colobus Monkeys leaping about in their world of tree tops is hardly restful, but to the young it seems like cosy rocking in the cradle. Among the primates, only the Gorilla baby, born in a tree nest, does not cling to mother but is supported by her hands. The little Mandrill tries to crawl when it is only 3 weeks old, and enterprising Baboon children climb impudently all over their mothers, holding themselves erect, and soon join a play group of their own age, romping and teasing one another and carrying stones on their backs, balanced proudly as if these were babies. A young Chimpanzee is physically and even psychologically superior to a human baby. Observations disclosed that a small Chimpanzee aged from 10 to 18 months had more understanding and a better memory than a human child of the same age. However, at 18 months the chimpanzee's receptive capacity was exhausted and the little human began to show his mental ascendency.

Above: Sacred Baboon (*Papio hamadryas*), Mandrill (*Mandrillus sphinx*), Drill (*Mandrillus leucophaeus*). *Below:* Tufted Mangabey (*Cercocebus aterrimus*), Young Baboon (*Papio* spec.), Congo Guenon (*Cercopithecus ascanius*).

"Africa is the home, not only of the biggest, cleverest, most beautiful and the most amiable monkeys of the Old World, but also of the ugliest." So wrote the famous German zoologist Brehm a hundred years ago. By the "ugliest" he meant the dog-faced varieties, for in his day, any creature which was distinguishable by both its head *and* its behind was considered revolting, indeed even depraved. Since Brehm's time Abyssinian Baboons, West African Mandrills and Drills have been given a place in zoology among those whose masculinity is visible in both front and hind quarters, like the buck and the lion. A remarkable thing about the young of these three larger ground-living monkeys is their distinctly anthropoid look, but as they grow older their features become more animal-like. Particularly startling is the change in appearance in the Mandrill. With sexual maturity the nose becomes vermilion-red, contrasting with the cornflower-blue swellings on the cheeks. This "neon-light advertisement" is important as it serves to keep the horde together in the green twilight of the rain forests where the black-faced Drills also roam. To be sure of a group following the right leader in case of hasty flight, the Mandrill has, as a further guide, light blue and violet markings on his red hind-quarters.

Above: Abyssinian Guereza or Colobus Monkey *(Colobus abyssinicus)*, Owl-faced Monkey *(Cercopithecus hamlyni)*, Patas or "Hussar Monkey" *(Erythrocebus patas)*. *Below:* Moustached Monkey *(Cercopithecus cephus)*, Mona Monkey *(Cercopithecus mona)*, Brazza Guenon *(Cercopithecus neglectus)*.

By the "most amiable" Brehm meant the Guenons, those graceful acrobats who swing about in the trees at all levels of the dense African forest. As their number is legion and the different species meet daily among the fruit trees and by the water holes, some impressive distinction is all important to preserve the purity of breed. Their little faces display a whole range of the inventiveness of nature, creating from a few colours an infinite variety of masks, whiskers and hair-do's. But we humans often confuse these hereditary characteristics with the changing expressions of the mimic. We forget that an apparently "melancholy goatee" or a "stoic owl face" may express innocent happiness just like the wily Punchinello. This anthropomorphic tendency is manifest in the name "Hussar monkey" for the Patas, whose moustache and fiery red coat call to mind a Hungarian cavalryman. Fortunately, hunters are hardly interested in the little quadrumanes with the exception of the black and white Colobus monkeys, whose decorative silky fur became their downfall because of a fashion craze. Although the Colobus monkey of the East African mountain forests is protected, Abyssinian poachers smuggle 3 to 4 thousand skins across the border into Kenya every month.

Of all the monkeys the best at showing its teeth is the brown Gelada *(Theropithecus gelada)*. When angry, it can even draw the upper lip back over its nose. Its own kind are as intimidated by this ferocious display as are leopards, and none would risk being bitten by those awesome fangs. The Geladas live in big hordes on the rocky cliffs between 10 and 12 thousand feet up in the North Abyssinian mountains. Their social life resembles that of the baboons, but in their colourfulness they are more like the drills, except that the red markings, which increase in intensity with excitement, are not on their hind-quarters, but on the chest, shaped like an hourglass, and a crescent on the throat. The Geladas' diet resembles that of the ground makakis. They scratch larvae from rock crevices, stick their hands into ants' nests and then lick off the swarming mass with relish. They also collect birds' eggs and hunt for small vertebrates. When they move stones to search for crawling insects, they are very careful to look first for any hidden snakes. At the time of the corn harvest, the troupe climbs down to about 6,000 feet where they meet the silver-maned Hamadryas, but as the hostile brothers only want to show off, their barking and baring of teeth seldom leads to a real fight.

It is generally accepted that the Chimpanzee *(Pan troglodytes)* is the most intelligent of the apes. This has been proved by the ratio of brain volume to body weight: Chimpanzee 25 ½ cubic inches/132 pounds, Gorilla 30 ½ cubic inches/550 pounds. Man 90 cubic inches/176 pounds. The natives of Equatorial Africa believe that the Chimpanzee is a sort of "man of the forest" and that it refuses to talk only because it does not wish to work like they have to. In fact, chimpanzees have all the necessary cords as well as mobile lips, but their "language" comprises only thirty primitive sounds. Furious outbursts of temper, as illustrated in the picture, are rare among these happy creatures, and the din they make in the forest signifies not only enjoyment but serves also to keep the horde in contact. The ear-splitting chorus is accompanied by a rhythmic hand clapping, stamping of feet, shaking of branches and drumming on hollow trees. Animal psychologists who lived for months among the Chimpanzees in the Gombe Reservation near Lake Tanganyika and the Budongo Forest in Uganda had to get used to this clamorous background. By observing how the apes use a stick for a tool or weapon these scientists hoped to find possible parallels which would help in speculations on the behaviour of prehistoric man.

Gorilla gorilla. In the Congo forest a young one sits among the aerial roots sucking the marrow from stalks picked by its parents...

In 520 BC when the Carthagenian navigator Hanno sailed down the West Coast of Africa with 30,000 warriors, he discovered and explored the Gulf of Guinea, but his courageous attempt to colonize was unsuccessful. However, the seafarers brought back skins of hairy "forest men" which they called "gorillas". These greatest of all apes were forgotten again until 1846, when missionaries furnished evidence of their existence and created a scientific sensation. From then on, every natural history museum wanted its gorilla skeleton and the great hunt for the man-apes began: from the virgin forests of the Cameroons, across the basin of the Congo River and as far afield as Uganda. In fear of the revenge of "King Kong", the hunters shot whole gorilla families to capture a single young one which never even survived transportation. To justify the massacre, these "heroes" invented atrocity stories of the rape of women and the murder of men, and drew imaginary pictures of hideous creatures over 6 feet high swinging clubs. The extermination of one of the most interesting primates nearly succeeded. It was only in 1925, when Baron Cartier de Marchienne, coined the slogan: "The world must be made safe for gorillas", that King Albert of the Belgians was inspired to organise a gorilla sanctuary which later became the nucleus of the Kivu (Albert) National Park.

...while the imposing father chases away intruders — (incidentally the expedition's photographers).

„Leave Ngagi alone and he'll leave you alone"; so say the natives who are well acquainted with this muscle-proud creature. Both the bearded Mountain Gorillas who haunt the Hagenia Forest at a height of 9,000 feet and their coast-dwelling cousins in the bamboo jungle like nothing better than a quiet family life. Unmolested by other animals, except now and then by a leopard trying to steal a gorilla baby, the troupe minds its own business. The young search for birds' eggs and berries while adults break off juicy bamboo shoots and stems of the giant wild celery. Because no branch could bear the 600-pound weight of the chief of the clan, he relies on the females and adolescents to climb to the tree tops and shake down the fruit. At dusk they all gather armfuls of leaves and twigs to bed down for the night. Compared to the roofed-in tree nests of the chimpanzees, which are also built only for one night, these gorilla mattresses are no works of art, and come the morning, the "gipsy camp" is left filthy and the dense forest swallows up the dark figures moving along on their padded soles and on the knuckles of their hands. Only when provoked a gorilla will rise to his full height, beat his chest and cheeks and rend the air with hair-raising bellows to frighten off the intruder, while the family of the furious monster prudently melts away into security.

To lure gorillas, bearers on safari imitate the plaintive cry of a young one beset by a leopard. Animal collectors hope in this way to bring an alarmed female into the open with her young; even then it is not easy to capture the quick-tempered little creature. Many a brave father Gorilla has tried to save a screaming young captive from the captor's sack, already being carried away through the forest. The first Gorilla to survive transportation to Europe came to the Berlin Zoo in 1876 and caused a great stir, but 80 years passed until a zoo gorilla in Ohio, U.S.A., bore offspring in 1956. The second gorilla child to be born in captivity, at the Basle Zoo in 1959, was the famous Goma, but it was 1961 before zoologists could observe the happy gorilla mother Achilla, at the same zoo, suckle and raise her offspring Jambo. The gestation period and circumstances of birth were similar to those of the human race, but the baby tried to sit up and crawl much earlier and teething began sooner. Already in the third month the gorilla mother was coaxing her child to move around on its own, but conditions in a zoo inhibit the development of all the phases of natural behaviour that occur in the wild, where vegetation and social life in the tribe play an important part. Thus observers report that gorillas carry their young up into the trees and so force them to climb and leap about while the whole family watches the performance with admiration or scorn, according to the result. Nevertheless, even if a gorilla child in a zoo does not learn all the skills needed for life in the wild, it guarantees the preservation of the species, especially until the newly independent States of Equatorial Africa give an assurance that they will enforce measures to protect the largest of all primates.

➤ A young gorilla impudently picnics in a "prohibited" banana plantation.

◄ Baby gymnastics at the Basle Zoo, Switzerland.
Mother Achilla arrived from the Cameroons in 1948, a young animal weighing 20 pounds. In 1954, she was joined by her mate Christopher, and on September 3rd 1959, she gave birth to the famous little Goma who had to be reared on the bottle. When Jambo arrived on April 14th, 1961, Achilla raised him herself; she is seen here playing happily with her three months old offspring.

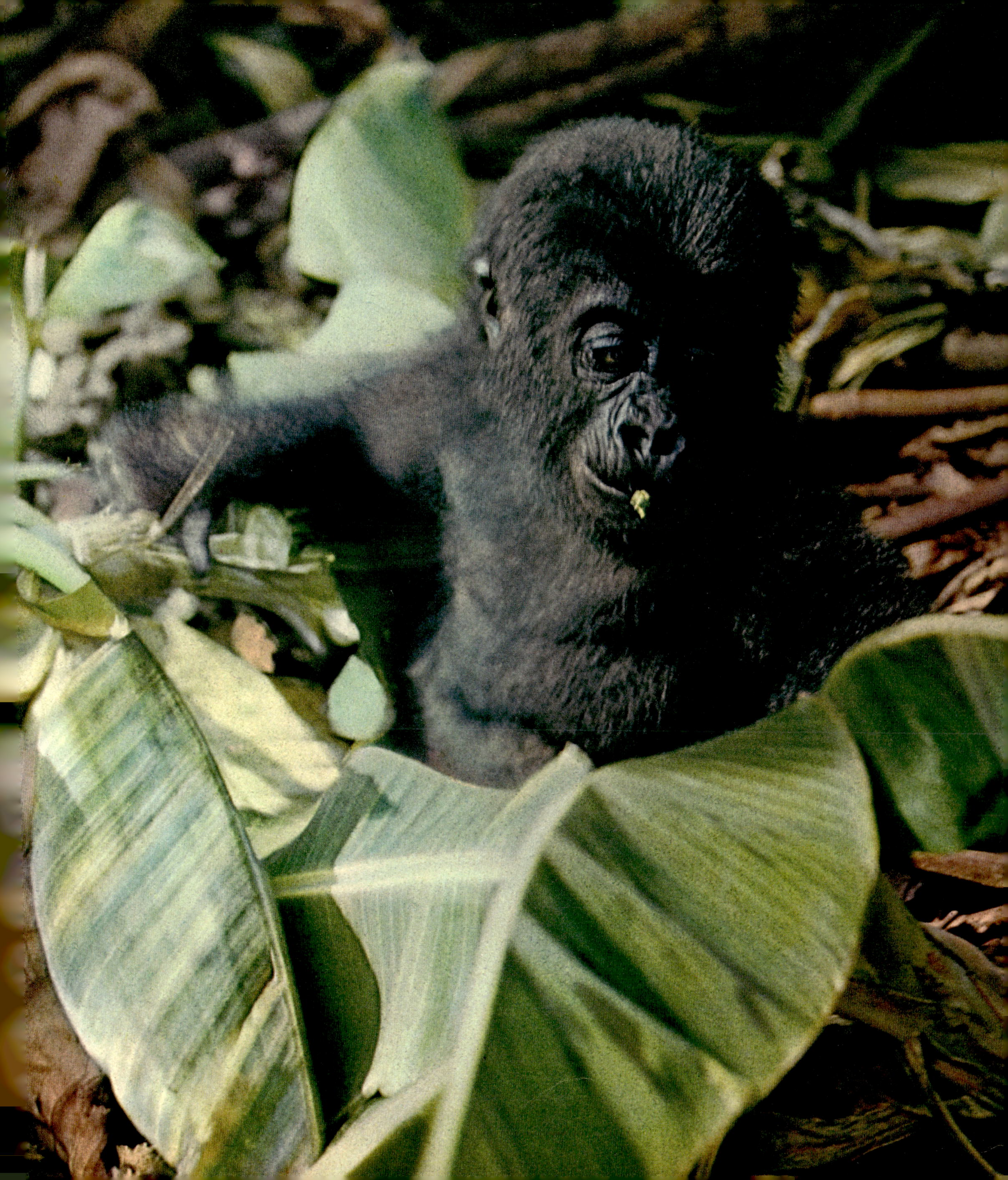

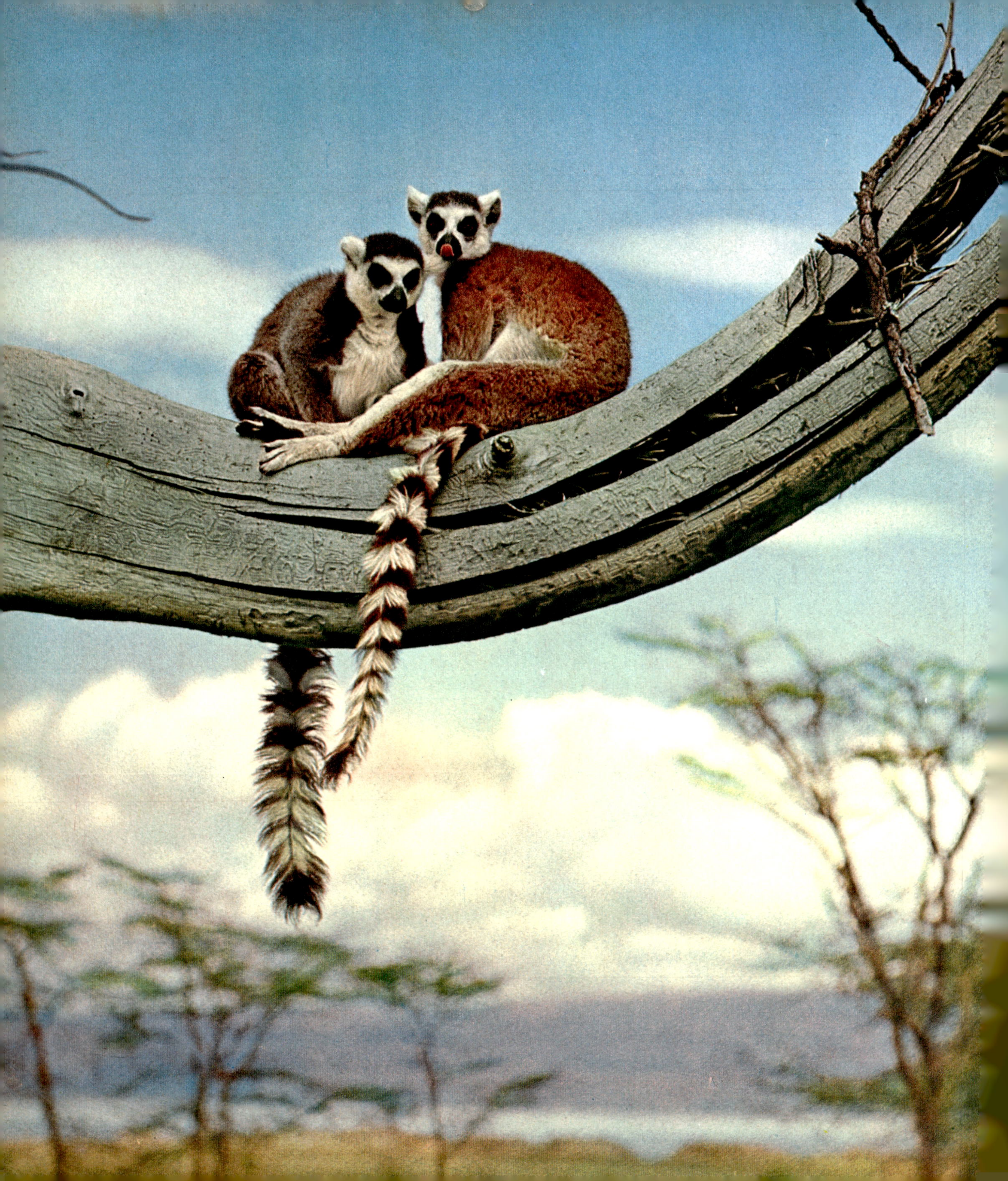

"Man and ape have common ancestors!" This was the thesis with which Charles Darwin, in 1858, shook the theological-philosophical edifice of the established conception of Creation. The opponents of the theory of evolution have long been silenced, but the earth still guards the secret of the origin of mankind. Every fossil find of primitive ape or prehistoric man adds only a twig to the genealogical tree of the primates; the roots vanish in the darkness of time. Present-day lemurs, which really should be called *Prosimiæ*, tell us very little, but it is in the ranks of their forebears that we find the outsiders which gave the primatial family new impulses. 75 million years ago, when the era of the saurians was coming to a close, the slow but constant specialisation among the prehistoric mammals began. Lemurs, which we consider the most primitive of all primates, were "in their day" the most evolved animals on earth. They roamed the forests of America, Eurasia, and Africa long before stronger species — cats, apes, and ungulates — made their appearance on the world stage. In time, the lemurs were crowded out by new enemies and competitors for food. Only nine species would have survived in Africa and Asia if a natural catastrophe had not made of Madagascar an island, a kind of Noah's Ark for the lemurian tribe. According to geologists the isthmus joining East Africa and India was submerged about 50 million years ago. The mythical "Gondwana Land" disappeared under the sea and since then only the island of Madagascar and some small archipelagoes rise above the Indian Ocean like peaks of a submerged mountain range. Separation from the Dark Continent was the salvation of the lemurs, who still make up one third of Madagascar's mammals. Only there were they spared the fight for survival against new forms of animal life; only there could they develop in peace and multiply. About 2,000 years ago, Hovas from Indonesia settled on the east coast of Madagascar, and much later the black Sakalava landed in the west of the island. Although these first hunters exterminated *Megaladapis*, the giant of the Lemur family, it was the goats, imported in 1513, which really menaced the lemurs. Within 200 years the goats had grazed the green island barren, and the *Prosimiæ* were forced to withdraw into remote virgin forests. Burning of scrub for land clearance and indiscriminate tree cutting accelerated the process of devastation, and to-day seven tenths of Madagascar is deforested. 21 lemur species survive in 13 small reservations. Will man, the most highly evolved of all primates, be wise enough to ensure the survival of his oldest relatives?

◄ A pair of Ring-tailed Lemurs *(Lemur catta)* on a high look-out. These pretty animals shun the forest and by day move in small groups through the bush of southwestern Madagascar. Although skilful climbers they search for their food on the ground like baboons.

➤ Three islanders and two continentals: 1 Lesser Dwarf Lemur *(Microcebus murinus)*; 2 Ruffed Lemur *(Lemur variegatus)*; 3 Sifaka or Monkey Lemur *(Propithecus diadema)*, all three Malagasy. 4 Great Black Bushbaby *(Galago crassicaudatus)*, from the Sotik region in Kenya; 5 Bushbaby or Moholi *(Galago senegalensis)*.

Rare photographs from the Madagascar forest reservations. Sifakas or Monkey lemurs *(Propithecus diadema)* surprised during an airy siesta...

In the security of their island home, far from the Dark Continent's leopards, servals, and venomous snakes, Madagascar's lemurs were free to evolve and specialise in every possible way. As vegetarians, insectivores, or nest robbers they chose their habitat without interference from stronger arboreal creatures. The smallest lemurs resemble mice or squirrels and some are not unlike climbing weasels or foxes. On this monkeyless island the long-tailed white Sifakas whose name derives from their cry "shee-fak", take the place of the guenons. They are cheerful sun worshippers and have little in common with the ghostly lemurs from whom they are descended. When their owl-eyed cousins wake up, the Sifakas retire to rest in the Didiera trees, but at dawn they are already climbing to the highest tree-tops for a snack of buds, blossoms, and leaves. At high noon, they come down to shadier levels to escape the heat and relax, combing their fur with their toes and dozing in the most precarious positions without ever tumbling off the branches. In the late afternoon, they enjoy a tour of the plantations to steal tamarinds and ripe mangoes. When caught at their misdeeds they vanish into the forest, springing from branch to branch, and covering distances of 20 to 30 feet between trees. As they leap, their tails trail behind like white banners. When pushing off from resting places they swing their powerful hind legs immediately forward, so as to seize the swaying branches on which they land simultaneously with hands *and* feet.

...and an Indri mother *(Indri indri)* carries her young pick-a-back through the entanglement of branches in the mountain forests.

The great Indri takes the place among lemurs of the apes among monkeys, and no one knows why it lost its balancing tail. Perhaps, at some intermediate stage in its development, the Indri used to live on the ground; perhaps an increase in weight forced it to modify its climbing technique so the tail became obsolete. The Malagasy called it "*babakoto*"— man of the woods — but when in 1787, the French scientist Sonnerat saw the natives pointing to it and calling out "indri, indri", meaning *look there, look there*, he believed this to be the creature's name. Many legends surround the Indri who may not be hunted because it bears a charmed life, and it was believed that if a spear were thrown, it would catch it and return it with unerring aim. But why do the *babakotos* live only in a certain forest region of Eastern Madagascar? Are they dependent on a particular kind of vegetarian diet which they can find only between the Bay of Antogil and the Masora River? During the day, they search for food and at dawn, at noon, and after siesta, they engage in a frightful howling chorus. Between these musical performances they hang at their ease from the branches, for their disproportionate hands and feet provide most useful hooks, particularly as they are able to spread their thumbs and big toes to an angle of 90 degrees; their other digits are all grown together so that their feet resemble those of a chameleon. Even more surprising is the hand of the rare Aye-aye, Madagascar's most startling nocturnal creature. Its "mummified" middle finger is a bony tool which it uses to dig grubs out of the bark.

Adventurous imps. The Moholi Galagos *(Galago senegalensis moholi)* are able to hold on to even a spiny euphorbia.

The last of the mainland lemurs are especially shrewd and well-versed in the vicissitudes of life, for their ancestors had to defy a host of enemies for millions of years. To-day's African Galagos have an advantage over their island cousins who are threatened by destruction of their habitat through tree cutting, since equatorial forests would blunt any axe! From Senegal to Mozambique there are nine different species of Galagos, sly banshees of the night with owl-eyes and bat-ears. The Moholis doing their gymnastics on a giant euphorbia are sharp-toothed little predators who crack beetles and locusts like nuts, but prefer eggs, young birds and the newborn of small mammals. On the ground they hop like miniature kangaroos and in the trees they bounce as though on springs, from branch to branch. When rapid movement is curtailed by lianas they weave through the darkness feeling their way with ultra-sensitive stubby fingers. Every now and then they coo like doves but at a certain hour of the night all the bushbabies begin to howl together like abandoned infants, so that even natives are deceived by these human, baby-like cries for help. But these "babies" are themselves parents, and many a female carries a young one, the size of a cockchafer, which clutches bravely to her fur and joins the chorus with its whimpering. As house pets they are rather unruly, being sometimes loving and sometimes snappy, but, in whatever mood, they love a lick out of the master's liquor glass.

Lazy-bones in the Congo Forest. A Bosman's Potto *(Perodicticus potto)* stares drowsily at the camera but is too sleepy to move away.

Apart from bushbabies the African rain forests harbour two species of primeval lemur: the foot-long Potto, whose habitat extends from Sierra Leone to Uganda, and the smaller, very rare Angwantibo of the Cameroons. Among the nimble *Prosimiæ* they represent the "sloths". It needs just one look to appreciate that the Potto is phlegmatic, for where it has made itself comfortable at dawn it is still to be found at dusk. It has sacrificed the index finger and the second toe so that its hands and feet act like pincers and give it a vice-like grip on vertical branches. When it settles down in a tree even the spiny neck vertebrae are wedged against the bark. It prefers to sleep in this airy position rather than in the confinement of a stuffy hole. Only when night falls does the woolly ball begin to move. Rubbing its amber eyes the Potto embarks in slow motion on the search for food. All its movements are lethargic and deliberate, first dangling from the branches and then creeping about so that it comes as a complete surprise to the watcher to see it suddenly overcome its phlegm and quickly seize a sleeping bird. However, the Potto usually avoids any undue excitement and is content to nourish itself with insects, fruit and honey.

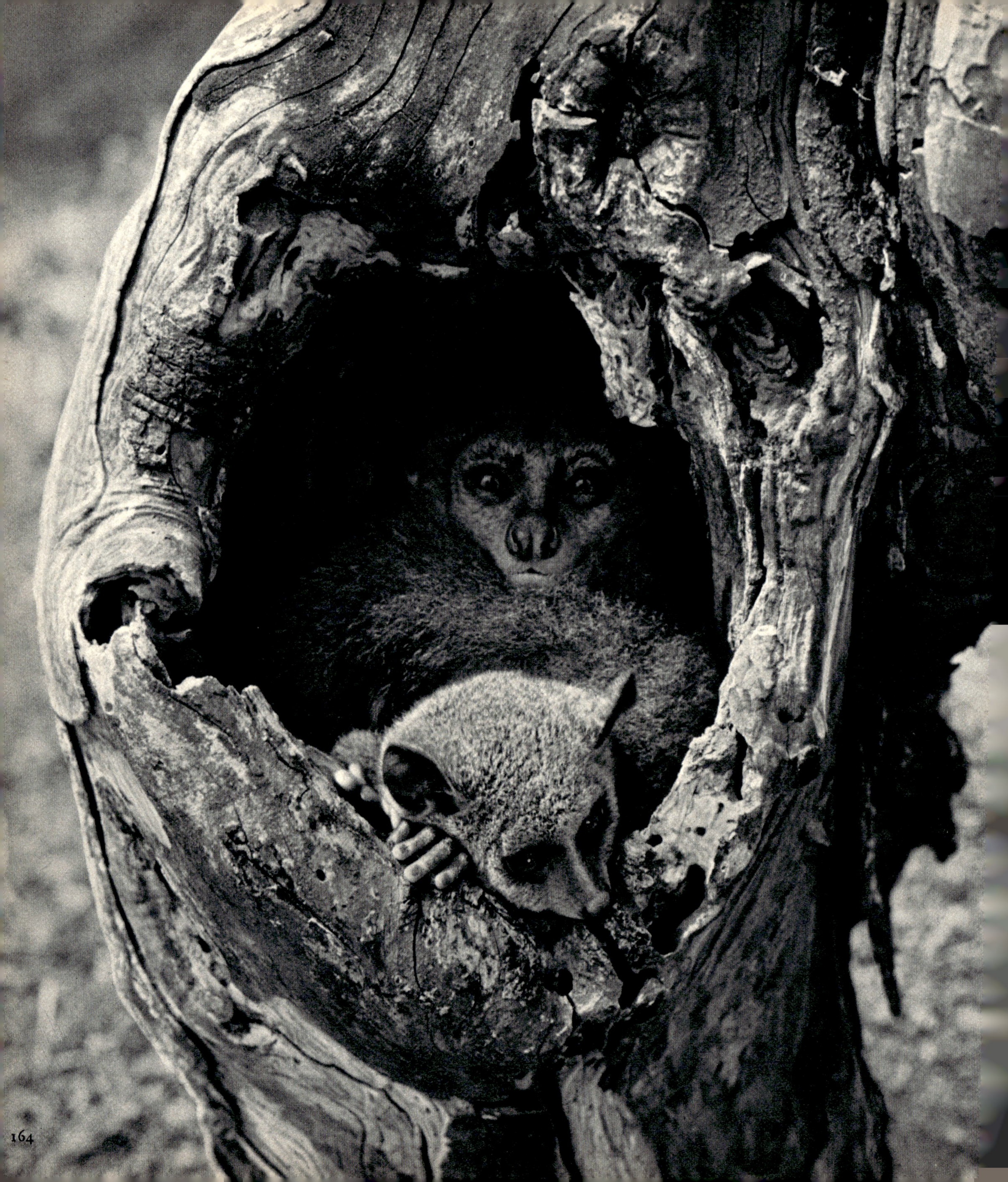

The extraordinary variety of lemurs is astounding in itself, but male and female Black Lemurs even wear different coats: he a black-a-moor and she in contrasting white and reddish brown. Hordes of these odd couples roam through the palm jungles of northwestern Madagascar and the small adjacent islands. They scramble about in daytime and on moonlit nights, munching leaves and fruit between mercurial bouts of play. When Malagasy natives and *makis* (as lemurs are called in the island) meet, there is terror on both sides, but while the *makis* only drop from the trees as if dead and then vanish in the undergrowth, the natives live in fear for days, expecting some disaster foretold by these "prophets of evil". In fact, Black Lemurs are far less aggressive than their cousins in eastern Madagascar, the Ruffed Lemurs *(page 159)*, who jump on the backs of marauding dogs and disturb the night with their bloodcurdling cries. The Ruffed Lemurs, like the Mouse Lemurs, Weasel Lemurs, and Dwarf Lemurs, are skilled nest-builders; the two last-named species sleep in their leaf-nests through the long drought period.—The African Galagos, however, are satisfied with a hollow in a tree. They wrap their tails round their heads and fold their thin ears like paper bags, in order not to see the light or hear the noises of day.

◄ Galagos awaking at sunset.

► A couple of Malagasy Black Lemur *(Lemurs macaco)*. In both pictures the flat finger nails can clearly be seen.

Pictures in medieval bestiaries or the results of unskilful taxidermy sometimes bestow on animals the most peculiar silhouettes and clumsy limbs, but an African Palm Civet looks somewhat out of shape even in this authentic photographic portrait. It belongs, with the Banded Palm Civet of Asia, to the most primitive viverrines of the Old World. Its dentition combines the characteristics of carnivores, frugivores, and prosimiæ. Although it could easily catch mice and plunder birds' nests, it prefers to live on sweet fruit and palm sap. The Palm Civet sleeps through the day, rolled up in a fork or hollow in a tree. At dusk, it climbs slowly about the branches or scurries headlong down the tree trunk, uttering plaintive cries, but its feeble voice is drowned by the croaking and squealing of the hordes of Tree Conies, primeval ungulates akin to the Rock Hyrax *(see page 139)*—which frisk noisily high in the tree-tops. This airy green world is also the home of the "gliders" among the African rodents, the Scaly-tailed Squirrels and Flying Dormice, able to plane for short distances by means of the parachute-like folds of skin stretched on either side between wrist and ankle. They have not as yet been photographed in the wild.

The African Palm Civet *(Nandinia binotata)* is nearly three feet long of which the tail is about half. The female usually carries her four kits on her back.

Fruit Bats photographed in the equatorial forest usually come out as dark dots on a leafy background or as smudgy shadows against the evening sky. Even in a zoo one has to wait a while until the handsomest of the *Chiroptera* wake up to peep out from under their flying membranes. Of the 1,000 bat species living mostly in the tropics the Fruit Bats are the most appealing because their fox-like faces are not disfigured by skin protuberances of devilish design. As fruit-eaters they do not need the hideous "radar equipment" which helps the moth-hunting varieties to detect insects. Only the Barking Hammer-heads of West Africa have grotesquely formed lips which enable them to suck out the flesh of soft fruit. From Africa to Polynesia, these large "flying foxes" are notorious, not as "demons", but as orchard robbers. When a horde of Fruit Bats has raided a plantation at night, there is nothing left to harvest, but usually they are content with the abundance of wild fruit. During the day they sleep suspended from the trees or in dark caves where deposits of guano-like excrement, 18 to 25 feet high, prove that the species has been frequenting the place over some thousands of years... After all, the order *Chiroptera* or flying mammals, which includes frugivores, insectivores, fish-eaters, blood-suckers and bird-catchers has inhabited the world for 60 million years.

African Fruit Bats, wingspan up to 3 feet. In contrast to the fingerless wing structure of birds, the bats' elongated finger bones provide the main support for the wing membrane

In the exciting play of equatorial forest life each dawn brings a change of actors. Where Fruit Bats, Galagos, and Palm Civets feasted at night, Guenons and a host of strange birds play the clown amidst the sunlit tree-tops in daytime. Many of the grotesque Hornbills, especially the white-crested species, like to follow the noisy gangs of monkeys to snap up insects flushed out by the "beaters"; but most of the Hornbills feed only on fruit and seeds. The strange protuberance or casque on the beak is hollow, hence not heavy, but it seems to give the "nutcracker bill" more power and probably serves also as an echo chamber for the characteristic laughter, trumpeting, and cawing. But the most surprising feature of the Hornbill tribe is their behaviour at breeding-time when the male immures the female in a hollow of a tree. As soon as she has settled in the nesting cavity her mate brings rotten wood and clay and she adds excrement as a binding medium to close the entrance. Eventually, only a small slit is left open through which she is fed by her mate; all would-be nest robbers are thereby frustrated!

An African Black-casqued Hornbill (*Ceratogymna atrata*) in the Congo Forest. This species of Hornbill grows to a length of 2 to 2½ feet. The naked skin around the eye and at the throat is blue. The beak of the young (*above left 1* ➤) has no casque.

Strange as it may seem, many a Hornbill mother endures 4½ months of voluntary seclusion. Immured in a tree hole, she moults, using the feathers to line the nest, incubates for three weeks, and then feeds the 2 to 4 young with tit-bits pushed through the opening by the male, who eventually looks quite bedraggled out of sheer effort. Only the females of the smaller yellow-billed species (2) break down the wall after 54 days and come out to help in the feeding, and the young immediately close the entrance again. — The chicks of Ground Hornbills, however, nestle for 82 days in perilously exposed hollows before they can follow their turkey-sized, long-legged parents into the savannah. — The most curious ground-living West African birds are the Bare-headed Rock-Fowl (5) which have been observed only rarely in Ghana, Togoland, and the Cameroons, in the overgrown rocky tracts of rain forests where they build their large pottery-like nests. — The habitat of the shy Congo Peafowl (6) is even more confined. The bird, unknown until 1937, lives only in the Ituri Forest. By contrast, the colourful arboreal Touracos (7, 8) are found everywhere. Ranging from giants 2½ feet high to dazzling dwarfs, they are unique in that they are the only birds whose colour runs when their feathers get wet, for the red turacin pigment is soluble.

2: Yellow-beaked Black Dwarf Hornbill *(Lophoceros flavirostrus)*. 3 and 4: Ground Hornbills *(Bucorvus abyssinicus & caffer)*. 5: Bare-headed Rock-fowl *(Picathartes gymnocephalus)*. 6: Congo Peafowl *(Afropavo congensis)*. 7: Giant Plantain-eater *(Corythaeola cristata)*. 8: Donaldson's Touraco *(Tauraco leucotis)*.

The mystery of bird migration between Europe and Africa is the more puzzling when one considers that only a few species of widespread songbirds are subject to the urge for intercontinental flight. For instance, the European Oriole is the only one among 70 species of Old World Orioles to fly across the Mediterranean. This rare visitor may be seen in Britain from April to June and leaves Europe in late August when he flies with the young of the season towards a new temperate summer in Southern Africa. On the way to winter quarters, European Orioles meet their African relatives, as for instance this Black-headed Oriole ➤ picking for insects in an Aloe flower. These flower spikes are also the meeting-places of the Sunbirds who help in the pollination of big-flowered tropical plants. While Orioles and Sunbirds proudly display their brilliant colours, the elegance of the black Widow Birds or Whidahs shows up in their silhouette. During the mating season, the sparrow-sized male sprouts a veritable comet's tail 6 to 18 inches long. Often half a dozen train-bearing admirers follow one inconspicuous female, and the chosen prince performs a whole repertoire of complicated aerobatics before his Cinderella. As is often the case in Africa, there are common as well as rare Widow species. The rare ones are those whose distribution does not exceed 150 square miles, because great climatic differences restrict their biotope. In this respect the Dark Continent holds the world record; 96 bird species are, as it were, geographical prisoners. Of these, 15 to 20 comprise only a few thousand individuals and some just a few hundred. This is one of the reasons why ornithologists all over the world envy their colleagues in Africa and dream of bird-watching safaris.

➤ A Black-headed Oriole *(Oriolus larvatus)* on an Aloe flower. Wankie National Park, Southern Rhodesia.

◄ Widow males from Kenya: *Above and centre:* Delamere's Long-tailed Widow Bird *(Coliupasser progne)*. *Below:* Pin-tailed Widow Bird *(Vidua macroura)*.

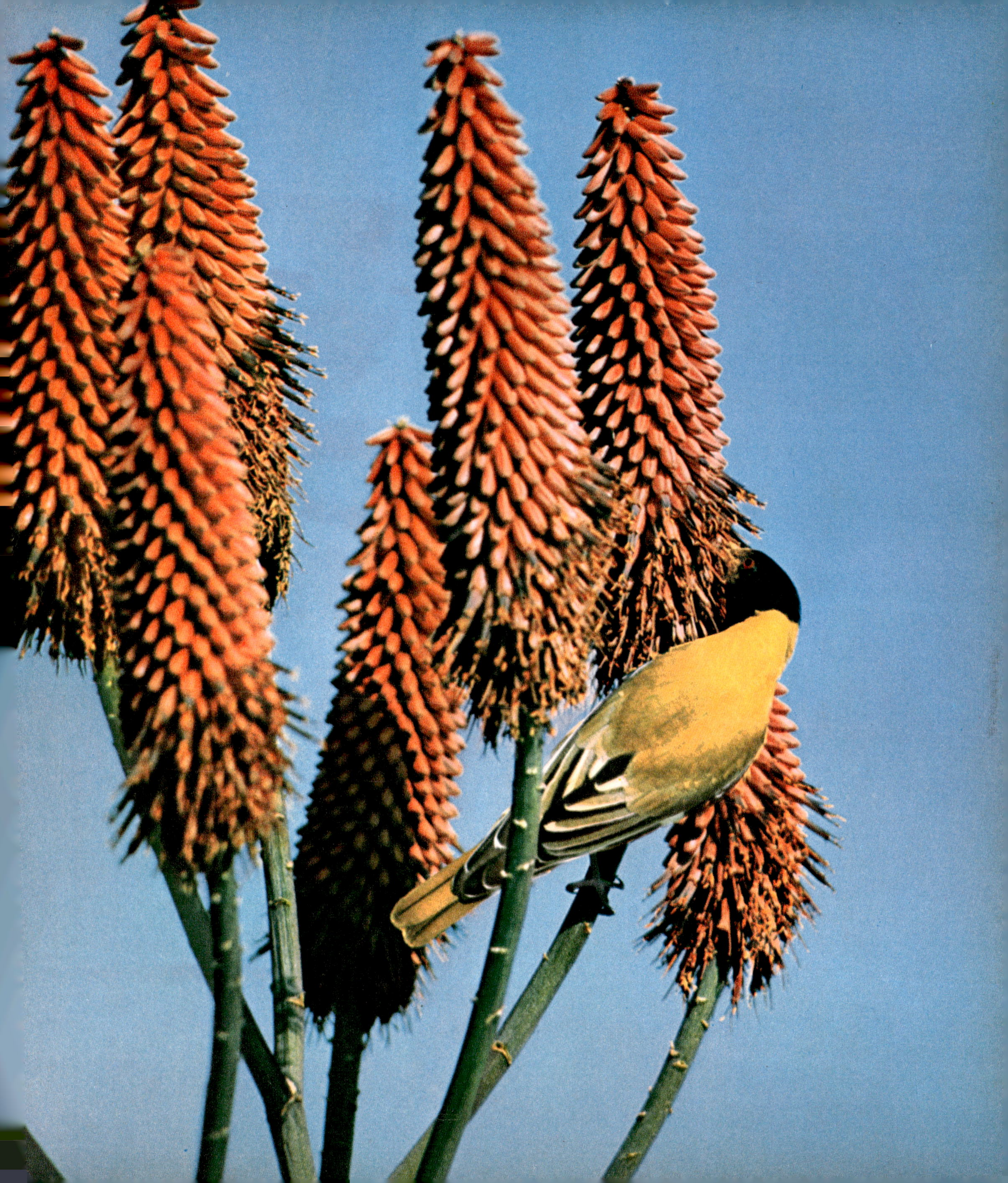

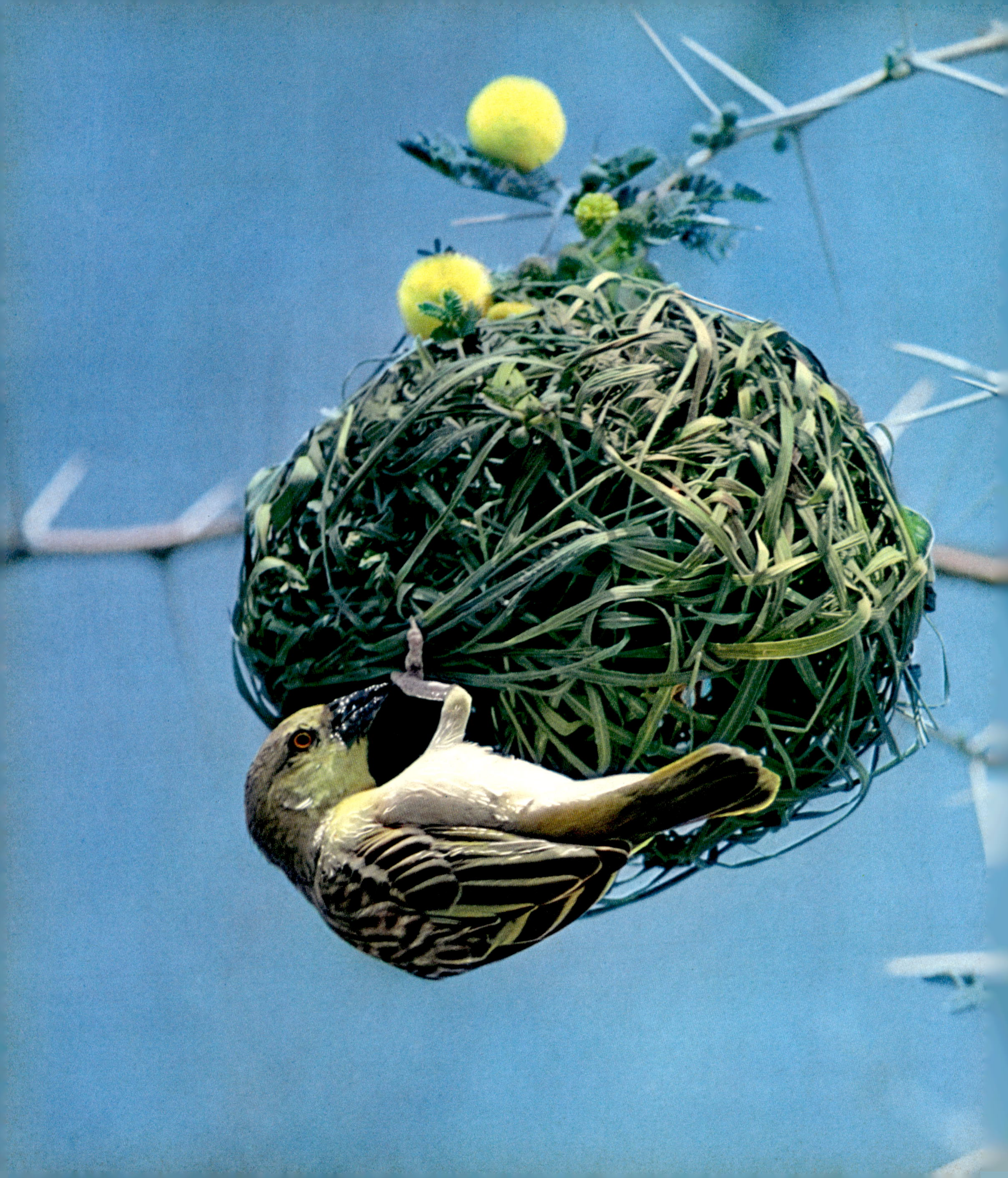

Birds' nests should be studied closely to appreciate fully their artistry. The male Weaver Bird chooses the most pliable material and then fixes loops of grass to a Mimosa bush. With his beak as his only tool he weaves stalk after stalk into the structure. As he works he has to hang on to the filigree with his claws and in his zeal he sometimes loses balance. Then he flutters nervously until he can settle again on the dangling unfinished structure. The Yellow-backed Weaver builds only a plain entrance hole; other species prefer long entrance tunnels, so that the finished nest resembles a chemist's retort. Some weave sharp thorns into the entrance as a protection against predators, and others use lumps of clay as ballast in their feather-light spherical nests so that the wind will not upset the cradle. But all this skill is wasted should tree snakes or climbing mammals steal the eggs. If only all birds would learn from the Cape Penduline Tit, who has invented a thief-proof nest. It weaves a pouch of plant fibre so tightly that even monkeys cannot tear it apart, and then leaves open a disproportionately large entrance hole... obviously an invitation to marauders. However, when egg robbers do reach down into it they find the sham hatchery always empty, for the cunning bird has built its nest with a double bottom. The big opening leads to a short cul-de-sac *(white dotted line on the photograph)*, while the actual inlet just above is always kept closed when the bird has left the nest or when it has slipped inside. The brood is safe in the bottom of the pouch, and even when the young can fly the whole family sleeps peacefully in the security of the most burglar-proof pendant nest in the bird world.

◀ A female Yellow-backed Weaver *(Ploceus jacksoni)* at her nest in a Mimosa bush.

▶ The nest of a Cape Penduline Tit *(Anthoscopus minutus)* in an Acacia tree. Transvaal.
Above: The actual entrance is closed. The white dots mark the cul-de-sac. *Below:* The photographer has opened the genuine entrance to demonstrate the bird's trick.

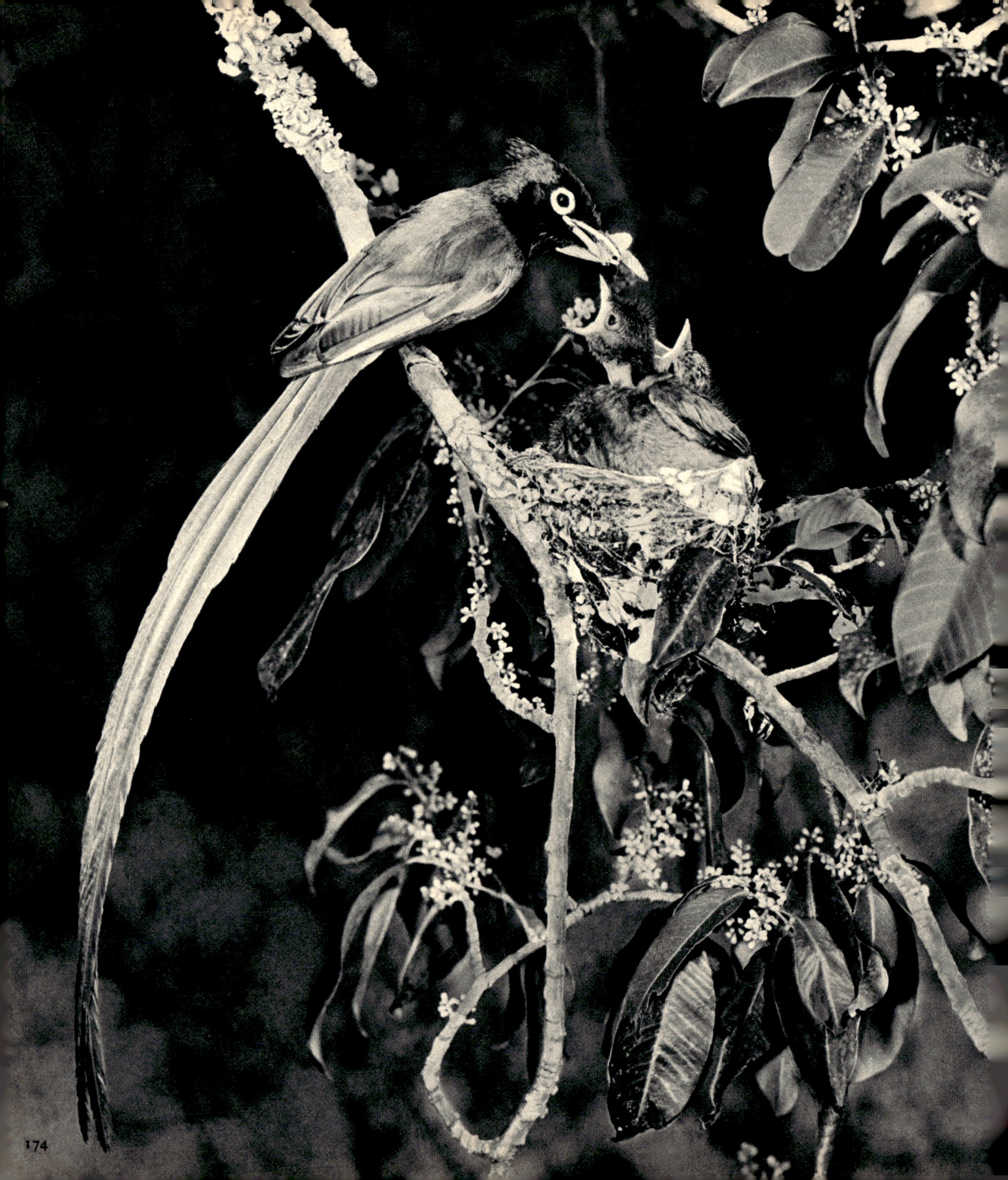

In Africa as elsewhere, bird lovers often wonder why, in many species, only the males display gorgeous plumage during the mating season, while in others both sexes are equally beautiful throughout the year. The latter are always *gregarious*, like the Long-tailed Mousebirds which move in groups, slipping through the densest thorn bushes in search of berries and seeds. However, when birds live in *isolated pairs*, the female is far more exposed to danger, and only the male wears conspicuous splendour, like the Paradise Flycatcher with its long tail feathers. If we take one view of evolution the male and female with insignificant plumage seem to be on the lowest rung. The visual distinction of the male is already a step upwards, but the highest evolutionary degree in the bird world is reached among those in which the beautiful display plumage is common to both sexes and has become a permanent characteristic of the species.

◄ Paradise Flycatcher *(Tchitrea viridis)*. A male at the nest in a Techlea tree *(Teclea simplicifolia)*, Kenya.

► Blue-naped Mousebirds *(Colius macrourus)* in a Mimosa tree.

Above the great rivers flowing through the semi-desert regions north and south of the tropics, the Carmine Bee-Eaters circle in twittering swarms. The beauty of the individual bird is lost in the mass of colour, as in one single colony on the upper Niger where ten thousand Carmine Bee-Eaters breed. They nest in close company on sandy river banks, digging out 5-foot long tunnels with their beaks. Whenever a bush fire occurs, Bee-Eaters appear to snap up escaping insects, and because of their daring dives into smoke and flame, they are called in French-speaking regions '*Oiseaux du feu*' = 'Fire-birds'. But these beautiful daredevils practise also a more relaxing hunting method: they often perch on the backs of antelopes and even on bustards. From these mobile hunting seats they catch every insect flushed out of the grass by their "mounts". Thus the young Bee-Eaters in the nesting tunnels are plentifully fed and grow quickly. As soon as they can fly the colonies empty. When drought threatens, the Carmine Bee-Eaters fly equator-bound from both north and south, there to find a new wealth of insect life in a more humid climate.

Green-headed Carmine Bee-Eater from the south *(Merops nubicoides)*. They breed in autumn and winter from Angola to Mozambique. Their northern relatives, the Carmine Bee-Eaters *(Merops nubicus)* nest in spring and summer from Senegal to Abyssinia.

◂ A breeding colony on the steep banks of the Savi River near Nyanyadzi, Southern Rhodesia.

▸ Close-up ²/₃ actual size. Both sexes wear this magnificent plumage during the whole year.

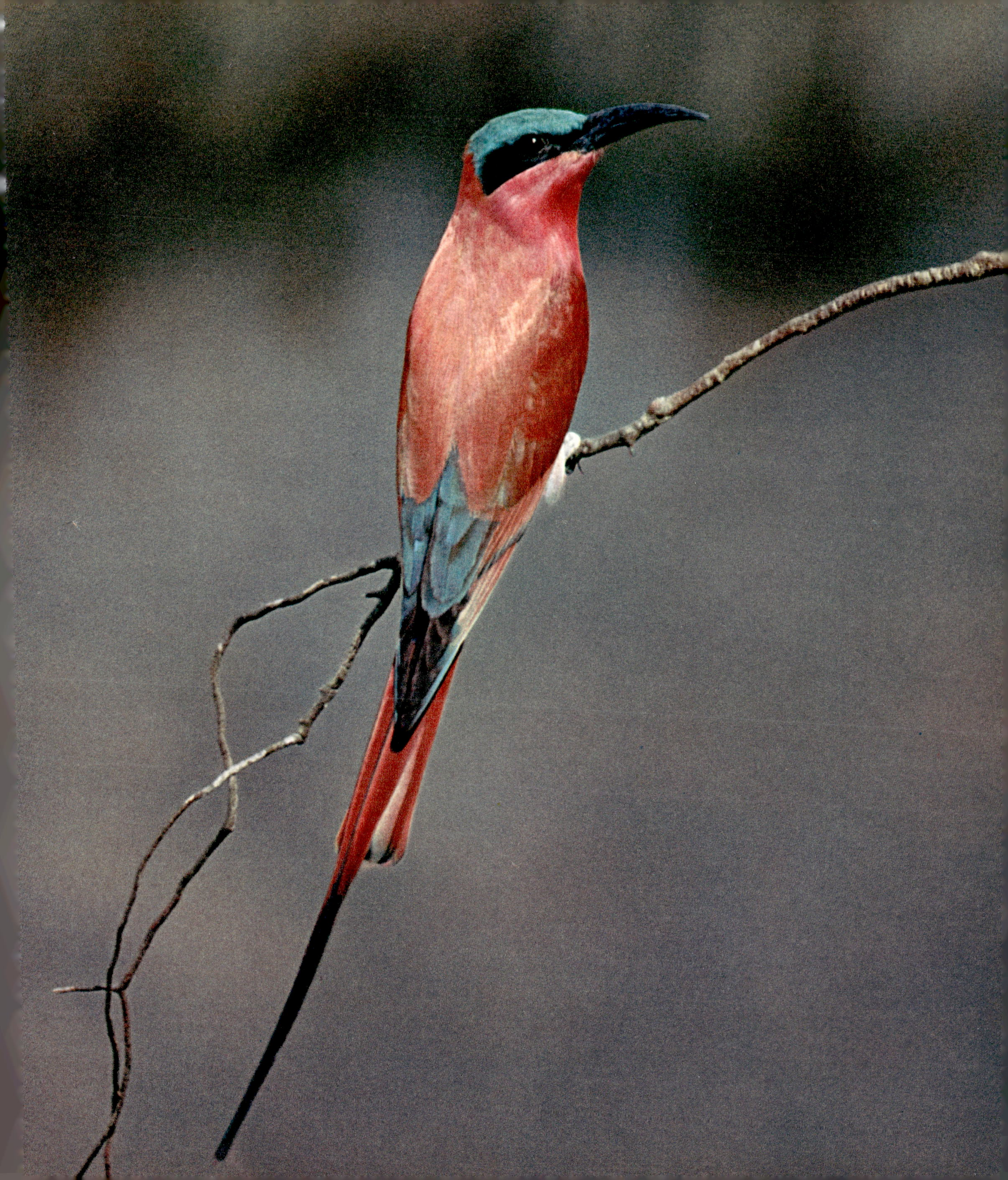

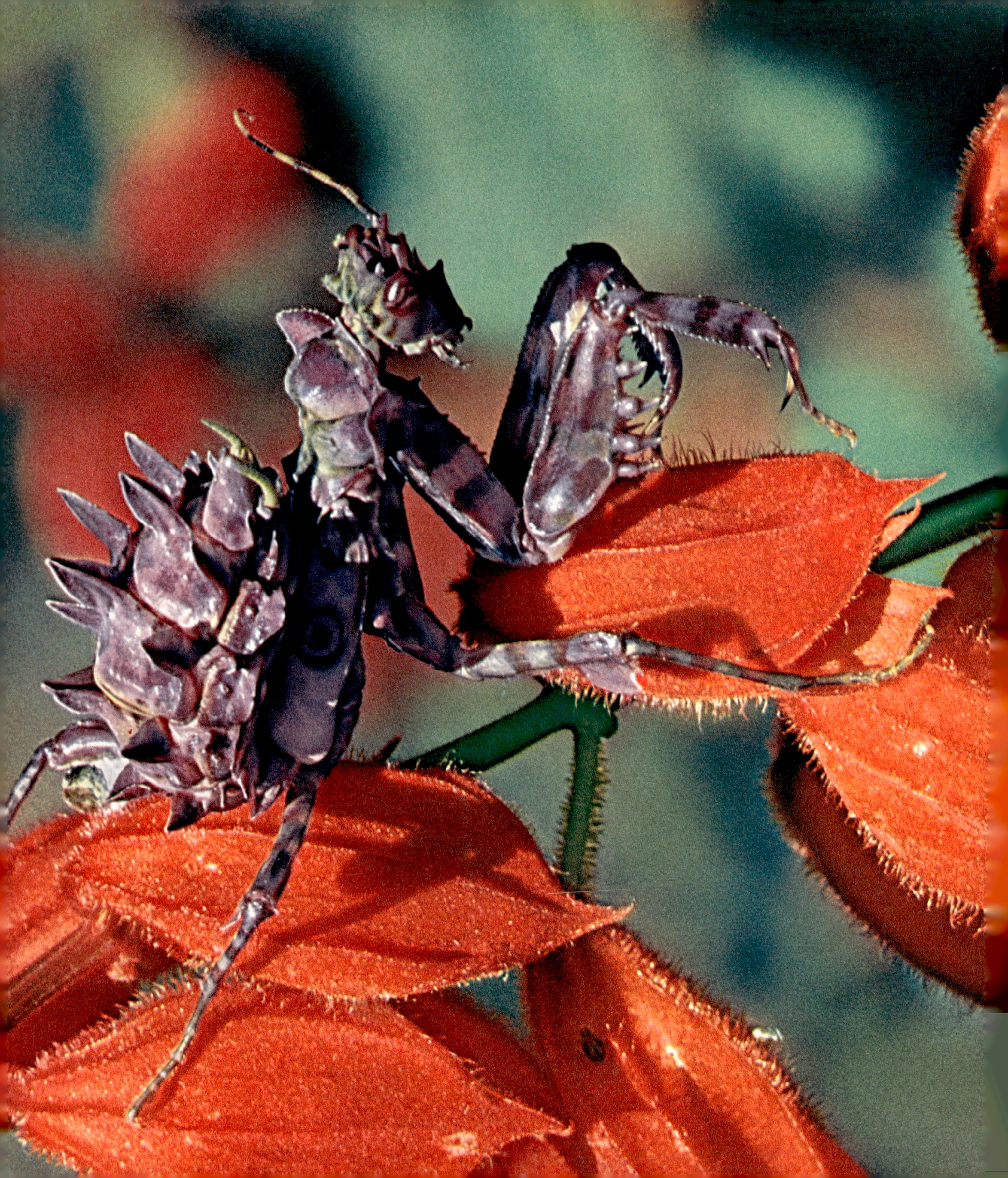

In terms of variety and numbers, the most successful conquerors of the Dark Continent are the insects. In deserts, steppes, mountains, and virgin forests they have adapted themselves to every possible condition — even the most unfavourable. The northern species which make up most of the life in the Sahara desert resemble the insects of southern Europe, although the "Saharians" are better conditioned to the "give and take" of a harder life. The bigger and more colourful exotic forms of African insects live only in the sub-tropics and tropics. To photograph these creatures is far more dangerous than taking pictures of lions from a car. Patient insect-observation is made difficult by ever-present venomous snakes and disease-carrying gnats. Besides, safari tourists want to bring home spectacular pictures of elephants and thus prefer to use a tele-photo rather than a close-up lens. Insect photography — a way to discover the bizarre in Nature — is everywhere still in its infancy... it is only just beginning in Africa where there are instinctive revulsions to be overcome in the face of frequently menacing insects.

◂ Southern Rhodesia. — The mauve larva of the mantis *Pseudocreobatra wahlbergii* likes to camouflage itself on lilac-coloured flowers. Here, against a red background, it feels unsafe and has raised its hindquarters aggressively. The wings, marked with a circle, are still undeveloped.

▴ Kenya. — The curious mantis *Phyllocrania paradoxa* which resembles a twig with dried-up leaves, stalking a locust.

Rhodesian Mantis in an attitude of watchfulness.

East African Mantis in her most impressive defence pose.

The Praying Mantis, of which entomologists differentiate 1,500 species, is surrounded by an aura of dignity and mystery. Only one species, the green *Mantis religiosa*, is sometimes found north of the Alps, but several species of the helmeted genus, *Empusa*, live on the shores of the Mediterranean. In Africa mantids lurk everywhere; bark-hued or soft-coloured species lie in wait, imitating twigs, leaves, and flowers. All are highly specialised predators whose deadly weapons are their forelimbs, raised as if in prayer. A mantis will wait motionless for hours for an insect to come so close that her long arms can embrace the prey, which is then pierced by the daggerlike spine on the middle section of the forelimb. She then devours her victim — locust, spider, bee or butterfly — throwing away now and then a meagre leg or the remnant of a wing, and all the while turning her triangular mask-like head this way and that on the look-out for danger. If she sees that a bird or chameleon has chosen her for its prey, she will try, although terrified, to scare away the enemy. Some species strike an alarming pose to frighten the adversary, others rub their jagged hind parts along the edges of their wings which creates a puffing sound. Such bluff usually proves in vain and the hunter, in turn, becomes the prey.

Pseudocreobatra wahlbergii depositing an egg mass.

Sudanese mantis *(Blepharopsis mendica)* on a Mimosa.

The female mantis is notorious as a husband-killer. Often she begins to nibble at her spouse even during copulation. The reason for this matrimonial ferocity has only recently been understood. Because of his small size and light weight, only the male is able to fly, but after fertilisation he has fulfilled his function. Thus it makes sense that he should become food for the female who cannot waste time stalking prey and must devote herself wholly to finding a secure place to deposit her cluster of eggs. Her efforts are often defeated by the parasite *Mantibaria manticida* whose tiny female settles on the thorax or wings of the mantis and waits patiently until her host starts to lay. Then the *Mantibaria* stabs her own eggs into the soft foam-like covering of the mantis nursery and assures for her progeny food and safety. But if all goes well the young mantids will hatch out as tiny replicas of their mother and begin immediately to hunt for aphids. Even when first hatched they possess all the complicated sensory organs: 2 facetted eyes, 3 auxiliary eyes and antennae, as well as the spined front legs of the adults; only the delicate wings are missing and will not develop until the nymphs have shed their skins many times.

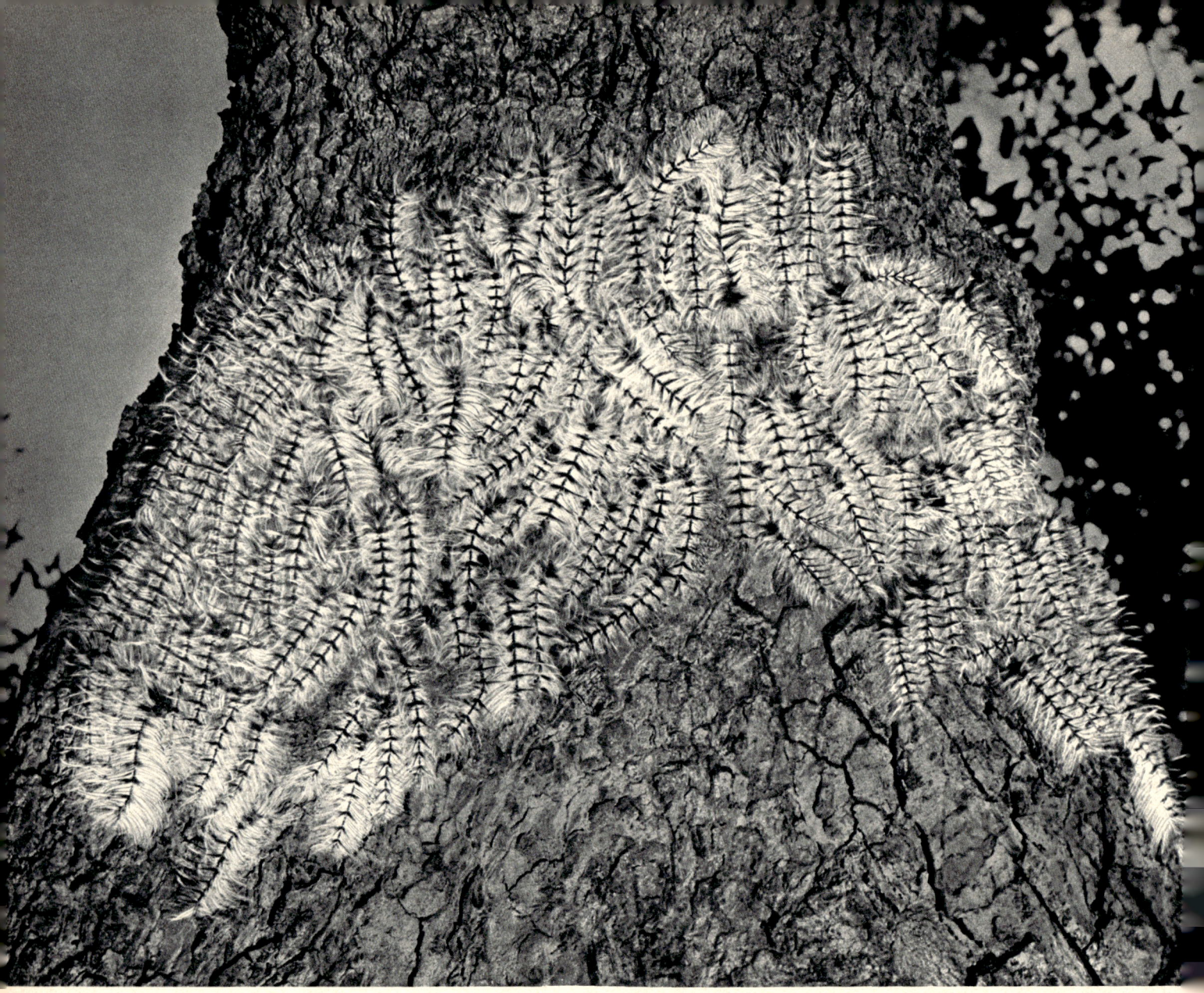

A colony of Lappet Moth caterpillars *(Pachymeta robusta)*, N. Rhodesia. – *Right :* a Bagworm Moth caterpillar *(Psycha* sp.*)*, Kenya.

The traveller who crosses 60 deg. of latitude expects to find fauna he has never seen before. His surprise is all the greater when he meets, beyond the equator, caterpillars and butterflies which do not differ greatly from those found "at home". Whereas the delicate rarities of lepidoptera are limited in distribution, the hardy, ordinary families are scattered world-wide. With their inherited characteristics as their only luggage, butterflies and moths moved out to colonize whole continents, and their progeny, to the north and to the south, have remained the same (colour variations excepted) in structure and behaviour. These Rhodesian caterpillars will become, after metamorphosis, small inconspicuous Lappet Moths, not unlike their European and American relatives, and the "bagworm" of Kenya behaves like our sacciferous larvae, glueing together a hide-away made from thorns. All African caterpillars are equipped with the same camouflage and defence mechanisms (poison hairs, secretions) which we observe in their northern relatives; for their diet they choose shrubs and trees belonging to similar plant families. The parasites which breed prolifically in the ideal conditions provided by "one-crop" economy in Africa create problems to be solved by agricultural chemistry.

Thirsty Swallowtails *(Papilio polycenes)*, White Pierids *(Pieris theuszi)* and other butterflies crowd together to suck up some moisture.

How lepidoptera dispersed during epochs of favourable climatic conditions is evident to-day from the observation of the migrations of Painted Ladies, Gamma Moths, Deathshead Moths and Convolvulus Hawk Moths which fly annually with the wind from North Africa to Europe. They appear in their millions in Spain and some even reach Iceland. Their mass emergence is a phenomenon induced by the short flowering period of arid zones which forces all insects to make the fullest use of the few weeks favourable to their propagation. So the Swallowtails and Pierids, which are seen in Europe only singly or in pairs, congregate here in swarms to suck rare traces of moisture from the drying earth. The Pierids which are fast fliers comprising 1,500 species are distributed all over the world. The blissfully fluttering Swallowtails and Parnassians are known in 600 different forms. The largest West African members of their family are the brown *Papilio antimachus* (up to 9 inches across) and the green-hued, black-veined *Papilio zalmoxis* (5 ½ inches across). — He who ponders over a butterfly collection often wonders why Nature has denied these soft-hued lepidoptera of Equatorial Africa the riot of colours she has granted to the flying gems of Madagascar, Indo-Malaya and South America.

Like Gulliver among the Lilliputians the Termite queen lies surrounded by her tiny servants. *Reduced. (For Termite hills see pages 144/145).*

Whereas among the bees and ants males have to forfeit their lives after fertilising a queen, a reproductive Termite couple together make their home in wood or in the ground and there the royal wedding is consummated. They shed their wings and together they care for the first offspring, who are able to work only after two months. As soon as the "family" of worker larvae has multiplied sufficiently to enlarge the termite home and provide service for the royal couple, the parents concentrate solely on propagation. Growth of the ovaries causes the abdomen of the ¾-inch long queen to swell enormously. In certain species she reaches the size of a banana. Lying nearly immobile, immured in the royal bed-chamber, she lives sometimes to the age of 20 years or more. From time to time the tiny king fertilises his monstrous spouse, and in a mysterious way the egg production of tropical species (10 to 30 thousand a day) is geared to the needs of the Termite state, depending on which caste is short of members: neuters, sexless workers who feed the rest with masticated wood pulp, nymphs who may develop into sexed insects with wings, soldiers, or in the case of the *nasuti*, warriors who exude a sticky defence secretion, as a kind of chemical warfare.

After an attack on a Termite state a tropical Ant *(Paltothyreus tarsatus)* carries off a stupefied Termite soldier. *(Enlarged.)*

No matter how bitterly Termite soldiers fight they are powerless against the strategically well-devised attacks of Warrior Ants. If an army of the notorious "Siafu", or Driver Ants *(Dorylis anomma)*, forces all the entrances simultaneously, the Termite state is lost, and the ensuing panic spreads to all small creatures over a wide area. Such ant armies consist of queen, eggs, larvae and pupae in their hundreds of thousands, and move like gypsies, with bag and baggage, through wilderness and settlement alike, and little on their path is spared. The whole insect world, many reptiles, and even small mammals are exterminated. Man protects himself and his cattle against this crawling horror with a wall of fire, but wild animals caught in the act of giving birth have often been devoured from within outwards. Where the Driver Ants have passed, nothing remains for the hyaenas and the vultures. Even waterways cannot stop the terrible advance. To cross small streams, soldier ants form living suspension bridges by locking their pincers into each other; should a river block their way thousands of bodies form themselves into great globes inside which the queen and the brood are protected and conveyed in safety. Even if numbers clinging to the outside are drowned, many others will reach new territories.

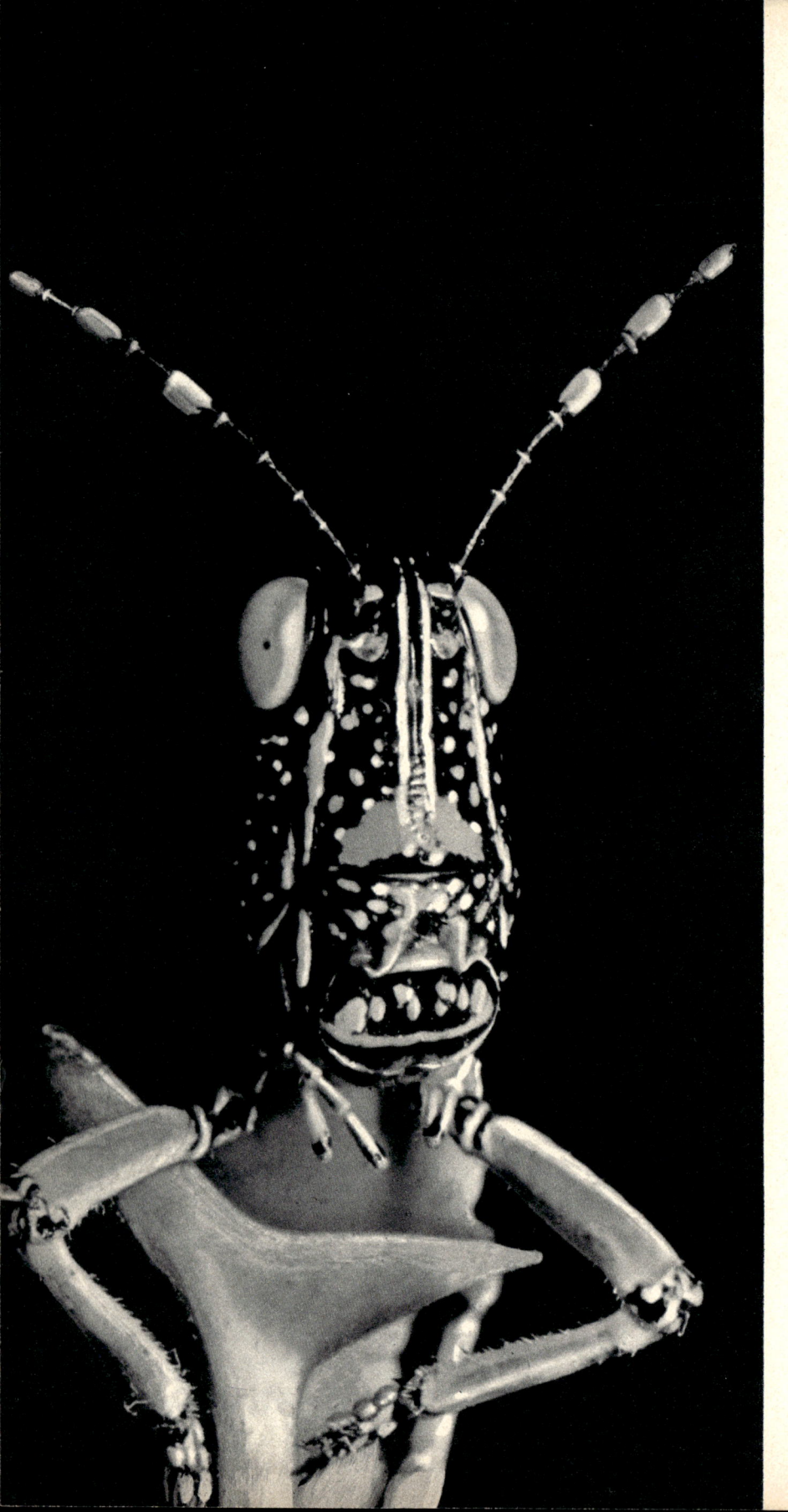

As with most people, native Africans have no love for insects, except for honey bees, although grilled locusts, ants, termites, caterpillars and beetle larvae appear on the menus of some tribes. Those species which threaten man's harvest or health are particularly detested. Because of this prejudice even the harmless species and man's allies, the pest destroyers, have to suffer. Only entomologists are unprejudiced in their study of the behaviour, life cycles and metamorphosis of these creatures which are so strange to most of us.

Here are seven famous, or notorious, African insects: on the left the rapacious locust, *Zonozerus elegans*, whose yellow and black head inspired African mask carvings. Then the monstrous bird spider devouring a chameleon (1). Her bite is supposed to cure rheumatism. The scorpion (2), a distant relative, could be her victim, too, but she would never dare to attack a 7-inch long giant scorpion. Only baboons are dexterous enough to pick them up and, with lightning speed, to tear off their venomous tail and pincers. — Number 4 is no knot on a branch but the small spider *Gasteracantha*. Finally, four beetles assert their needs; the Rhinoceros beetle (number 3) loves rotting wood, the Goliath beetle, as big as a fist, and its cousin *Mutsora sp.* (5) live on tender blossoms, but the Tiger beetle is carnivorous and its larva (6) is a highwayman who lies in wait for insects in an earth tunnel. The Sacred dung beetle or Tumblebug *(Scarabaeus sacer)* (7) works hard to roll pills of dung for itself and its larva (8). Because the ancient Egyptians took its dung pills for symbols of the world it is the only insect to whom monuments have been erected. The Romans transposed this symbol to the "Divine Scarabaeus" who rolls the golden sun ball in the sky.

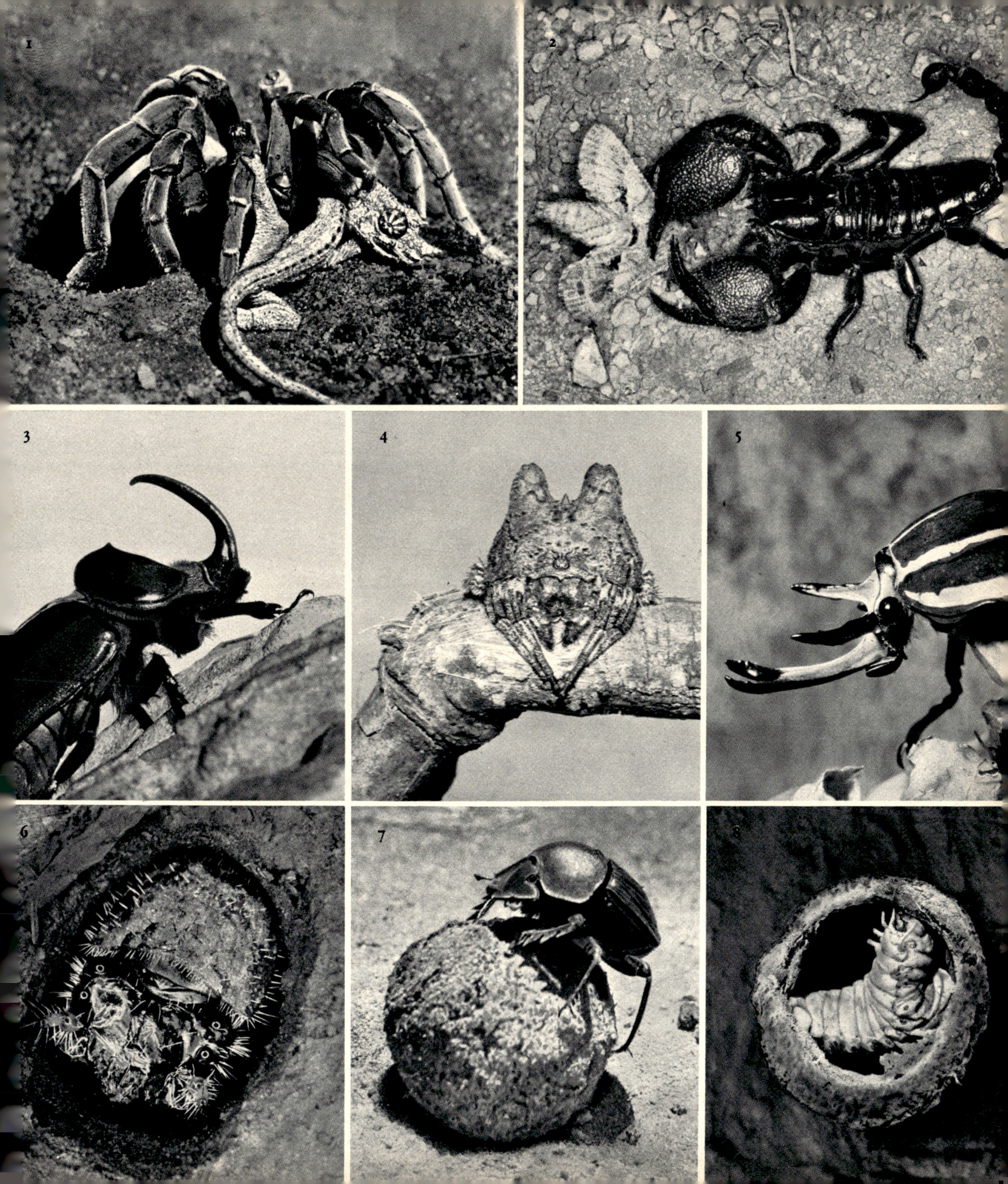
1
2
3
4
5
6
7

1. The Leopard Tortoise *(Testudo pardalis)* grows to 19 inches. 2. The Egyptian Spiny-tailed Lizard *(Uromastix acanthinurus)*, 19 to 20 inches

One of the most important elements in the life of reptiles is constant heat. Africa would be swarming with tortoises were it not for the scores of plunderers that rob their egg caches; the few baby tortoises that finally hatch hardly suffice to ensure the continuity of their species. The sluggish vegetarian land tortoises with their variously patterned, high-domed shells, browse quietly in the steppes and even on the fringe of deserts where their needs are satisfied by the fruit and young pads of the fig cactus. But rivers and ponds of tropical Africa hide a host of rapacious fast-swimming turtles; the most conspicuous among them are the *Trionychidae*, heavyweights whose soft carapace is covered with skin. The strangest among freshwater turtles are the small black *Pelomedusae*, which cannot retract their snakelike heads and necks, but have to turn them sideways.—Turtles and tortoises can withdraw into their shells as into a fortress and close all the openings with horned limbs or hinged flaps, but this heavy armour is a hindrance to their movements on land. Just as antedeluvian, if a little more practical, is the scaly coat of the Girdle-tailed lizards (3) or Sungazers. When menaced they roll up and bite their own tails, thus presenting to the enemy a spiny ball which is best left alone. The 16-inch long Giant Sungazer flattens itself to the ground and thrashes with its spiny tail so furiously that a tenacious adversary soon gets a bloody nose.

3. The giant Girdle-tailed Lizard or Sungazer *(Cordyllus giganteus)*.   4. The agile Atlas Lizard *(Agama bibroni)*. 16 inches.

The Girdle-tailed Lizards are predators who pounce on small reptiles and insects, but the Egyptian Spiny-tailed Lizards live on blossoms, dates, and leaves (2). They dig tunnels 6 feet long under the desert sand where they seek, according to prevailing outside temperature, coolness or warmth, or fall in times of drought into a cataleptic state. They, too, defend themselves by a violent lashing of their tail but because of the absence of spikes they cannot stay on the defensive; they jump up and down in their fury and bite savagely.—(4) The most agile of all the small African reptiles are the *Agama* Lizards which can make long jumps and run upright for short distances. They are part of the scenery in all native villages, welcome as vermin-killers who begin their day's work when the geckos finish their night shift. They glide through the huts seeking the company of fly-pestered humans but will never allow themselves to be caught. Wherever a male Agama suns himself, a few insignificant greyish-brown females congregate to admire the 16-inch long swain with his beautiful red head; yellow throat and steel-blue body. The hotter the sun shines the more colourful the male Agama becomes.

In very early times snake bites led man away from the state of primitive fatalism and brought about his first steps towards the art of healing. But in Africa to-day deaths from snake bite still claim more victims than does modern traffic. Many serum institutes already do indispensable work, and local people help to supply *snake parks* with venomous snakes for the production of serum. Nevertheless, in cases of emergency the specific antidote is rarely on hand. The most dreaded villains are the Black and Green Mambas, whose deep bite causes death through paralysis of the respiratory system. The Egyptian Cobra or Asp *(Naia haie)*, sacred to the ancient Egyptians was Cleopatra's instrument of suicide, and the black-necked Spitting Cobra aims its poison into the eyes of the enemy, causing temporary blindness. The more sluggish Gaboon Vipers and Puff Adders are less aggressive, although they emit very powerful venoms which decompose the blood of the victim. Such chemical aids to hunting and digestion are used mainly to catch small mammals; only when man steps unexpectedly on a snake or comes too close to its hiding place will it defend itself against apparent danger.

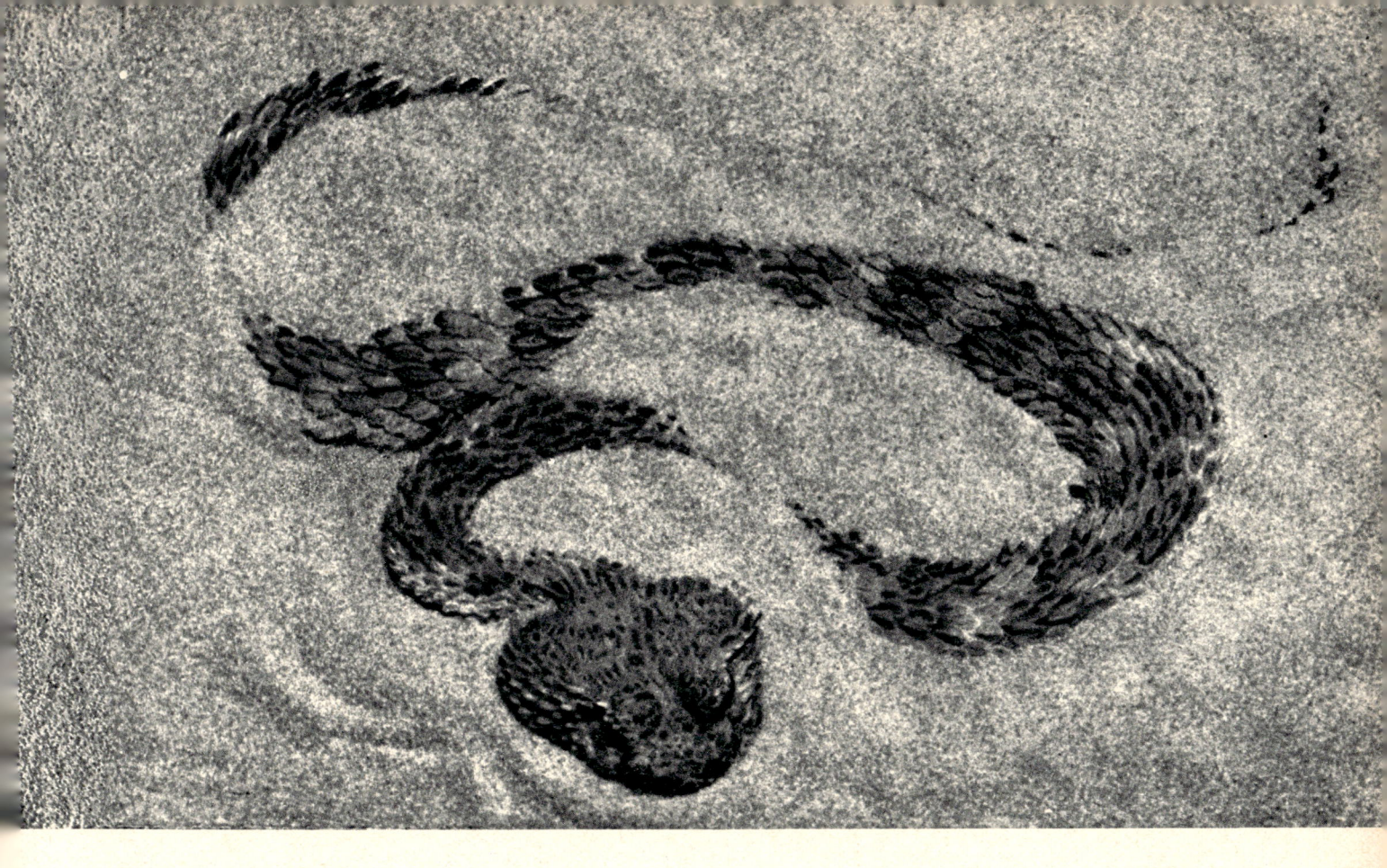

Death waits buried in the desert sand in the shape of the dangerous Horned Vipers *(Cerastes cerastes, above)* and Sand Vipers. Compared to these the Egg-eating Snake *(Dasypeltis scaber)* is a harmless wayfarer. Specially equipped to consume birds' eggs, it even gulps large "finds" whole, for in its oesophagus sharp cutting edges, protruding from the vertebrae, break eggshells to bits. — But the most astonishing swallowing act is accomplished by the huge African Python *(Python sebae, below)*, which lies inert after feeding and is shown here having swallowed a calf. These primeval, non-poisonous, constricting snakes measure 10 feet by their 7th year. As the females fast for 3 to 6 months annually while guarding their 100 eggs, the males grow much quicker. At 20 years of age, wrapped in 18 feet of valuable skin they weigh over 200 pounds.

South African Dwarf Chameleon *(Chamaeleo pumilus)* with young which in this species hatch almost as soon as the eggs are laid.

Although the majority of chameleons live in Madagascar, the original home of this bizarre reptile family is presumed to have been East Africa. History does not relate whether they reached Madagascar across the isthmus which once joined the isle to the mainland, or travelled on uprooted trees, but of 66 chameleon species only two migrated to Asia and one to Southern Spain. There are giants and dwarfs among them; the smallest measures only 3½ inches, and a 2-foot long giant can catch even small birds and mice with its sticky tongue. Every move of the lethargic chameleon is in slow-motion tempo; the tongue alone works with lightning speed. Only the electronic flash and high speed film have made it possible to photograph the act of "tongue shooting" in all its phases. In repose, the tongue is drawn back into the mouth, wrapped round the hyoid bone, and held by strong longitudinal and circular muscles. The moment the muscles come into action the tongue is released; a thick pad appears for a fraction of a second between the lips, gets longer and longer until its objective is reached, then the prey is sucked up and vanishes instantly into the mouth. Often this sticky lassoo is as long as the creature's body and can be aimed with precision at a distance of 12 inches.

Camouflaged among the leaves, an East African viviparous Chameleon *(Chamaeleo bitaeniatus)* catches a locust.

The chameleon is best known for its proverbial ability to change colour, but it is far more effectively camouflaged by its sloth-like immobility. It remains motionless for hours or moves so phlegmatically that insects are unaware of the stalking hunter. Chameleons are far more conspicuous to the human eye than is generally supposed, for they cannot possibly adapt themselves to every surrounding colour pattern. The light and dark colour cells lie in two layers under the skin and act by dilation or contraction of their pigment content. Light, moisture and temperature have a *direct* effect on the skin and reduce the camouflage so that the animal appears lighter at night, darker at sunrise and variegated in bright daylight. Beside these involuntary colour changes there are those induced by visual stimulants and moods. The chameleon's eye "signals" the brain to transmit to the colour cells the imitative conditions, but fear or anger can disrupt the camouflage instantly when agitation creates a contrasting alarm pattern. A grey chameleon turns black with rage, a green one yellow, and a furious motley chameleon suddenly develops leopard spots on a white background. At the same time, the creature swallows air to distend its capacious lungs and puffs out its body in an effort to scare away the attacker.

Many male chameleons with their fantastic head ornaments of horns, helmets, cockscombs or "elephant's ears", resemble miniature dragons. Small wonder that Malagasy and Negroes attribute all sorts of magic powers to the strange climbing reptiles. In Kenya the Kikuyu tribe see in every chameleon the reincarnation of an ancestor; others believe that the little sorcerers are maleficent creatures whose touch brings death. To the primitive mind it is not only the colour change that is quite incomprehensible and the source of an archaic fear, but also the threatening hiss and especially the "evil eye", which follows the watcher everywhere. In 350 B.C. Aristotle recorded the observations of an Alexandrian student thus: "*The eye turns in a circle. It looks in all directions and sees everything it wishes.*" The chameleon's field of vision is restricted by the tiny peep-hole in the protecting eyelid, but the almost unlimited movement of each eye in every direction more than compensates for this disadvantage. Moreover, the movement of each eye is independent of the other, so that a menaced chameleon can look sideways or forward for an escape route and at the same time concentrate on the pursuer behind. As no brain can cope simultaneously with two separate visual images, the chameleon, like those who squint, has to obliterate one image momentarily from its mind, in other words, it sees with the left eye while the right eye changes position, and vice-versa. This monocular vision with heterochronous action enables the chameleon to follow the flight of an insect all round itself without betraying its presence by movements of its body. Only when the insect has settled is the chameleon ready to shoot out its tongue, focusing both eyes to obtain binocular vision.

◄ 1: *Chamaeleo* sp. looking upward and downward at the same time. 2: Three-horned Chameleon *(Chamaeleo johnstoni)* looking sideways, and 3: downward. 4: Casqued Chameleon *(Chamaeleo africanus)* looking forward when releasing its tongue.

➤ A Three-horned Chameleon in the volcanic Nyragongo region, Kivu Province, Congo (Léopoldville) Republic. The colour photograph shows clearly the pincer-like toes. Once the chameleon anchors itself with its toes and prehensile tail even force cannot pull it off the branch. In battle the horns can pierce the softer parts of a rival's head.

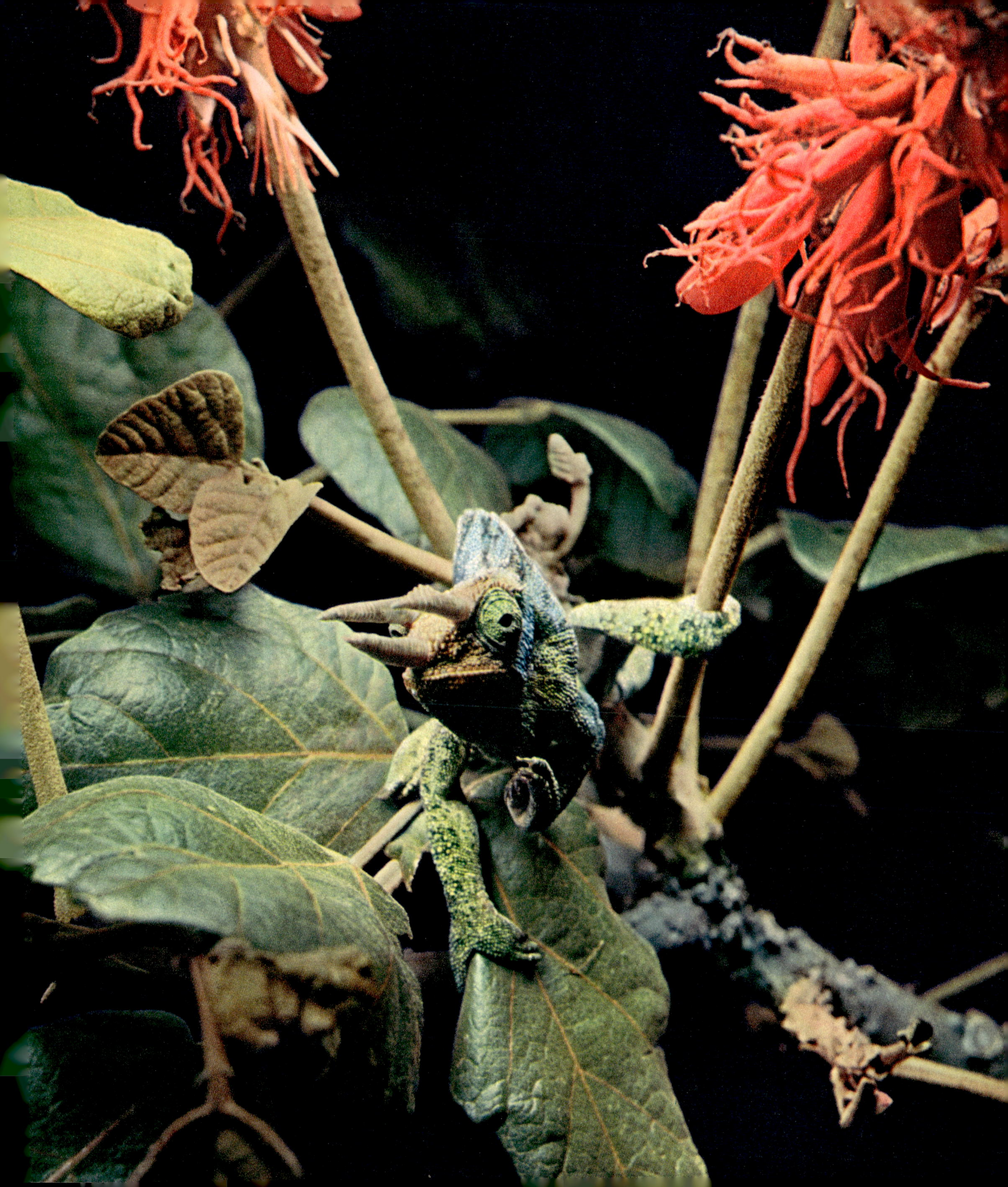

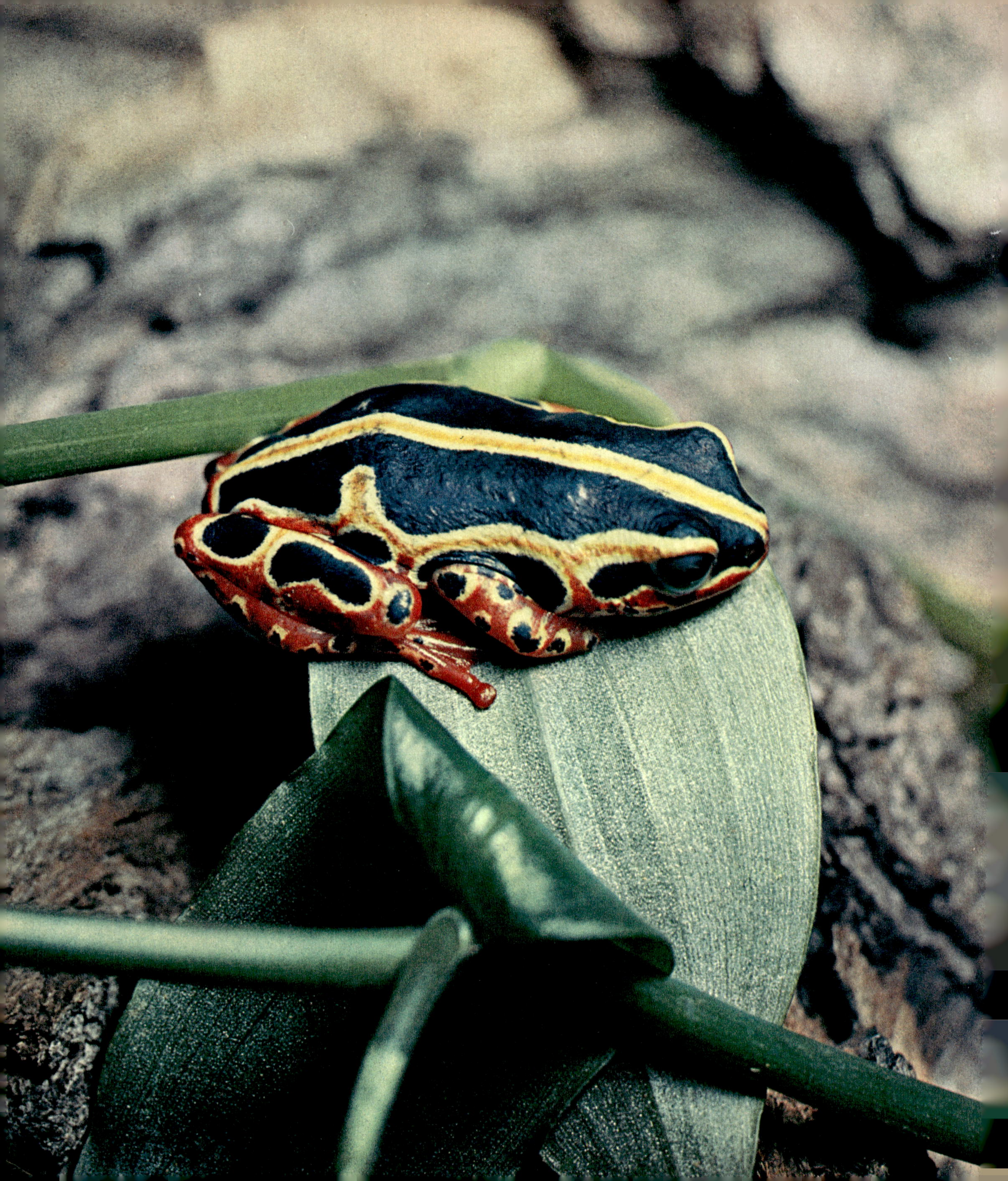

Hot and humid tropical forests are a paradise for frogs. While the little tree frogs call their cheery "tchik-tchik" from the highest branches, an ear-splitting croaking concert resounds in the undergrowth. Some, like the *Hyperolius*, are as colourful as butterflies; others wear a more modest coat but have unusual breeding habits. The *Chiromantis* hang their foam nests on twigs over the water, and the *Hylambates* hop around for weeks with their eggs in their mouths. Among ground-living species there, too, are oddities, like the Hairy Frogs from the Cameroons, which sprout villous girdles around the loins and thighs during the mating season. In Mozambique, the brachycephalic toads, round as balls, gambol in search of termites, their favourite food. The giants among African amphibians are the 10-inch long Goliath frogs and Leopard toads which can swallow mice whole. Outside the tropic belt many species must aestivate during periods of drought, but the clawed frog runs no such risk — it lives in the great lakes and just never goes on land. As it lacks a tongue, the frogs' normal hunting apparatus, it catches small crayfish and water larvae with its fingers and stuffs them into the mouth with its hands. It uses its clawed toes as weapons of defence, but to little purpose, though, if it has wriggled into a net, for Negroes, too, like frogs' legs as a delicacy.

◂ African coloured frog of the species *Hyperolius* (enlarged).

Above: Striped Tree Frog *(Hyperolius melanoleucus)* from West Africa (natural size).
Centre: Leopard Toad *(Bufo regularis)* from Kenya, up to 10 inches long.
Below: Clawed Frog *(Xenopus laevis)* which has become famous through the Xenopus pregnancy test.

A fish which can walk on land and climb trees — the Mud Skipper *(Periophthalmus koelreuteri)*. Length 7 inches.

Clumsy, primitive armoured amphibians were the first vertebrates which ventured out of the sea onto dry land, 300 million years ago. It is only in rock strata 150 million years "younger" that fossils of the first fine-boned frogs have been found. In spite of the evidence offered by fossils, a real appreciation of events during such tremendous lapses of time surpasses our imagination. But even to-day, there exist creatures which still demonstrate some of the prehistoric phases of evolution. Certain kinds of fish which live close to tropical coasts have adopted an amphibious way of life only during late geological times. The lumpsuckers can exist for short periods out of the water, but their close relatives, the mud skippers, can make excursions on land lasting for hours. Atmospheric oxygen, absorbed through the skin, has become so vital to them that they asphyxiate if confined to the water. Their pectoral fins have developed into rudimentary limbs with joints, and the ventral fins function as sucking discs. They can heave themselves onto dry land, and at low tide climb up the roots and branches of the mangrove trees. Like frogs they are protected from dehydration by a skin mucus. Thus the Mud Skippers hunt insects in the shade of leaves and at high tide return to the water.

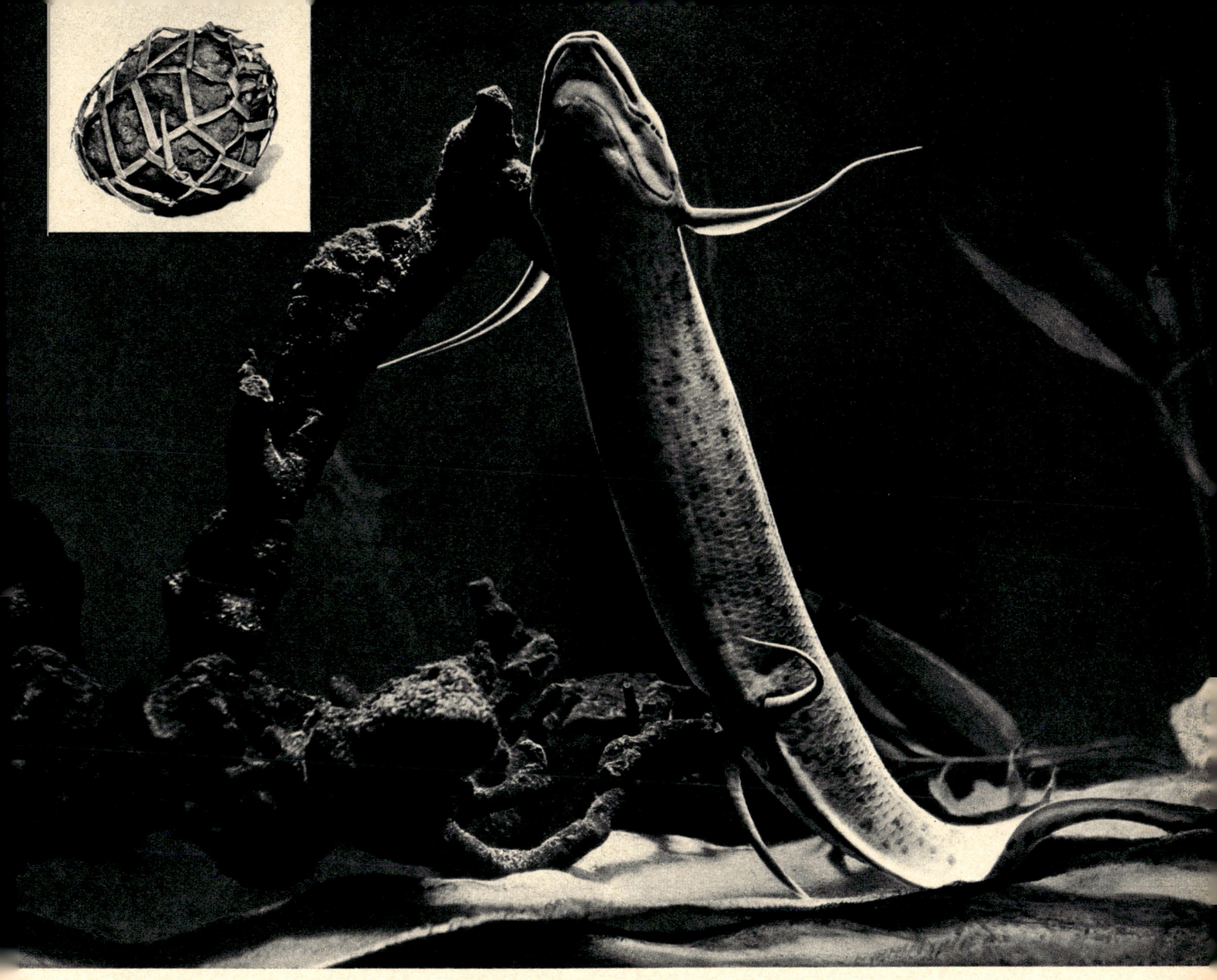

A fish which can breathe on land for six months: The African Lungfish *(Protopterus annectens)*.

When the earth was still young the life of many primitive freshwater fish was jeopardised by the drying up of rivers and lakes, caused by landshifts. The ancestors of the Lungfish were able to survive the periods of drought because their swim bladders developed into rudimentary lungs. In other primeval fish species such adaptation went even further and the fins turned into limbs, giving the fish the ability to move on land. Some, eventually, became amphibians, but some lung-breathers retained their fish form; a living example of this phase of evolution is the 6-foot long African Lungfish. During the rainy seasons it inhabits the shallow waters of flooded marshes and breathes through its gills. When the dry season begins, it digs itself an 18-inch hole in the mud, then rolls up into it and exudes around itself a viscous slime which hardens into a protective "cocoon". Thus it lives for nearly 6 months, breathing through a small opening and consuming its own fat. The natives find "Kamongo", as they call this fish, easily by the airholes in the sun-dried clay soil. They dig the "canned" fish out and carry them to market in sisal nets *(above left)*. The buyer needs only to soak the clay ball to obtain a huge, tasty meal.

The aggressive Reticulated Moray Eel *(Lycodontis tessellata)*. Up to 5 feet long.

The Mail-cheek Fish *(Tetraroge spec.)* usually hides among seaweed.

Forcipiger longirostris which pokes into every crevice with its "forceps".

Long-Fin Butterfly Fish *Heniochus acuminatus*, 4 inches.

Between the Tropics of Cancer and Capricorn an incredi͏̈ alone is the home of over 1,000 colourful species of fre with local specimens and cosmopolitan fish as well, the al is still more interesting as there the fish of three oceans plankton, the few kinds live in huge shoals. On the eas minerals and plankton, provide quite a different environr ten times as many species but in relatively small numbe importance. These ten examples from the kaleidoscope o͏̈ expect to experience. He should only watch without to too small, too beautiful or too poisonous to be put int Reticulated Moray Eel but the Leopard Trigger Fish w sensations of warmth and cold, ca͏̈

◂ Bat Fish *(Platax pinnatus)* which grow to 25 inches in length.

The poisonous Leopard Trigger Fish *(Balistes conspicillum)* 1½ foot long.

Trigger Fish *(Balistes undulatus)* with dorsal spine erect.

The Toby *(Tetrondon spec.)*, inflating itself.

A blue and yellow Angel-Fish *(Pomacanthus spec.)* from the Red Sea.

f fish abound. The inland waters of Equatorial Africa
, but around the tropical coasts where the nets teem
varieties is stupendous. The situation in South Africa
died. On the cold Atlantic side, rich in minerals and
varm waters of the Mozambique Current, deficient in
o the specialisation of life in the coral reefs there are
so many varieties visual distinction is of paramount
n waters give an idea of the joys or fears a diver may
d catch with circumspection, for most coral fish are
pan. Of those illustrated here it is not the notorious
ost dangerous. When eaten, its poison reverses the
y blindness, and is often fatal.

The orange-yellow Blaasop *(Canthigaster valentini)* 8 inches. ➤

Fish, which are the oldest vertebrates in the world, have had a long time to perfect all the defence methods later used by land mammals. Long before porcupines existed there were porcupine fish. Seven varieties of these spiny creatures inhabit the coral reefs along Africa's southeastern coast. With their indestructible tooth-plates they crush the hard coral branchlets and up to a pound of coral lime can accumulate in their stomachs. The porcupine fish in a good temper is normally just portly, as in the picture, but when danger threatens it swallows so much water that it turns into a ball of spines that can choke any predator. Caught in this condition, the porcupine fish spits out the water in distaste and sucks itself full of air instead. When thrown back into the water it floats belly upward. On the banks of the Nile, the Congo and the Niger children often play waterball with the less spiny *Fahaka* which can also inflate itself. The smooth-skinned toby *(see page 201)*, who also swims along the East African coastline, is another prize air-swallower. Neither the porcupine nor the toby is edible because of their diet of coelenterates, for, although immune to the poison themselves, they retain the toxic substances in their bodies.

A pair of Porcupine Fish (*Diodon maculifer*) surrounded by an abundance of floating eggs. Older specimens measure up to 20 inches.

In the labyrinth of coral reefs a hunted fish has time to inflate itself or vanish into a crevice, but in the open seas there is one course only — rapid flight. It is not given to many to seek safety outside their own element, but fear lends wings to the *Cypselurus*. Chased by tunny, dolphins, or porpoises, the flying fish swims upwards at 18 m.p.h., pierces the surface of the water with pectoral fins folded, then instantly spreads these "wings". It can increase its velocity by vibrating the tail, 50 times a second, and reach 40 m.p.h. Under its own power the *Cypselurus* could hardly fly 2 feet, but when borne along by the sea wind, it covers some 200 yards in 12 seconds. The glittering fish has no control over its flight, and can change direction only by a new thrust off the surface, taking to the air if predatory fish are below it and diving to find protection in its own element if pursued by frigate birds. Often a few inches suffice to provide escape from the enemies of both environments. The unforgettable spectacle of flying fish, leaping porpoises, and the aerobatics of sea birds break the monotony for ships' passengers cruising in tropical waters, but who can picture the prehistoric winged dragons with their 24-foot wingspan sailing over the primeval ocean?

Cypselurus spec., 10 to 20 inch. long flying fish, and many other varieties flee in swarms from ships in African coastal waters.

Red fire-fish, devil fish, dragon-fish, firework fish: these are only a few of the names given to one and the same creature which is both admired and feared by fishermen and skin divers from the Gulf of Suez to Madagascar and the Far East. Young fire-fish are transparent and almost invisible, but the mature, 8-inch long specimens are among the most striking inhabitants of the coral reefs. When they glide through the water with fins extended, they call to mind magnificently emblazoned ships with all sails set, their trailing filaments like waving pennants, and the devilish heads resembling the prow of a galleon. There is something bold and challenging about the behaviour of the fire-fish, because every threat of attack gives the creature an opportunity for the most impressive defence manœuvres. The long feathery pectoral fins enable it to stem the current and, by quick movements of its tail, the fire-fish stands on its head or swims sideways so as to bring the poisonous spines to bear. Eighteen of these weapons are distributed in the dorsal, ventral, and pectoral fins. Two jabs, and a human being will suffer excruciating pain; smaller creatures are paralysed instantly by the powerful venom. But more dangerous still is the fire-fish's ugly relative, the Stingfish who lurks in the shallow pools left by the ebbing tide. Its spines can penetrate bathing shoes, and because the poisonous contents of two gland sacs are, at the slightest touch, emptied into these spines, their pricks are as fatal as snake bites.

➤ Fire-Fish *(Pterois volitans)* among sponge-covered coral in the Red Sea near Hurghada, Egypt. At rest the Fire-Fish uses its floating streamers as "bait" for small fishes. While hunting, it suddenly spreads its fins to drive its terrified prey into a cul-de-sac.

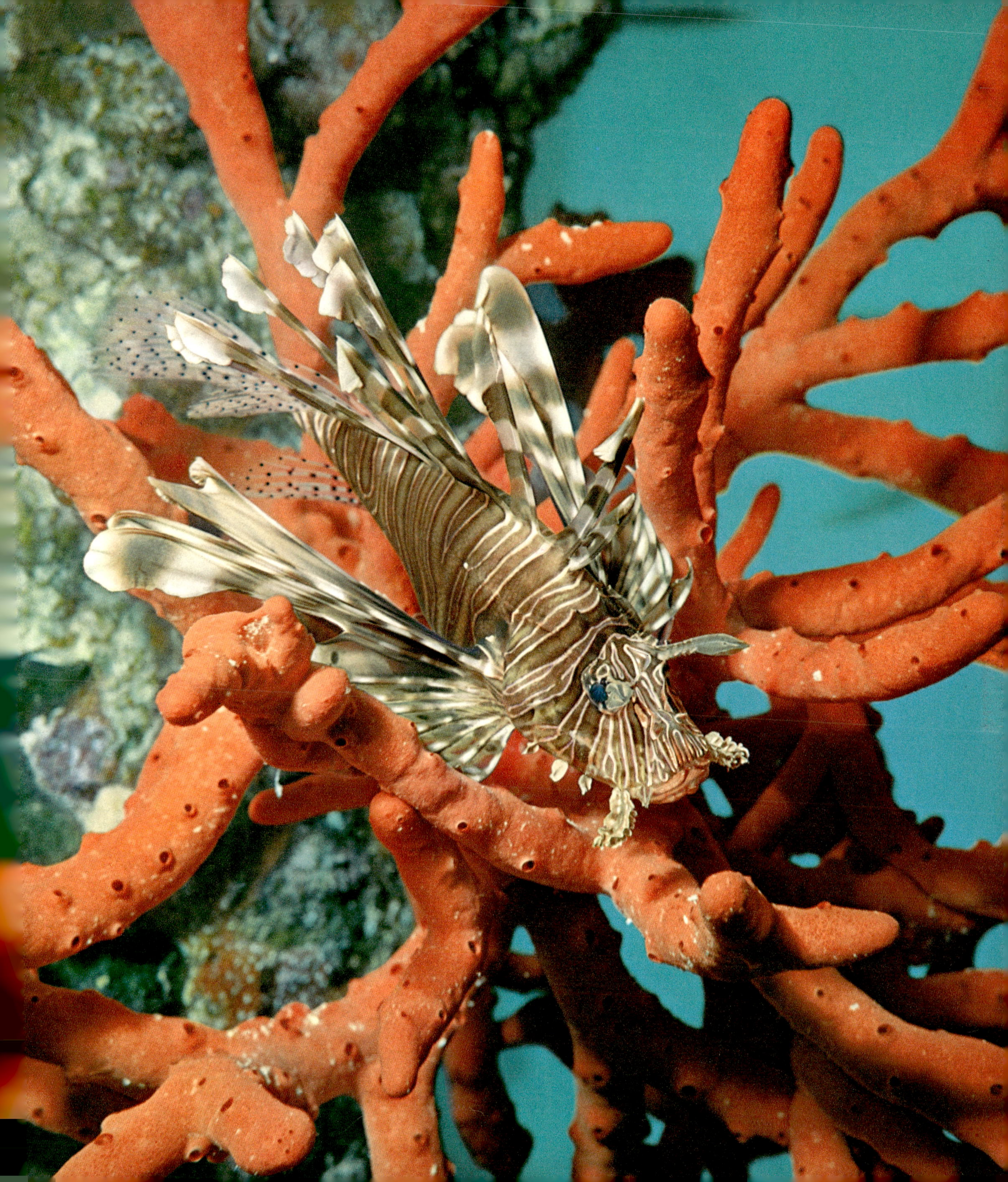

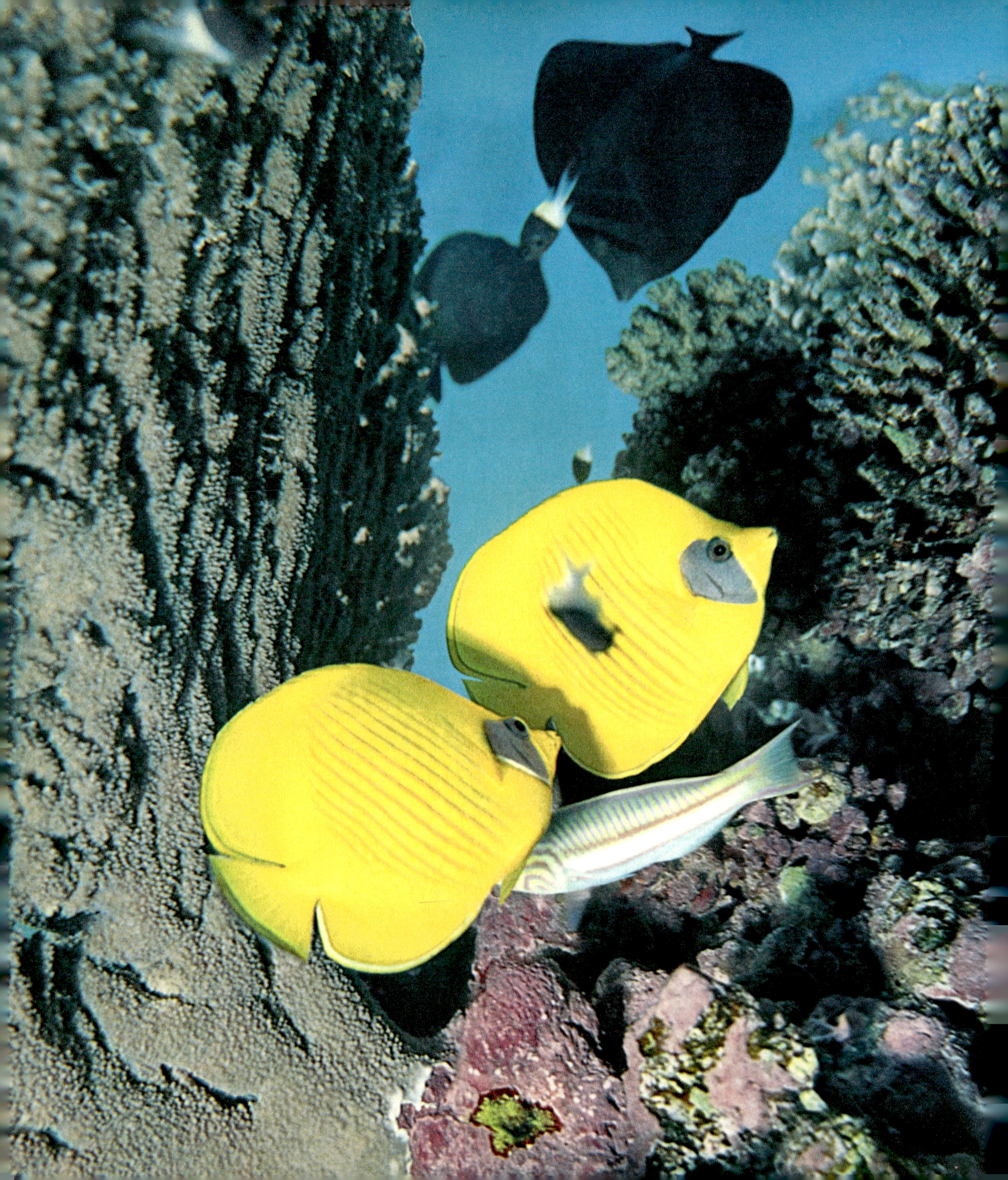

Nature adorns her most delicate tropical creatures with all the colours of the rainbow. In the green virgin forests, the splendours of her palette scintillate on the wings of birds and butterflies, but in the luminous blue of the sea the colours of the coral reef fish seem to glow as if freshly squeezed from tubes of oils. To find such beauty on land, the naturalist must travel to the Equator, but the skin diver need only take a trip to the Red Sea or the Caribbean. There, he can watch shoals of slender fish whipping past with military discipline, or Angel-Fish gliding along in magnificent solitude. Restless inhabitants of grottoes scurry from dark caves and vanish into apparently endless corridors, only to reappear at another window of the coral palace. Disc-shaped Butterfly Fish swim like lovers side by side. The skin diver following them might think he was witnessing a silent squabble, but if the couple seem to separate in a huff they always come together again through some mysterious signal. From Port Sudan to Durban, 19 varieties of these 5 to 12-inch long Butterfly Fish have been found, and it is still uncertain how many colour variations the Indian and Pacific Oceans shelter, especially as the young change colour and form as they grow. To-day, underwater photography reveals the beautiful reality, while just a few decades ago, textbooks showed only illustrations of specimens faded in alcohol. Ichthyologists classify the Butterfly Fish among the *Chaetodontae* or bristle-toothed, which, with their pointed mouths suck all sorts of small creatures out of crevices and coral pores. They are not very fast swimmers because balancing their disc-shaped body is difficult, but the rounded dorsal fin conceals powerful spines with which the fish anchors itself to rock clefts when danger threatens, and then even force cannot remove it. The smallest of the coral fish seek still greater safety. The *Amphiprionidae*, clownfish or "demoiselles", 3 to 5 inches long, are in symbiosis with the big sea anemones *Stoichactis*, a flower-like coelenterate, often 3 feet across, which actually live on fish. The little "lodgers" exude secretions which locally neutralize the paralyzing effect of their host's tentacles and, in gratitude for protection, they bring bits of food, and clean the sand and dirt out of the anemone. Other sea creatures, too, know how to make use of the stinging properties of sea anemones. Small boxer crabs gather minute actinia and brandish them in their pincers as weapons of defence. The fry of horse mackerel shelter under the umbrella of jellyfish. The hermit crab often equips itself with double armour; it uses an abandoned whelk shell as a house and plants two or three sea anemones on top.

◄ Butterfly Fish *(Chaetodon spec.)* in the Red Sea near Hurghada at the exit of the Gulf of Suez. ▼ "Demoiselles" *(Amphiprion polymnus)* shelter between the tentacles of a sea anemone.

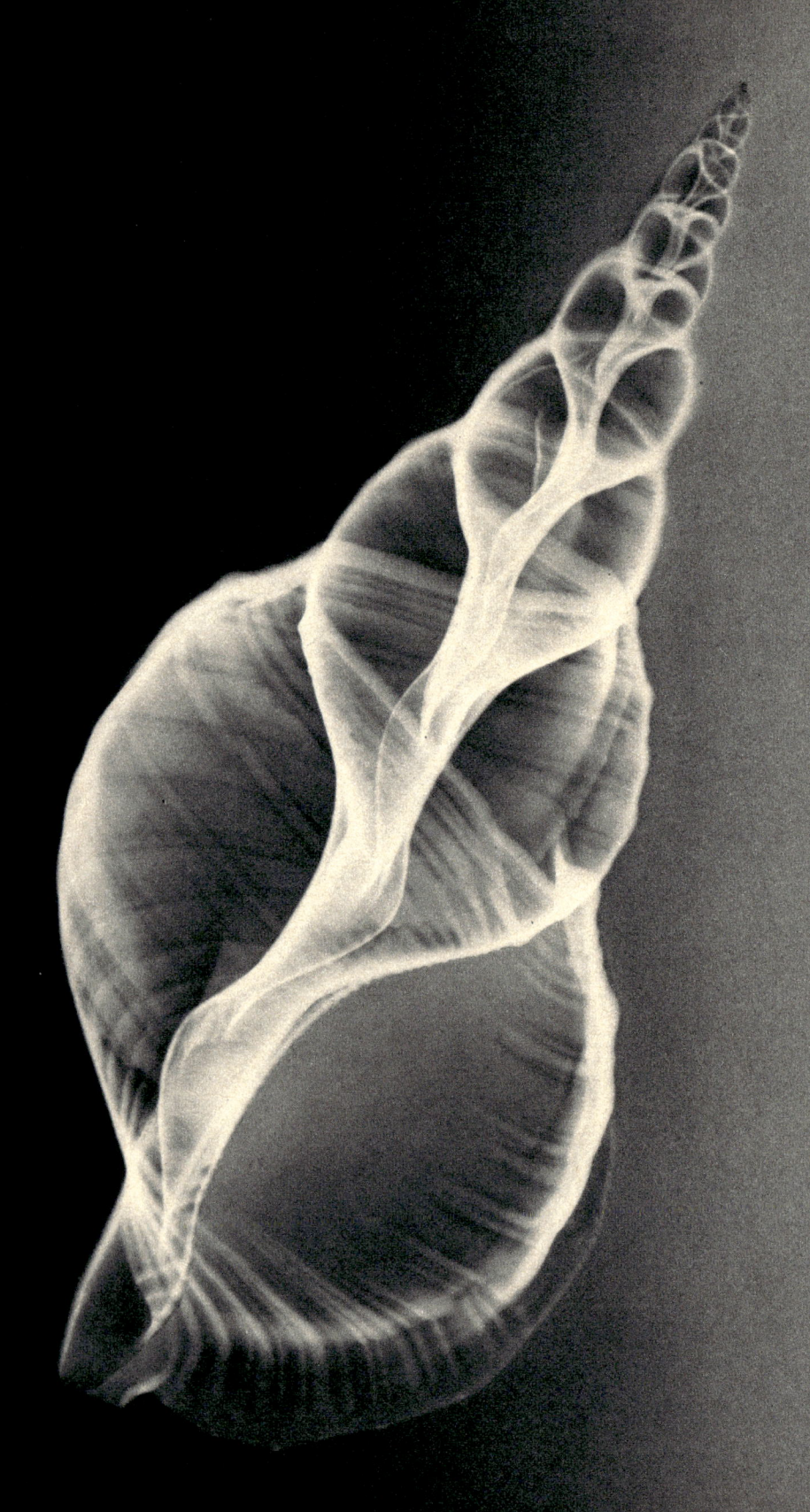

Anyone who shrinks from donning mask and snorkel to see the performance in the *"Theatrum Mare Indicum"* should at least take a look at low tide. Wearing stout rubber shoes as protection against sharp coral and poison spines, one can discover a multitude of shells of exquisite shapes and bizarre designs, far more beautiful when inhabited than when lying empty and mostly damaged on a beach. All the snails left in the puddles keep their operculum closed to avoid drying out, and will search for food only when the tide comes in again. Vegetarian Scorpion Shells browse among the algae, big Tritons seek decomposed animal matter, and carnivorous Bishop's Mitres attack sedentary bivalves, secreting an acid which, drop by drop, "drills" open the shell of their prey. Other carnivorous sea snails open mussels with their calcareous outgrowths, or kill naked molluscs with the poisonous stylets of their tongues. Some are able even to open sea urchins with a corrosive secretion of sulphuric acid. As their ways of life differ, so also do their homes. But what is the origin of these geometrical structures? Shells are built up from organic substances and carbonate of lime exuded from glands in a fold of the skin called the "mantle". If the mantle is active on both sides, two symmetrical shell halves develop; if activity is confined to one part of the mantle, a spiral is formed. Heredity governs the secretion of mineral matter and pigments, and alternating periods of growth and rest create the curious spines and varied patterns. But the exact cause of these rhythms is still a complete mystery.

◄ An X-ray photograph of a Triton's Horn *(Charonia tritonis)*, 14 inches long, which, since ancient times, has been used as a bugle from the Thyrrhenian Sea to the Pacific Ocean.
► Five shells from the Indian Ocean, 5 to 6 inches long.

Scorpion Shell *(Lambis chiragra)*.

Spindle Shell *(Fusinus tuberculatus)*. Mitre *(Mitra mitra)*.

Aulica scapha, a carnivorous snail.

Edible Harp Shell *(Harpa ventricosa)*.

209

The shells of snails and mussels and the articulated carapaces of crabs and crayfish are Nature's ways of protecting vulnerable marine creatures. Another means is the rigid armour of the colourful Trunkfish which live in a "box" formed by hexagonal bony plates, with small openings for the eyes, mouth, and the boneless propeller fins. Nevertheless, these angular creatures can swim quite fast to escape an inquisitive skin diver, but they prefer to rest on rocks or coral branches, moving only lips and pectoral fins to accelerate their rate of breathing, which seems to be constricted by their rigid box-like structure. When hungry they propel themselves about slowly on the sea bed, head downwards, digging for minute molluscs and crustaceans, and are often followed by small fish snapping at floating scraps. Trunkfish are rarely pursued by marine predators, for some of them, including the Horned Cowfish ➤, excrete a toxic slime. In spite of their apparent clumsiness Trunkfish carried by warm sea currents often make long journeys. Sometimes they are thrown ashore on tropical beaches, and such finds have puzzled ichthyologists for the contrasting colours and spot patterns of the fish vary according to age, and young Trunkfish have often been wrongly classified as newly-discovered species. In souvenir shops of ports in the tropics they hang from the ceiling as dried and faded "mobiles", and in South Africa their desiccated "boxes" are used as hygroscopic "weather prophets". Some coastal natives cook them whole and spoon the white meat right out of the "box".

➤ The blue white-spotted Trunkfish *(Ostracion lentiginosum)*, 10 inches long, found in both Indian and Pacific Oceans, is borne with the Mozambique Current as far as East London.

➤ The Horned Cowfish *(Lactoria cornutus)* grows to 18 inches and with age acquires a tail as long as its body. It, too, lives in the coral reefs of the Indian and Pacific Oceans and is well-known to the natives of the East African coast from Mogadiscio to Mossel Bay. Aquarium dealers sell 7-inch long specimens for £30 ($85).

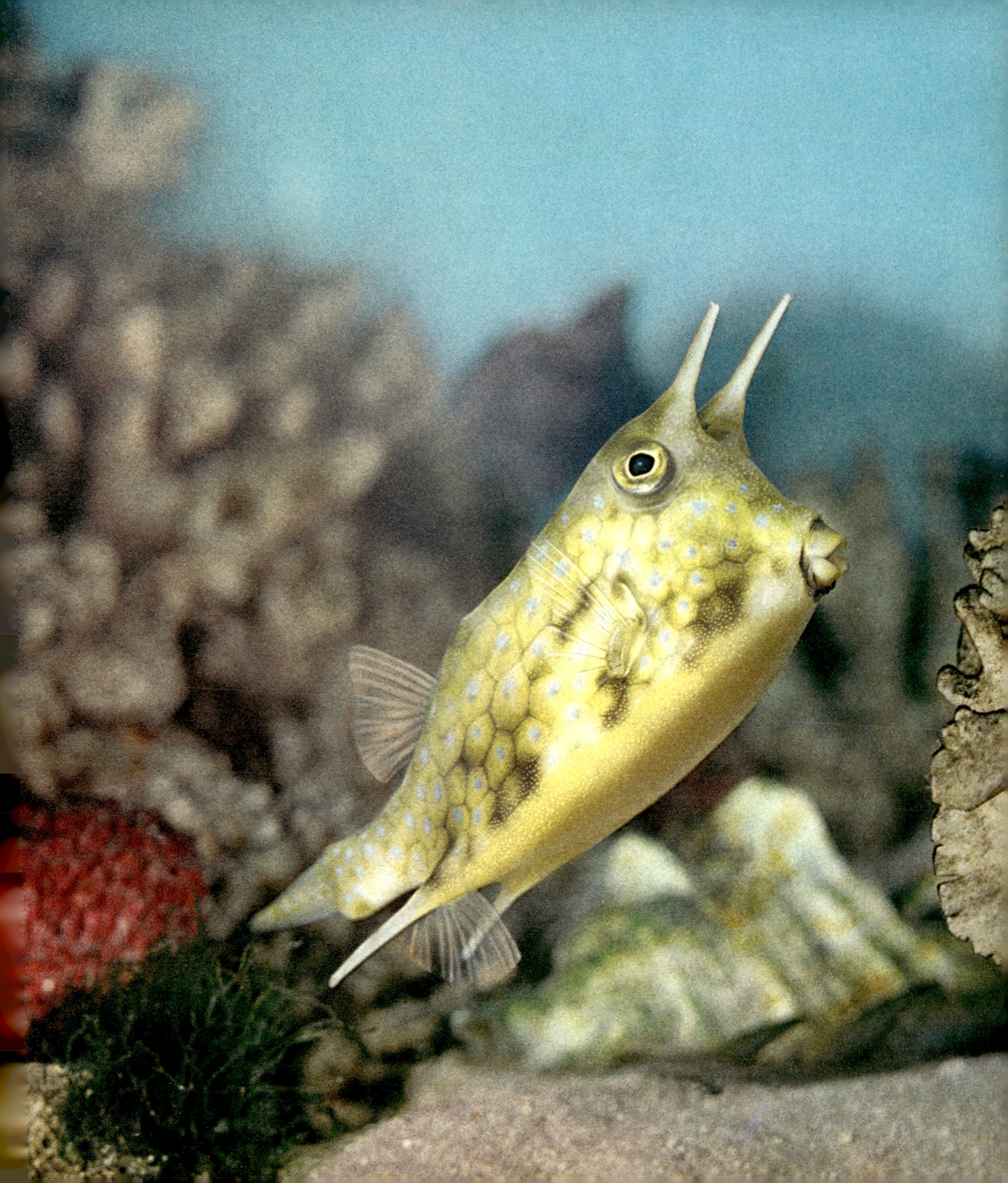

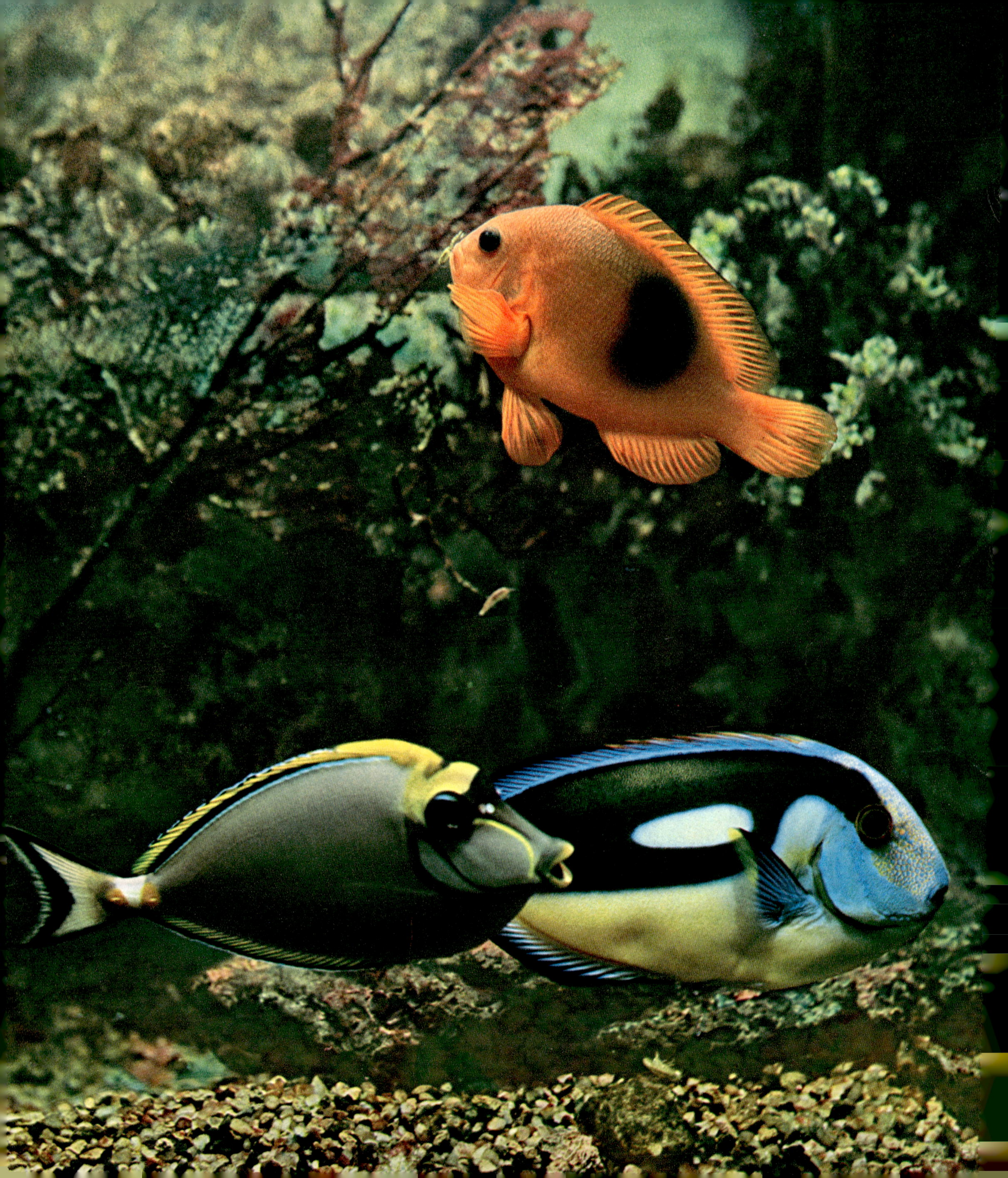

As a source of information for the ichthyologist, the Mozambique Channel is a veritable gold mine. For instance, on a single scientific fishing expedition the nets brought in 52 species hitherto unsuspected in East African waters and 12 kinds which had never been described by marine biologists. Thus the number of known fish varieties, now some 30,000, grows from year to year. That the increase is reported mostly from the African side of the Indian Ocean is due to the fact that four marine research stations have been established there, on the islands of Zanzibar and Nosi-Bé, in Lourenço Marques, and at Durban. All four of them are famous for their studies of the region's primeval fish: the fringe-fin, LATIMERIA CHALUMNAE SMITH *(see below)*, which roused world interest, when caught in 1938 at the mouth of the River *Chalumna*. By a fortunate coincidence this specimen came into the hands of Miss *Courtenay-Latimer*, curator of the East London Museum, who passed it on to the ichthyologist, Professor *J.L.B.Smith*. Why should a 5-foot long, nearly decomposed fish waken such interest? It was as though, after 50 million years, someone had been raised from the dead. Fossil finds have revealed that 350 million years ago these primeval crossopterygians, or fringe-fins, lived in the waters of all continents, but in the younger rock strata no further evidence of their existence appears. Thus it was assumed that these *coelocanths* had become extinct with their relatives, the *Rhipidistia*, the very founders of the first family of land vertebrates. However, the re-discovery of a single contemporary fringe-fin did not unravel the mystery of its way of life. Handbills printed in English, French, and Portuguese distributed among East African fishermen offered a reward of £100/$300 for every specimen caught, but the Second World War brought other problems to the fore, and it was not until 1952 that another fringe-fin was netted at a depth of 500 feet near *Anjouan*, one of the Comoro Islands. On instructions from Dr. *D.F.Malan*, then Prime Minister of the Union of South Africa, the fish was flown by military plane to Durban, to Professor Smith, who named it MALANIA ANJOUANAE SMITH. The fishermen of the Comoro Islands must have wondered at all this fuss, for they had known the sensational creature, which they call *Komessa*, for generations. The flesh, tasting of blubber, is so repugnant that they are not at all pleased when a cyclone drives a *Komessa* into their nets. So long as some see without knowledge and others know without seeing, Nature will divulge her secrets only little by little.

◄ Three "recent" types of coral fish from the Indian and Pacific Oceans whose development began only at the end of the Mesozoic period. Above: Red Demoiselle *(Amphiprion ephippium)*. Below left: Unicorn Fish *(Naso lituratus)*. Right: Surgeon Fish *(Paracanthurus theutis)*, so-called because of the two sharp erectable spines on the tail with which they "skin" their enemies as with a scalpel. These two live in the Mozambique Channel. Their disc-like transparent young drift with the current as far as the Cape of Good Hope.

Neither big-game fishermen nor divers ever see the giants of the oceans — blue whales 110 feet long, whale-sharks 70 feet long or giant squids 60 feet across — but with luck ships' passengers in African waters may see leaping devil-rays 24 feet across and marlins from 9 to 14 feet. Bold underwater photographers visit the winged *Manta* ➤ in its home in the depths, for this huge plankton feeder is quite harmless provided divers do not venture too near. Only its strength makes it dangerous. A harpooned devil-ray can pull quite big a boat for hours, and by leaping suddenly and landing on a craft, has often capsized it and submerged the crew under its great winged body. — A roving swordfish chasing shoals of mackerel, spurred on by its enthusiasm to speeds of 30 m.p.h., can pierce a small boat. The rostrum of the spearfish is not strong enough for such performances, but from California to New Zealand the formidable marlin are the favourite game-fish of wealthy sportsmen. In recent years East Africa has lured marliners to her shores, boasting safaris in two elements with this slogan: "Lion *and* Marlin Adventures!"

◄ A leaping Marlin *(Makaira herscheli)*. It is one of the biggest "modern" bony fish and may weigh as much as 1,000 pounds.

➤ A Devil-Ray *(Manta birostris)* in the Red Sea near Port Sudan; on the underside of this big cartilaginous fish, two Suckerfish *(Remora remora)* travel as stowaways.

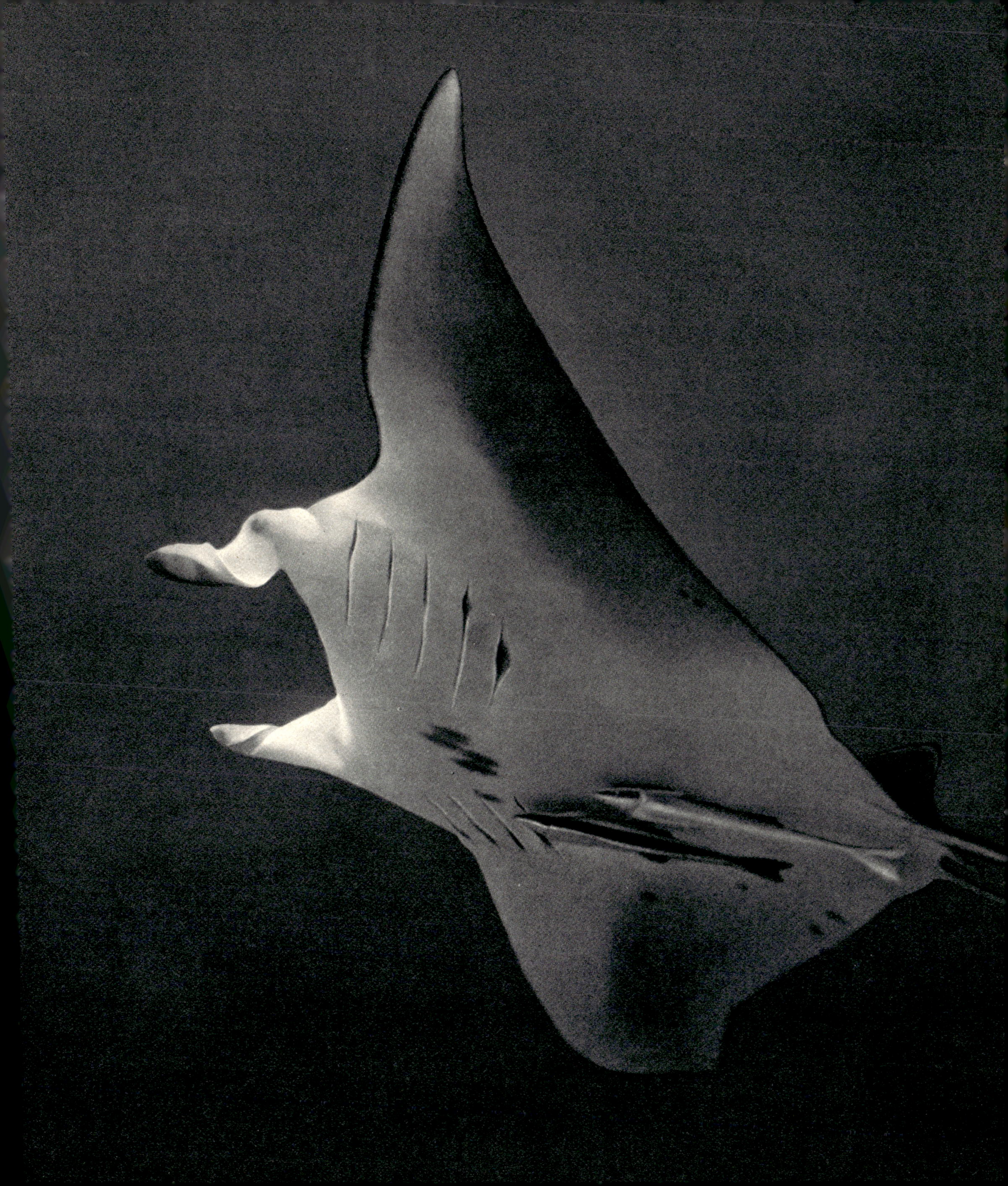

One of the most primitive rays is the 12-to-20 foot long Sawfish *(Pristis pectinatus)* accompanied here by five Remoras.

Although sharks and rays are close relatives, they are bitter enemies, and it is not surprising that the usually placid rays have been provided with a formidable anti-shark defence. The 15-foot wide sting-rays have a long poison-barb at the base of the tail. From time immemorial coastal natives have used these barbs as spear heads. The huge sawfish carry a sharp-toothed, double-edged sword. They use this "snout" extension to comb the algae and ooze at the bottom of the sea for molluscs, but in self-defence they can inflict terrible wounds on an attacking shark, which then falls victim to its own kin. Frequently sawfish from the Atlantic and Indian Oceans venture up the estuaries of African rivers to nose about in the brackish mud and often tear fishermen's nets. As it is believed that an angry sawfish can cut a man in half, they are feared by bathers; panic breaks out on some South African beaches if a harmless sawshark, barely 3 feet long, is sighted. These small, degenerate ground sharks can be identified by the lateral gills, whereas the true sawfish has ventral gill openings. The females of both species give birth to fully developed young whose saw teeth are hidden in a fold of skin so as not to injure the mother. Many sharks and rays are viviparous. In some the first embryos to hatch eat the other eggs. The most primitive forms of cartilaginous fish are oviparous, attaching their eggs to corals, where they cling for months as so many "mermaids' purses".

Atlantic Sharks *(Charachinus* spec.*)* off the coast of Mauretania. Their dorsal fins, visible from a distance, are a signal of danger to bathers.

Of about 250 shark species which hunt in the seven seas, 90 varieties live in African coastal waters. The biggest — the giant whale-sharks — in spite of their great size (70 feet) are harmless plankton feeders and only rarely come into collision with ships, while basking on the surface. The smallest live in the great depths, and off the Cape 1½- to 2-foot long Lantern sharks, showing luminous areas on their bellies, have been caught at a depth of 3,500 feet. The majority of these torpedo-shaped cartilaginous fish are medium-sized, from 3 to 6 feet long. There are spotted blunt-toothed shell-fish crackers, and fast-moving sharp-toothed fish-hunters, both of which get caught in their hundreds in drag-nets off the Cape. They are processed into fish oil and meal or are canned, although canned shark is unpopular because all sharks are detested as man-eaters. South Africans hate above all the dangerous river sharks, and the tiger sharks which come up the estuaries now and again to hunt for crocodiles. However, the greatest danger to divers, to the ship-wrecked, and to careless bathers are the blood-thirsty hammerheads (20 feet), blue sharks (24 feet), and the great white sharks (40 feet). Will these carnivores hinder the progress of submarine technology and the exploitation of the continental shelves? So many other mammals — whales, dolphins, seals, sea-otters, manatees, and dugongs — were able to return to the sea 50 million years ago; surely *Homo aquaticus* of the 21st century, too, will be able to find a place there despite the sharks.

Flying over Seal Island, east of Cape Town, where Cape Fur Seals *(Arctocephalus pusillus)* congregate in their hundreds.

"Only hope can sail round this cape." So said seafarers in olden times, and that is why they sought to reach India by the west rather than round this dangerous southernmost point of Africa. But the Cape fur seals, experts at riding the waves, have always been masters of the storm-whipped seas around the Cape of Good Hope. During their bachelorhood, these South African fur seals roam far afield, but in the breeding season huge herds move northward to congregate at the ancestral birth-places, between Cape Cross and East London, where they stay for four months. To-day, these remote and rocky islands are protected by nature conservation laws which limit the slaughter of seals, and sealskin coats from South Africa have become a rarity on the world market. 80% of all furs come from the Bering Sea. — But why do these cold-loving seals not migrate to the icy waters of the Antarctic where their relatives live? What draws them to Africa? They follow the cold water current which is diverted at the Cape and then, flowing north to the Equator, is known as the Benguela Current. Furthermore, ice-cold undercurrents surge up to the surface off the coast of South West Africa. Although 700 miles closer to the Equator, the water temperature at Walvis Bay is much lower than at Port Elizabeth, which benefits from the warm Mozambique Current.

Along the southwestern coast, where the Cape Cormorants *(Phalacrocorax capensis)* enrich every rocky island and even an artificial isle.

Sea currents influence the climate far into a continent. Where oceans are warm evaporation is high, and moisture-bearing winds favour lush vegetation; but near the cold Benguela Current, evaporation and rainfall are so scant that Africa's southwestern coast is now a desert beside a sea rich with fish. This phenomenon occurs only here and along the coasts adjacent to the Humboldt Current (Peru-Chile), and only in these two areas do dry winds preserve the thick layers of bird droppings, known locally as "white gold". The Incas used *guano* as nitrogenous manure, but in the Old World this magic compound was unknown until the 19th century, when its discovery caused a "guano boom". In 1845 alone, 450 ships dropped anchor off the small South West African island of Ichaboe, and 6,000 seamen feverishly collected the droppings of generations of Cape gannets and cormorants. The old deposits having been exhausted, the harvest of new ones now belongs to the State. But an inventive carpenter from Swakopmund began in 1930 to build a wooden island, fixed with driven piles, which he later enlarged to 20,000 square yards *(above)*. Here 90,000 cormorants present him during the mating season with 900 tons of high-quality guano. Once the birds which "laid the golden eggs" fly off with their young into the vastness of the Atlantic, the annual harvest — worth £ 20,000 / $ 60,000 — is collected.

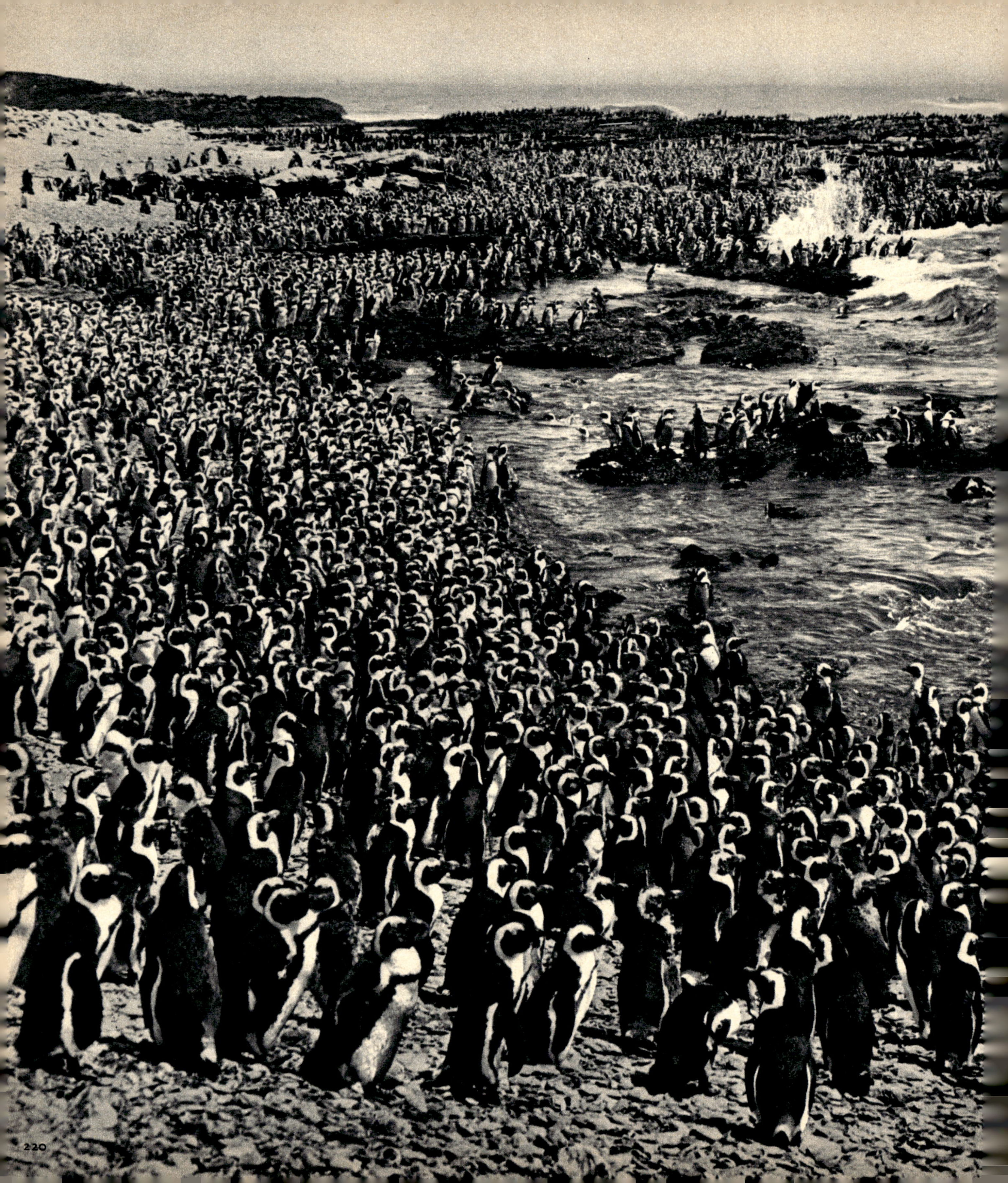

Cape Province, land of extremes! Here, in a small area, the traveller finds concentrated the impressions of a journey through 72 degrees of latitude. For the geologist, antarctic and tropical epochs meet, and in the region of Port Elizabeth the zoologist finds, separated only by 30 miles, penguins *and* elephants. It is significant for the fate of the fauna as a whole that the number of penguins is still higher than the population of the neighbouring town, while only 34 Cape elephants survive in the Addo National Park. The struggle for the harvest of the sea has hardly begun, while the battle for the good earth is coming to an end.

Since when has this southern land, which has its seasons reversed, was alternately covered by sea or submerged under an armour of ice, which once flourished with tropical vegetation and then, in the interior, became a parched desert — since when has this been a rallying-point for penguins... Are these *pikkewijne* which have never seen snow and ice reminders of the last South African glacial period? Or did their forebears reach the rocky coast much later, swimming from the Antarctic? We know nothing of their early migrations in these southern waters, and can only guess that their remote ancestors were capable of flight and reached the Antarctic archipelagoes by way of the air. Then, living close to a sea rich with fish, with no predators from which to escape in flight, their wings gradually atrophied and turned into flippers. "Flightless birds are the greatest anomaly in Nature", said Darwin. Where else can one find 50,000 ostriches a n d one million penguins? Nowhere but in this unique corner of the world, the surprising land of the Cape.

◂ Jackass Penguins *(Spheniscus demersus)* in Algoa Bay near Port Elizabeth. Other penguineries of equal importance are Dassen Island near Saldanha Bay, north of Cape Town, and Halifax Island in Luderitz Bay. Outside the breeding season penguins swim and dive in the vast oceans between Cape Cross and Lourenço-Marques. Only when moulting begins do they come ashore, since their tattered plumage would absorb too much water. It is for this reason that not only breeding pairs but also bachelor birds leave the sea. As soon as the eggs are hidden in holes in the ground or between stones, the egg collectors from the Department of Agriculture arrive. Nevertheless, 5 weeks later thousands of fluffy chicks hatch out. After 3 months, when the young can swim, the colony empties, and it's time for another guano harvest.

INDEX OF CONTRIBUTORS

The editors and the publishers wish to express their thanks to the photographers whose work is reproduced in this volume, and to the many scientists and institutions who have supplied precious information, in particular to Dr. W. Huber and Dr. H. Sägesser of the Natural History Museum, Berne.

BIBLIOGRAPHY:

Joy Adamson, «Living Free». – «Africana», years 1962/63, in particular the works by Lesley Clay, R. Hewitt Ivy, F. & V. Reynolds, Alan Root, Dr L. D. Vesey-Fitzgerald, John van Zyl. – David Attenborough, «Zoo Quest to Madagascar». – David Armitage Bannerman, «The Birds of West and Equatorial Africa». – «Brehm's Tierleben», Bearbeitung von Wilhelm Bardoff. – Edouard Le Danois, «Les Poissons». – François Edmond-Blanc, «Le Grand Livre de la Faune africaine et de sa chasse». – Prof. Dr Lutz Heck, «Tiere in Afrika». – Julian Huxley, «The Conservation of Wild Life and Natural Habitats in Central and East Africa». – «Orion», Zeitschrift für Natur und Technik, years 1958/59, articles by Dr Dieter Backhaus, Dr H. v. Boetticher, Prof. Dr Günter Niethammer, Dr Ferd. Stahrmühlner, Dr Georg Steinbacher, Hans W. Schomber. – Prof. Dr Adolf Portmann, «Die Tiergestalt». – Dr Austin Roberts, «Birds of South Africa». – Peter & Philippa Scott, «Animals in Africa». – Prof. J.L.B. Smith, «The Sea Fishes of Southern Africa». – Hans-Wilhelm Smolik, «Das grosse illustrierte Tierbuch». – «Das Tier», vols. 1–3, information given, among others, by James W. Atz, Prof. Dr Bernhard Grzimek, C.A.W. Guggisberg, Dr C. Hofbauer, Dr Erna Mohr, Maurice Ryan, Peter Ryhiner, Wilhelm Schack, J.B. Shenton, Prof. S.L. Washburn & Irves de Vore, Herbert Wendt. – Union Internationale pour la Conservation de la Nature: Bulletin 1961/62 and Atlas des Réserves naturelles dans le monde, «Derniers Refuges». – «La Vie des Bêtes», in particular articles by: André Cauvin, René Guillot, Aimé Michel. – Fritz Walther, «Entwicklungszüge im Kampf und Paarungsverhalten der Horntiere», Jahrbuch des Georg-von-Opel-Freigeheges, Band 3.

Seventy wildlife photographers of two continents have contributed the results of their patient work to this collection:

AERO FILMS & AERO PICTORIAL Ltd., London W. 1: 2–3
AFRICAN LIFE PUBLICATIONS Ltd., Nairobi/Kenya: 133
Toni ANGERMAYER, München 9: 86 (a, b), 150 (a) – Tierpark Hellabrunn
ATLAS PHOTO, Paris, Photos Jean Dragesco: 89, 96, 97, 105, 217
David ATTENBOROUGH, Richmond/Surrey: 160, 161
Des BARTLETT, ARMAND DENIS PRODUCTIONS, Nairobi/Kenya: 13, 14–15, 24, 25, 26, 30, *43*, 46, 48, 49, 61, 75, 76 (b), 84, 86 (f), 98–99, 100, 101, 102, 110 (a), 111 (a, c), 112 (a), 113 (b), 116, 120, 122, 123, 124, 125, 127, 128, 130, 134, 135, 136, 138, 139 (b, d), 140, 142, 143, *158*, 159 (4, 5), 164, 170, *171*, 174, 179, 181 (a), 182, 184, 187 (1, 2, 6, 8), 197 (b)
BERINGER & PAMPALUCHI, Zürich: 87 (b, c), 150 (b), 151 (e), 165, 167, 200 (9) (Zürich Zoo)
R. A. BOURLAY, Greendale/S. Rhodesia: 17, 76 (a), 141, *177, 178*, 180 (1), 187 (3, 4)
Alice BROWN, Nairobi/Kenya: 29, 38, 57, *90*, 117
Gerhard BUDICH, Berlin: 194 (a)
Ilse COLLIGNON, Photo-Agentur, München 23: 21 (Photo Peter Butler), 44 (Photo Conte Federico Patellani)
COMET PHOTO AG, Zürich: 27, 56 (Photos B. E. Lindroos), 28, 79 (Photos Jack Metzger)
CONZETT & HUBER, Zürich: 11, 45, 52 (Photos E. Schulthess)
Jean DRAGESCO, Le Vésinet (S. & O.), France: 63, 77 (a), 87 (a), *89*, 96, 97, 105, 109 (a, b), 148–149 (centre), 217
Ed van der ELSKEN, Amsterdam: 55
Foto FEUERSTEIN, Schuls: 193, 194 (b, c), *195*
FONDATION INTERNATIONALE SCIENTIFIQUE, Bruxelles, by POPPER Ltd., London: 6, 47, 70, 113 (a), 114, 137, 142 (below), 144, 146, 147, 154, 155, *157*, 163, 168, 169 (1, 4, 6)
FOX PHOTOS Ltd., London: 86 (e), 190 (top), 220–221
René GARDI, Bern: 65, from «Blaue Schleier – rote Zelte».
Gerhard GRONEFELD, München 9: 103, 187 (7)
Klaus H. HARCK, Tsumeb, Afrique du Sud-Ouest: 186
Prof. Dr Lutz HECK, Wiesbaden: *20*
Dieter HINRICHS, München 13: 18
Foto HOEFLINGER, Basel: 106, *196* (Basel Zoo)
Prof. Rolf ITALIAANDER, Afrika-Archiv, Hamburg: 190, 191 (bottom), from «Geliebte Tiere», Georg-Westermann-Verlag
J. S. KARMALI (from Frank W. Lane): 41
G. E. KIRKPATRICK (from Frank W. Lane): 192
Jürg KLAGES, Zürich: 74–75 (bottom), 150 (c), 151 (b, c), 152
Elsbeth KNÖLL-SIEGRIST, Basel: 32, 71, 88, 149 (right), 150 (d), 151 (a), 156, 198, 199, *207* (Basel Zoo)
Prof. O. KOENIG, Biol. Station Wilhelminenberg, Wien: 139 (a)
Frank W. LANE, Ruislip/Middx., England: 22, 23 (Photos S. R. Pelling); 41 (Photo Karmali); 42, 87 (f); 192 (Photo G.E. Kirkpatrick); 214 (Photo O. J. Sprungman); 216 (Photo Hugo Schröder)
B. E. LINDROOS/COMET, Zürich: 27, 56
Werner LUETHY, Bern: 154 (d)

Aldo MARGIOCCO, Genova-Bolzaneto: 185, 187 (5), 189 (4), 203
John MARKHAM, F.R.P.S., London N. 14: 169 (5, 8)
Jack METZGER/COMET, Zürich: 28, 79
Wolfgang MEYERHOFF, Oberhausen-Sterkrade: 215
MINISTRY of INFORMATION & LABOUR, Khartoum/Sudan: 64
NATURHISTORISCHES MUSEUM BERN: 209
Archiv Prof. Dr Günter NIETHAMMER, Bonn: 219 (top)
OKAPIA TIERBILDER G.m.b.H., Frankfurt am Main: 9, 10, 12, 33, *34*, 82 (top), 83 (bottom), 87 (e), 92, 104, 121, 139 (c), 148 (left), 150 (f), 159 (1), 169 (7), 180 (5), 183, 200 (1), 201 (1), *211*
Jacques F. ORMOND, Genève: 110 (b, c), 111 (b)
Conte Federico PATELLANI: 44 (by Ilse Collignon, München)
Klaus PAYSAN, Stuttgart: 112 (b), 145, *172, 175*, 181 (b)
S. R. PELLING (from Frank W. Lane): 22, 23
D.C.H. PLOWES, Umtali/S. Rhodesia: 95, *108*, 173, 176
PONTIS-PHOTODIENST, Charlotte Plessner, München-Pasing: 54 (Photo Andreas Ramer)
Paul POPPER Ltd., London E.C. 4: 4, 5, 6*, 7, 16, 35, 40, 47*, 58–59, 66, 69, 70*, 72, 74, 78, 85, 94, 109 (c), 113* (a), 114*, 118, 126 (top), 137*, 142* (bottom), 144*, 146*, 147*, 150 (e), 154*, 155*, *157*, 159 (2), 162, 163*, 168*, 169* (1, 4, 6), 197 (c), 201 (3)
* Photos: Fondation Internationale Scientifique
Victor ROEDELBERGER, Zürich: 188 (2), 201 (2), 204, *212*, (Zürich Zoo)
ROENTGENINSTITUT, Dr A. Eggli & R. Bütikofer, Bern: 208
Alan ROOT, Nairobi: 8, 36, 37, 60, 62, 77 (b), 91, 119, 129, 132, 166
Wilhelm SCHACK †, by Mme Mariana Schack, Pretoria, Republic of South Africa: 50–51, 67, 68, 86 (c, d), 169 (2)
Hugo SCHRÖDER (from Frank W. Lane): 216
Emil SCHULTHESS, Zürich (from Conzett & Huber): 11, 45, 52
Günter SENFFT, Darmstadt: 197 (a)
Ludwig SILLNER, Nürnberg: 201 (4), *205, 206*
SKY FOTOS Ltd., Johannesburg: 218, 219
Dr W. SPILLMANN, Zug: 169 (3)
Ormal J. SPRUNGMAN (from Frank W. Lane): 214
Paul STEINEMANN, Basel: *19* et 120; no. 120 from: «Geheimnisvolle Zoo-Kinderstube», Orell-Füssli-Verlag
ULLSTEIN-BILDERDIENST, Berlin-Tempelhof: 115, 191 (top and centre), 199 (inset), 213
Peter VOGEL, VDB, Berne: 209
Fritz WALTHER, Dipl. Psych., Eppenhain/Taunus; photographs from the Georg-von-Opel Reservation for Animal Research, Kronberg/Taunus, no. 80, 81, 87 (d), and from the Frankfurt am Main Zoo, no. 82 (bottom), 83 (top)
Wolfgang WEBER, Frankfurt am Main: 73 (drawings after a documentary film by Wilhelm Schack †)
G.J.F. WILLIAMSON, Portsmouth, England: 31, 39, 53, 126, 131
John W. WINISTOERFER, Zürich (Photo Jannie van Niekerk): *107*
Walter WISSENBACH, Herborn/Dillkreis: 188 (1)
G. WOLFSHEIMER, Sherman Oaks: 200 (2, 3), 201 (5), 202, 210

Numbers in italics refer to colour plates

This English version is based on the Swiss original editions:
"PARADE ANIMALE" / "BELAUSCHTE WILDNIS"

ALPHABETICAL INDEX OF ILLUSTRATIONS

Aardvark 142
Aardwolf 143
Acinonyx jubatus 40, 42, 43, 122
Addax nasumaculatus 87
Aepyceros melampus 21, 79, 86
Afropavo congensis 169
Agama bibroni 189
Alcelaphus buselaphus 131
Ammodorcas clarkei 87
Amphiprion ephippium 212
—*polymnus* 207
Anastomus lamelligerus 104
Anhinga rufa 110
Antelope, Addax 87
— Beisa 87, 127
— Black-heeled 21
— Eland 86
— Marsh-buck 88, 89
— Roan 76, — Sable 76
Anthoscopus minutus 173
Antidorcas marsupialis 20
Ants, Tropical 185
Aonyx maculicollis 137
Arctocephalus pusillus 218
Ardea melanocephala 111
Ardeotis kori 103
Aulica scapha 209

Badger, Honey 125
Balaeniceps rex 102
Balearica pavonia 97, 108, 109
Balistes undulatus 201
—*conspicillum* 201
Bat, African-fruit 167
Bateleur 115
Beetle, Goliath 187
— Rhinoceros 187
— Sacred Dung 187
Bee-eater 176
Bellicositermes 145, 184
Blepharopsis mendica 181
Blesbok 87
Bongo 129
Bubulcus ibis 5, 77, 100, 102
Bucorvus abyssinicus & caffer 169
Buffalo, Cape 5, 60
— Dwarf 60
Buphaginae 76, 77
Bushbaby 159
Bustard, Giant 103
Butterfly, Swallowtail 183
— Pierid 183

Camel 64, 65
Camelus dromedarius 64, 65
Canis lupaster 119
Canthigaster valentini 201
Carcharinus spec. 217

Cerastes cerastes 191
Ceratogymna atrata 168
Cerccoebus aterrimus 150
Cercopithecus aethiops 29, 148
—*ascanius* 150, —*cephus* 151
—*hamlyni* 151, —*mona* 151
—*neglectus* 151
Chaetodon spec 206
Chamaeleo africanus 194
—*bitaeniatus* 193
—*johnstonii* 194, 195
—*pumilus* 192
Chameleon 192, 193, 194, 195
Charonia tritonis 208
Cheetah 40, 41, 42, 43, 122
Chimpanzee 153
Civet 135, — Palm 166
Civettictis civetta 135
Coelocantha 213
Colius macrourus 175
Coliuspasser progne 170
Colobus abyssinicus 151
—*caudatus* 149
Connochaetus taurinus 72
Cordylus giganteus 189
Cormorant 6, 219
Corythaeola cristata 169
Crane, Crowned 97, 108, 109
Crocodile, African 7, 45, 46
— Blunt-nosed 44
Crocodylus niloticus 7, 45, 46
Crocuta crocuta 117
Cubitermes 144
Cypselurus spec. 203

Damaliscus albifrons 87
Darter 110
Dasypeltis scaber 191
Diceros bicornis 52, 53, 54, 77
—*simus* 50–51
Dik-dik 128
Diodin maculifer 202
Dispholidus typus 91
Drill 150

Eagle, Cape Sea- 112
— Crowned- 113
— Long-crested 113
— Vulturine Fish- 114
Egret, Cattle 5, 77, 100, 102
Eland 86, 130
Elephant 2–3, 14–15, 17, 18, 19, 55, 56, 57, 58–59
Ephippiorhynchus senegalensis 111
Equus quagga boehmi 12
—*chapmani* 72, 73, 74
—*granti* 75, — *hartmanni* 74
Erythrocebus patas 148, 151

Fennec 139
Fish, Angel- 200–201, Bat 200–201, Blaasop 200–201, Butterfly 207, Coelocanth 213, Cow- 210, Demoiselle 207, 213, Devil-ray 214, Emperor- 200–201, Fire- 204, Flying- 203, Lung- 200 to 201, Marlin 214, Mud-skipper 200–201, Muraena 200–201, Porcupine- 202, Remora 214, Saw- 216, Shark 217, Surgeon- 213, Trigger- 200–201, Trunk- 210, Unicorn- 213
Flamingo 8, 9, 98–99
Flycatcher, Paradise 175
Forcipiger longirostris 200
Frog 197
Fur Seals 218
Fusinus tuberculatus 209

Galago, Great 159
— Moholi 162
Galago crassicaudatus 159
Galago senegalensis 159, 162, 164
Gasteracantha 187
Gazella dama 63
—*dorcas* 80, 81
—*granti* 84
—*thomsoni* 12, 62
Gazelle, Dama 63, Dorcas 80, 81, Grant's 84, Llama 87, Thomson's 12, 62, Waller's 78, 83, 87
Genet 121
Genetta genetta 121
Gerenuk 78, 83
Giraffa camelopardalis 10, 14–15, 23, 66, 67, 68, 69, 77
Giraffe 10, 14–15, 23, 66, 67, 68, 69, 77
Gnu 103
Gorilla 154, 155, 156, 157
Gorilla gorilla 154, 155, 156, 157
Guenon, White-nosed 150
— Brazza 151
Gypohierax angolensis 114
Gyps africanus 24
—*ruppellii* 24

Haliaëtus vocifer 112
Hammerheads 101
Hare, Jumping 138
Harpa ventricosa 209
Hartebeeste 131
Helogale undulata 141
Heniochus acuminatus 200
Heron 111

Hippopotamus 6, 16, 48, 49, 100, 101
Hippopotamus amphibius 6, 16, 48, 49, 100, 101
Hippotragus equinus 76
—*niger* 76
Hornbill 168, 169
Hunting-dog, Cape 118
Hyena, Spotted 117
Hyperolius 196, —*melanoleucus* 197
Hyrax, Cape 139
Hystrix galeata 136

Ibis, Glossy 7
— Sacred 111
Impala 21, 79, 86
Indri 161
Indri indri 161

Jackal 22, 39

Klipspringer 87
Kob, Uganda 86
Kobus defassa 86, —*kob* 86, 133
— *leche* 4
Kongoni 131
Kudu, Greater 61, 86
— Lesser 132

Lactoria cornutus 211
Lambis chiragra 209
Latimeria chalumnae 213
Lemur, Black 165, Lesser Dwarf 159, 165, Monkey 159, 160, Ring-tailed 158, Ruffed 159
Lemur catta 158
— *Macaco* 165
— *variegatus* 159
Leopard 30, 31, 32, 33
Leptailurus serval 123
Leptoptilos crumeniferus 116
Limnotragus spekei 88
Lion 13, 21, 22, 35, 36, 37, 38, 39
Lithocranius walleri 78, 82, 83, 87
Lizard, Atlas 189
— Girdle-tailed 189
— Spiny-tailed 188
Locust 94, 186
Locusta m. migratorioides 94
Lophiomys 139
Lophoaëtus occipitalis 113
Lophoceros flavirostis 169
Loxodonta africana 2–3, 14–15, 17, 18, 19, 55, 56, 57, 58–59
Lycaon pictus 118
Lycodontis tessellata 200
Lynx caracal 120
Lynx, Desert 120

223

Makaira herscheli 214
Mandrill 150
Mandrillus leucophaeus 151
— *Sphinx* 150
Mangabey, Tufted 150
Manis gigantea 144
— *tetradactyla* 146
— *tricuspis* 147
Manta birostris 215
Mantis, Praying 178, 179, 180, 181
Marsh-buck 88, 89
Mellivora capensis 125
Merops nubicoides 176, 177
Microcebus murinus 159
Mitra mitra 209
Mongoose 141
Monkey, Colobus 149, 151
— Gelada 152
— Green or Vervet 29, 148
— Mona 151
— Moustached 151
— Owl-faced 151
— Patas 148, 151
Moth, Bagworm- 182
— Lappet- 182
Mousebird 175
Mutsora sp. 187

Naja haje 190
Nandinia binotata 166
Naso lituratus 212
Nyala 85, 86

Okapi 70, 71
Okapia johnstoni 70, 71
Openbill 104
Oreotragus oreotragus 87
Oriole 170
Oriolus larvatus 171
Orycteropus afer 142
Oryctes sp. 187
Oryx, East African 127
— Scimitar 63
Oryx algazel 63
— *beisa* 127, — *gazella* 87
Osteolaemus t. osborni 44
Ostracion lentiginosum 210
Ostrich 105, 106
Otter, Finger- 137

Pachymeta robusta 182
Paltothyreus tarsatus 185
Pan troglodytes 153
Pangolin, Giant 144
— Long-tailed 146
— Tree 147
Panthera leo 13, 22, 34, 35, 36, 37, 38, 39, 60
— *pardus* 30, 31, 32, 33
Papio anubis 26
— *cynocephalus* 27
— *hamadryas* 150
Papilio polycenes 183

Paracanthurus theutis 212
Pea-fowl 169
Pedetes surdaster 138
Pelecanus rufescens 6, 25, 110
Pelican 6, 25, 110
Penguin 221
Periophthalmus koelreuteri 198
Perodicticus potto 163
Phacochoerus aethiopicus 126, 127
Phaeton aethereus 110
Phalacrocorax 6
— *capensis* 219
Philetairus socius 93
Phoeniconais minor 8, 9, 98, 99
Phoenicopterus antiquorum 98, 99
Phyllocrania paradoxa 179
Picathartes gymnocephalus 169
Pieris theuszi 183
Plantain-eater 169
Platalea leucorodia 96
Platax pinnatus 200
Plegadis falcinellus 7
Ploceinae 90, 91
Ploceus cucullatus 92
— *jacksoni* 172
Pomacanthus spec. 201
Porcupine 136
Potto, Bosman's 163
Pristis pectinatus 216
Procavia 139
Propithecus diadema 159, 160
Proteles cristatus 143
Protopterus annectens 199
Pseudocreobatra wahlbergii 178, 181
Psycha sp. 182
Pterois volitans 204, 206
Pteropinae 167
Python sebae 190, 191

Quelea quelea 55
Quelea, Red-tailed 55

Rat, Crested 139
Ratel 125
Remora remora 215, 216
Rhaphicerus campestris 134
Rhinoceros, White 50, 51
— Black 52, 53, 54, 77
Rhynchotragus guentheri 128
Rock-fowl 169

Sagittarius serpentarius 112
Scarabaeus sacer 187
Scopus umbretta 101
Scorpion 186
Secretary bird 112
Serval 123
Shells, Bishop's Mitre 208, Conch 208, Harp 208, Spindle 208, Triton's Horn 208
Shrew, Elephant 139
Sifaka 159, 160
Situtunga 88, 89
Snake Bird 110

Snakes, African Python 191, Egg-eating 191, Egyptian Cobra 190, Horned Viper 191
Spheniscus demersus 220–221
Spider, Bird-eating 187
Spoonbill 96
Springbok 20
Squirrel, Spiny 140
Steinbok 134
Stephanoaëtus coronatus 113
Stork, Marabou 116
— Saddlebill 111
— Shoebill 102
Struthio camelus 105, 106, 107
Suricate 124
Suricata suricata 124
Syncerus caffer 5, 60

Tauraco leucotis 169
Taurotragus eurycerus 169
— *oryx* 86, 130
Tchitrea viridis 175
Terathopius ecaudatus 115
Termites 145, 184, 185
Tetraroge spec. 200
Tetrodon spec. 201
Testudo pardalis 188
Theropithecus gelada 152
Threskiornis aethiopica 111
Tit, Penduline 173
Toad, Leopard 197
Tortoise 188
Touraco 169
Tragelaphus angasi 85, 86
— *imberbis* 132
— *strepsiceros* 61, 86
Tropic bird, White-tailed 110

Uromastix acanthinurus 188

Varanus niloticus 47
Vervet 29, 148
Vidua macroura 170
Vulpes zerda 139
Vulture 23, 116
— African 24
— White-backed 24

Wart-hog 126, 127
Waterbuck, Lechwe 4
— Red 86
Weaver birds 91, 100, 173
— Layard's 92
— Sociable 91, 93
Wolf, Egyptian 119

Xenopus laevis 197
Xerus erythropus 140

Zebra, Chapman's 14–15, 72, 73, 74
— Grant's 75, Boehm's 12
— Grevy's 75
— Hartmann's 74
Zonozerus elegans 186

ROTOGRAVURE AND COLOUR-HELIOGRAVURE:
VERBANDSDRUCKEREI LTD BERNE
Printed in Switzerland